D1170911

Schinkel's Berlin *A Study in Environmental Planning*

"Foremost among the numerous attributes of this richly gifted man, I would rank his high ethical dignity, his rare moral strength and his even more distinguished characteristics of unselfishness and extraordinary kindness of heart."

–Gustav Friedrich Waagen

Karl Friedrich Schinkel, 1781–1841
(Portrait by Franz Krüger, 1836)

SCHINKEL'S BERLIN

Harvard University Press, Cambridge, Massachusetts, 1972

A Study in Environmental Planning *Hermann G. Pundt*

Library of Congress Catalog Card Number 75–172325
SBN 674-79095-2
Printed in the United States of America

To My Beloved Wife

Preface

German scholars can proudly list more than four hundred publications by or about one of their country's outstanding architects of the nineteenth century—unfortunately, few of them are in English. The enormous corpus of existing literature dealing with the life and work of Karl Friedrich Schinkel is crowned by the scholarly achievement of the late Paul Ortwin Rave. From the 1930's until his death in 1962, he was engaged in the compilation and publication of all available data pertaining to Schinkel's career. Largely because of his efforts students everywhere can consult the multivolume *Schinkel Lebenswerk* series and find the results of exhaustive research—careful and comprehensive analyses, reliable facts, and thorough documentation—handsomely presented. Under his guidance and largely by his pen, these many splendid volumes treat almost every aspect of Schinkel's work.

Yet, Rave himself acknowledged that he had only provided the groundwork for the critical studies and more penetrating analyses of Schinkel's unique contribution to the history of architecture which were sure to be written in the future. One area in particular was not so much ignored as overlooked owing to the historian's persistent tendency to concentrate on works of architecture as individual monuments. As a state architect in a growing European capital, Schinkel had been vitally concerned with the total context of his architecture and recognized the necessity of relating his new buildings to their surrounding environments. Thus, by extension, he became an environmental planner. Until now the superior quality of his architecture has overshadowed this broader dimension of his work, and the vagaries of time, war, and progress have destroyed or diminished his urban environmental schemes.

In attempting to re-create the physical context of Schinkel's well-known architectural works, I have concentrated primarily on the area of central Berlin, where, in the early decades of the nineteenth century, he tried to create a harmonious and organic urban environment. The record he left of nearly four thousand drawings, fortunately still preserved in his Museum am Lustgarten, and numerous written statements of various types have been the primary sources for this investigation.

In the course of my research I benefited from the brief conversations I was fortunate enough to have with Professor Rave in Berlin in 1960 and also from more extensive and prolonged discussions with the very knowledgeable Dr. Goerd Peschken, many within the very buildings we both admire. During these meetings he provided not only the keen observations of a trained architect, but also unique insights into the character of Schinkel, the man.

In the final preparation of this study I also enjoyed the generous assistance of the staff of the Staatliche Museen zu Berlin (DDR), especially Dr. Gottfried Riemann, whose warm hospitality made the study of countless drawings in the Schinkel collection a pleasant experience. I should also like to express my appreciation to those who helped in a number of significant ways: Dr. Vera-Maria Ruthenberg of the Staatliche Museen zu Berlin (DDR); Dr. Ekhart Berckenhagen and Dr. Brigitte Wenzel of the Staatliche Museen, Kunstbibliothek (West Berlin); Dr. Dorothea Trepplin of the Hochschule für Bildende Künste, Bibliothek (West Berlin); Dr. Helmut Börsch-Supan of the Verwaltung der Schlösser und Gärten, Schloss Charlottenburg (West Berlin); and Dr. Liselotte Camp of the Bayerische Staatsgemäldesammlungen, München. I was especially gratified by the interest shown in this work by Dr. Margarete Kühn, whose untiring efforts on behalf of the preservation of Germany's architectural heritage will be appreciated by many future generations.

I should also like to acknowledge the assistance of Mr. James K. M. Cheng, who skillfully drafted the new maps and plans; Dr. Alan B. Galt, who scrutinized the passages translated from the German; and especially Mr. Simon A. Davis, who contributed numerous suggestions improving the clarity and readability of the text. For their faithful help throughout many years of study and research, I am also grateful to Herrn Dipl.-Ing. Lutz Simon, Oberregierungs-Baurat, Donauwörth, and my brother, Friedrich Karl Pundt.

Finally, I should like to acknowledge my indebtedness to three fine teachers: Professor Ernest A. Connally, who provided the initial stimulus for this research and who has continually supported it; Professor James S. Ackerman, who encouraged its continuation and suggested its publication; and Professor Eduard F. Sekler, whose perceptive criticism and thoughtful suggestions have been especially appreciated. The gratitude I feel for the sustained encouragement and knowledgeable assistance which I received from my wife cannot be expressed in words.

Funds which helped toward the completion of this work were contributed by the Department of Fine Arts, Harvard University, and by the Graduate School Research Fund, University of Washington, Seattle.

Contents

Illustrations

Dimensions are given in millimeters, and height precedes width.

Schinkel's Berlin *A Study in Environmental Planning*

Introduction

Karl Friedrich Schinkel ranks among the best-known neo-Classical architects of nineteenth-century Europe. A contemporary of Leo von Klenze of Munich, Charles Percier and Pierre François Fontaine of Paris, and John Nash of London, he attained an eminent international status after having been the student, protégé and associate of a number of distinguished men in his own land of Prussia. As a youth, he received sound training under David and Friedrich Gilly, highly respected architects in Berlin at the turn of the nineteenth century. Early in his career the diplomat, scholar, and connoisseur of art, Wilhelm von Humboldt, became one of his principal mentors. As early as 1816, Goethe recognized Schinkel's potential as an artist and an architect, saying that one can only wish that "such a rich talent may be granted an equally broad sphere of action."[1]

Schinkel would indeed find a wide range of activities as the most successful of Prussia's state architects. He held increasingly important official positions from 1810 until his death in 1841. As a civil servant he demonstrated outstanding organizational skills as well as the ability to reconcile aesthetic aspirations with economic realities. His clarity of thought, decisiveness of action, sense of total commitment, and loyalty earned him the trust and support of his sovereign, Friedrich Wilhelm III, King of Prussia (1797–1840).

In addition, his superior abilities as an architect ensured the respect and admiration of his professional contemporaries. The Parisian architect, Jakob I. Hittorff, was moved to compare him to Michelangelo—a most flattering appraisal.[2] Leo von Klenze, writing from Munich, praised him as a great artist whose sensitivity and exquisite Grecian designs proved "that one can build in the spirit of the Greeks on the barren sands of the Mark Brandenburg just as well as along the banks of the Ilissos, as long as one has a free mind and a free will."[3] Others were especially impressed by his modesty and lack of pretense—qualities that were coupled with a stubborn determination to realize his architectural conceptions and to accept no compromise when matters of principle were involved.

While men of his own time judged Schinkel as a superior classical architect as well as a competent landscape painter, future generations would view his capabilities in somewhat more complex terms. For instance, Walter Curt Behrendt, in a study of Alfred Messel in 1911, wrote that he considered Schinkel to be the chief representative of the so-called "theoretical-academic and rationalist" branch of Berlin's building tradition—an assessment which ignored his more important contributions.[4] About the same time, Adolf Loos reminded his colleagues of Schinkel's important place in the continuing process of renewal which he felt architecture must undergo when he wrote that "each time that architecture departs from its great example—time and again misled by the petty ones, the ornamentalists—the outstanding architect is close at hand who will lead it back to antiquity. Fischer von Erlach in the south, Schlüter in the north, were rightfully the great masters of the eighteenth century. And at the threshold of the nineteenth stood Schinkel. We have forgotten him. May the light of this towering figure fall upon our coming generation of architects!"[5]

A decade later, Sigfried Giedion saw in Schinkel's work stylistic qualities of Romantic-Classicism and considered his designs as representative of the most progressive ideas of the period. Still later, Nikolaus Pevsner emphasized Schinkel's positive attitude toward modern building technology.[6] Other critics of the first half of the twentieth century continued to interpret his importance to modern architectural thought as "protofunctionalist" in theory and Franco-Prussian rationalist in practice.[7] Among professional architects such men as Peter Behrens, Walter Gropius, and Mies van der Rohe not only spoke highly of Schinkel's achievements, but also continued his legacy as an architect and a humanist. It is perhaps fitting that the last work of the long-established master of "modern classicism" should be an important public building in West Berlin, the Neue Nationalgalerie. Referring to his design in 1963, Mies noted that "the final solution for the utilization of the site permitted a building of clarity and precision, which, I believe, will stand in harmony with the tradition of Schinkel in Berlin."[8]

At present, the ever-increasing interest in total physical environments and the diminishing fascination for buildings as individual statements of structure are not only forcing architects to broaden their scope of vision and participation; they are also redirecting historians in their attempts to interpret the past. In regard to Schinkel and his relevance for a new generation in the last decades of our century, a revaluation of his work appears urgently needed. A limited number of recent essays have already suggested that a concern with a broad context of environment, rather than with monuments as self-sufficient entities, was more evident in his work and thought than past histories have revealed.[9]

It remains now to determine to what extent and with what degree of success Schinkel was able to create or improve urban environmental scenes. Since he projected and executed numerous architectural designs and planning schemes for the civic center of Berlin, it seems logical that this study should concentrate on his efforts there. His work as a planner cannot be finally evaluated, however, until other aspects of the place and the period have been scrutinized. The early parts of this study summarize the environmental character of Berlin prior to Schinkel's time and treat those aspects of his training and experience which presumably affected his development as a planner of urban environments.[10] The Appendix lists the important events in Schinkel's life chronologically and includes a résumé of his works and projects. It was devised especially for the non-German reader and is intended to be an easily accessible source of information, much of which could only be found heretofore in numerous German tomes.

I Berlin before Schinkel's Time

Schinkel arrived in Berlin in 1794. He had spent his boyhood in Neuruppin, an important garrison town in the Mark Brandenburg, but Prussia's capital was to become his home for life. Though Berlin was the center of Prussia's political and cultural life, it possessed neither the cosmopolitan air of Paris nor the size and worldliness of London. During the early part of the thirteenth century it had been no more than an insignificant settlement on the eastern periphery of the loosely bound medieval German empire, and, as late as the reign of Friedrich II (1740–1786), its principal importance was the fact that it housed the monarchy's largest garrison within a ring of customs walls and gates.

The wide spectrum of men who had shaped its destiny ranged from merchants and margraves to kings and conquerors. Their ambitions and, at times, their shortcomings had determined the development of its historical role and cultural life. They had also patronized the creation, expansion, and often the destruction of an ever-expanding urban environment, the peculiar characteristics of which presented problems still unsolved by the nineteenth century. Yet, within Schinkel's lifetime this city would be transformed into a major European capital and aspire to cultural eminence.[1]

In examining the composition of Berlin's urban topography, four basic components are readily apparent: a river, an island, a building, and a

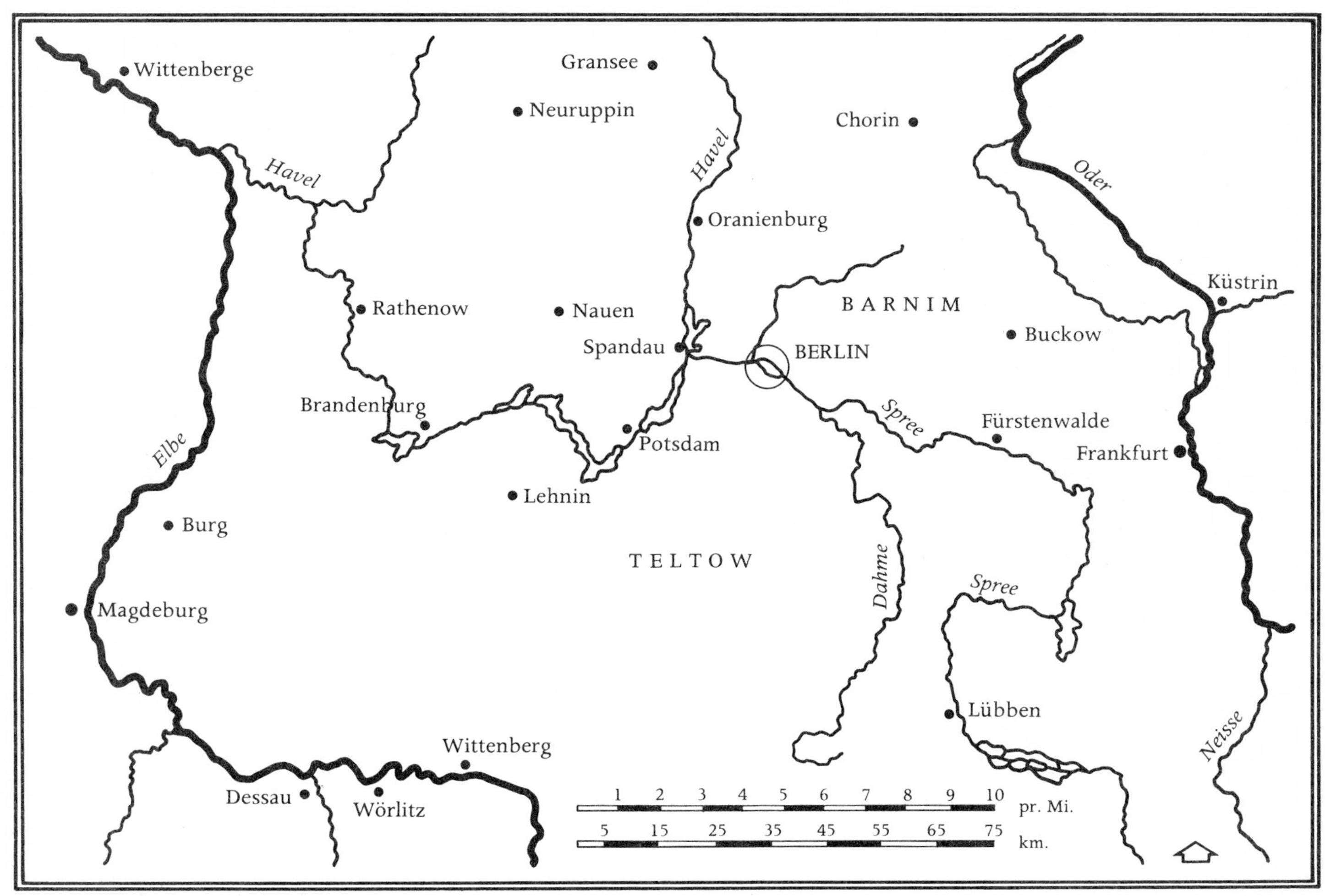

1. Mark Brandenburg between the Elbe and Oder rivers.

Berlin before Schinkel's Time

street. The river is the Spree, Berlin's principal natural environmental feature (Figure 1). Geographically, the Spree is located between the Elbe and the Oder rivers, and it has served historically as the commercial link between the province of Schlesien (Silesia) in the southeast and the Mark Brandenburg in the north. As it flows northwestward toward its confluence with the Havel River near Spandau, it cuts through the plains of Barnim and Teltow where it twists in its marshy riverbed to create a large, elongated S curve (Figure 2). Here, on the right bank of the Spree, an Askanian margrave of the twelfth century decided to found a new town, and its Rhenish and Dutch colonists called it *to dem Berlin*, a phrase which means, literally, "a bend in the river."

The Spree is also indirectly responsible for Berlin's second most impor-

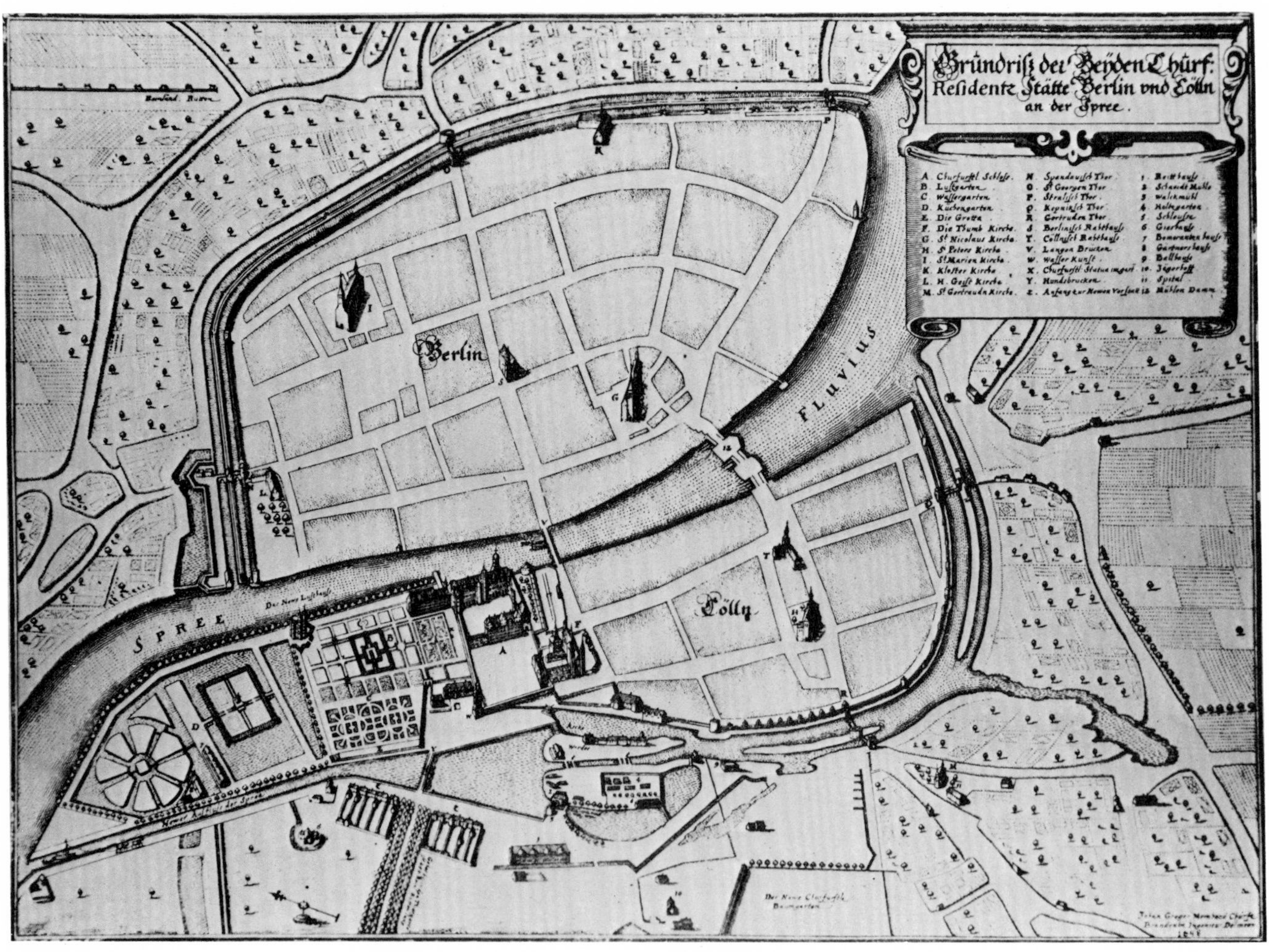

2. Johan Gregor Memhard. Map of Berlin and Cölln, 1648.

Berlin before Schinkel's Time

tant geographical component, an island with irregular contours determined by the flow of the river and one of its minor branches. It measures about 1.7 kilometers in length and 260 meters in width at its center. Gradually narrowing downstream, its elongated point to the north originally consisted of swampy meadows and ponds.[2] Toward the south the island widens, and its soil is more secure. This was the site of medieval Cölln, originally a settlement of Wendish river pilots and fishermen. It is generally acknowledged that the founding of Cölln antedates that of Berlin by several years; its first surviving document is dated 1237, while Berlin possesses no records prior to 1245. Although the Mühlendamm across the Spree had connected them since early times, Berlin and Cölln remained semi-independent communities as late as 1710.

It is almost impossible to determine more accurately the physical features of these two towns during the first four hundred years of their existence.[3] Only with the appearance of the first extant city plan in 1648 can an investigation begin. Johan Gregor Memhard's map (see Figure 2) clearly shows the curving river and the long, narrow island. It also records the two additional landmarks upon which the future of Berlin's planning was to hinge.

The first of these, a large building complex completely spanning the island at the northern boundary of Cölln, is identified as the "Churfürstliche Schloss." The original fortified castle on this site, constructed by the Hohenzollerns in 1443–1450, had been replaced between 1538 and 1540 by a Renaissance château.[4] Memhard carefully delineates this palace with its courts, gardens, and auxiliary buildings. The southwest corner of the complex is defined by the palace chapel, the Thumb-Kirche (marked *F* on the plan). Directly north of the palace lies the Lustgarten, or ducal pleasure garden, which had been redesigned only seven years before Memhard drew his plan. This formal section of the palace grounds was composed of ordered, geometric patterns in the Dutch fashion. Further north was the Küchengarten, which provided the palace kitchen with fresh vegetables. At the very tip of the island Memhard shows a wheel-like pattern, which consisted of triangular-shaped raised fields separated by drainage canals to avoid flooding. The layout of these gardens, as well as the appearance of dikes and canals on the island and surrounding the area of old Berlin, suggest the work of Dutch planners and engineers. Memhard himself, though Austrian by birth, had been trained in Holland and was one of several architects from the Low Countries who had entered the service of Prussia during the reign of the Great Elector, Friedrich Wilhelm (1640–1688).[5]

Fifty years after Memhard had so carefully drawn the Renaissance château with its extensive grounds, Andreas Schlüter was commissioned to expand it. His Baroque palace, in area as well as location, corresponded closely with the site of the old château, its wings and courts stretching across the entire width of the island.

Finally, Memhard's map of 1648 is the earliest record of Berlin's fourth major planning component, the Unter den Linden, which appears as a tree-lined road approaching the island at an oblique angle from the west. It must be made clear at the outset that the importance of this avenue goes far beyond its symbolic significance as Prussia's *via triumphalis*. In the context of Berlin's history of urban planning, this avenue served as the base line for every major expansion program, while it also presented a specific paradox in its physical relationship to the palace, the island, and the river. For these reasons alone, one cannot speak of nineteenth-century planning efforts in central Berlin without first examining the character of this major artery.

The historical beginning of the Unter den Linden in 1647 was of a humble sort. Friedrich Nicolai, the eighteenth-century chronicler of Berlin's history, summarized the event in a single sentence: "Located beyond the secondary branch of the Spree River and to the right of the Hundebrücke, an avenue extended to the Tiergarten; planted with 2000 nut and linden trees in 1647, it measured 250 *rheinländische Ruten* [942.50 meters] in overall length."[6] This description, written in 1786, is almost identical to the note Memhard wrote alongside the avenue on his map of 1648. Although he did not attach enough significance to this recently created *allée* to include it in his reference table of important historical and architectural landmarks, this graphic representation of the Unter den Linden in the earliest known survey of the capital still reveals two important points.

First, it is clear that the avenue had not been planned to effect a connection between the old sections of Berlin on the right bank of the river, the newly developed palace area on the island, and the gradually expanding residential suburbs to the west. Rather, it appears that the road had originally served as a connecting link between the palace and the ducal hunting grounds, the Tiergarten, west of the cities. In addition, the drawing reveals a peculiar orientation of the road in relation to the palace. If the center line of the avenue is continued toward the east, across the Hundebrücke (named after the ducal hunting dogs), it meets the palace at an acute angle of about thirty degrees. Along this imaginary extension it appears that sections of the palace have been reduced in height, as if to accommodate a view from an upper-story window of the domestic wing down the Unter den Linden. Since the avenue served as a tree-shaded route from the palace to the hunting grounds of the Tiergarten, it seems plausible that the planner may have attempted a direct visual link between the ducal properties as well.[7] If this is true, then the original siting of one of the most critical streets in Berlin was based on a purely personal, albeit princely, decision rather than on considerations of service and future expansion of the municipalities.

If Memhard's drawing of 1648 recorded primarily the two-dimensional aspects of the urban scene, another contemporary graphic document focused on the pictorial qualities of the city. Caspar Merian's panoramic view of Berlin and Cölln of 1650 (Figure 3) illustrates the picturesque and semirural nature of the Prussian capital at that time. The skyline is dominated by medieval church spires and the central complex of the

3. Caspar Merian. View of Berlin and Cölln, 1650.

palace. As was typical of the period, the major buildings are identified by letters keyed to a reference table. Several parts of the palace complex are singled out, including the exterior stairtower of the central section which is labeled *D* and described as "the Wendelstein, which can be ascended on horseback." As in Memhard's record, Merian's view shows that the sections of the palace west of the tower and the ducal apartments were kept low and could thus afford an unobstructed view along the newly planted Linden avenue. Merian, however, not being a surveyor as was Memhard, is not concerned with indicating the proper relationships between parts of the city scene. Thus, the tree-lined avenue appears not to lead directly to the Hundebrücke, and its visual connection with a particular part of the palace is not readily apparent. The value of Merian's *veduta* is in its pictorial effects and in the rendering of individual elements within their urban setting.

The original Linden avenue, as we have seen it in the graphic records of Memhard and Merian in the middle of the seventeenth century, existed for no longer than about a decade. The ambitious construction of a "modern" fortification system between 1658 and 1675 eliminated the original avenue forever. Only the surveyor's center line remained as a vestige of the old road, but this remnant would soon serve as a base line for the expansion of the suburbs toward the west.

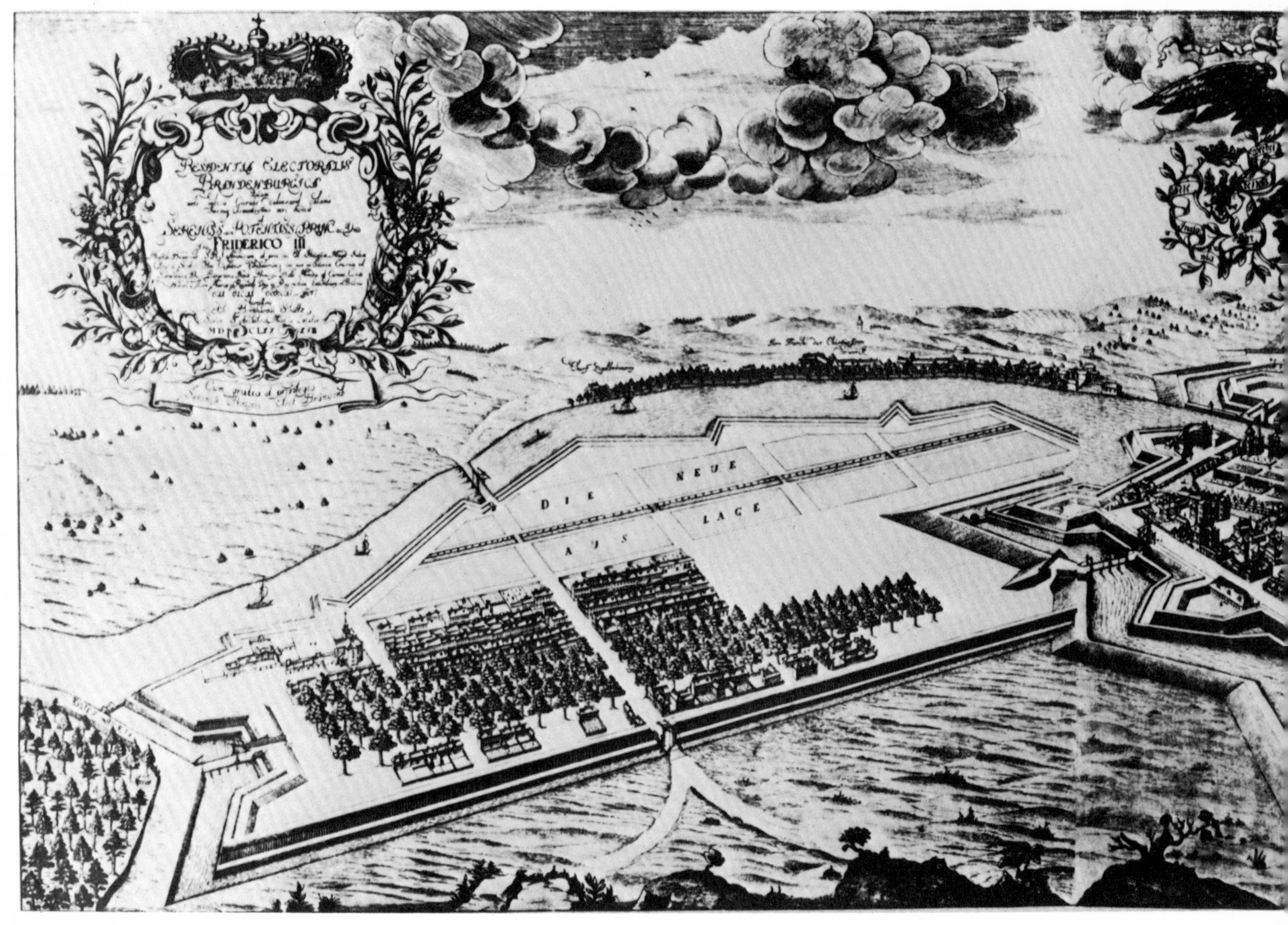

4. Johann Bernhard Schultz. Aerial view of Berlin, Cölln, Friedrich-Werder, and Neustadt, 1688.

Berlin before Schinkel's Time

In 1688, the year of the accession of Friedrich III, Johann Bernhard Schultz recorded the topography of the expanding residential cities (Figure 4). His minutely detailed aerial view shows the old quarters of Berlin and Cölln in the center of the composition and, toward the western edge in the center foreground, Friedrich-Werder, a semi-independent community which had been founded and developed after 1660. Surrounding these three ducal municipalities is an extensive fortification system, composed of thirteen wedge-shaped bastions with concentric walls and moats. Caspar Merian's portfolios of city views document the fact that substantial fortifications, such as those at Berlin, were an essential part of European urban structures during the second half of the seventeenth

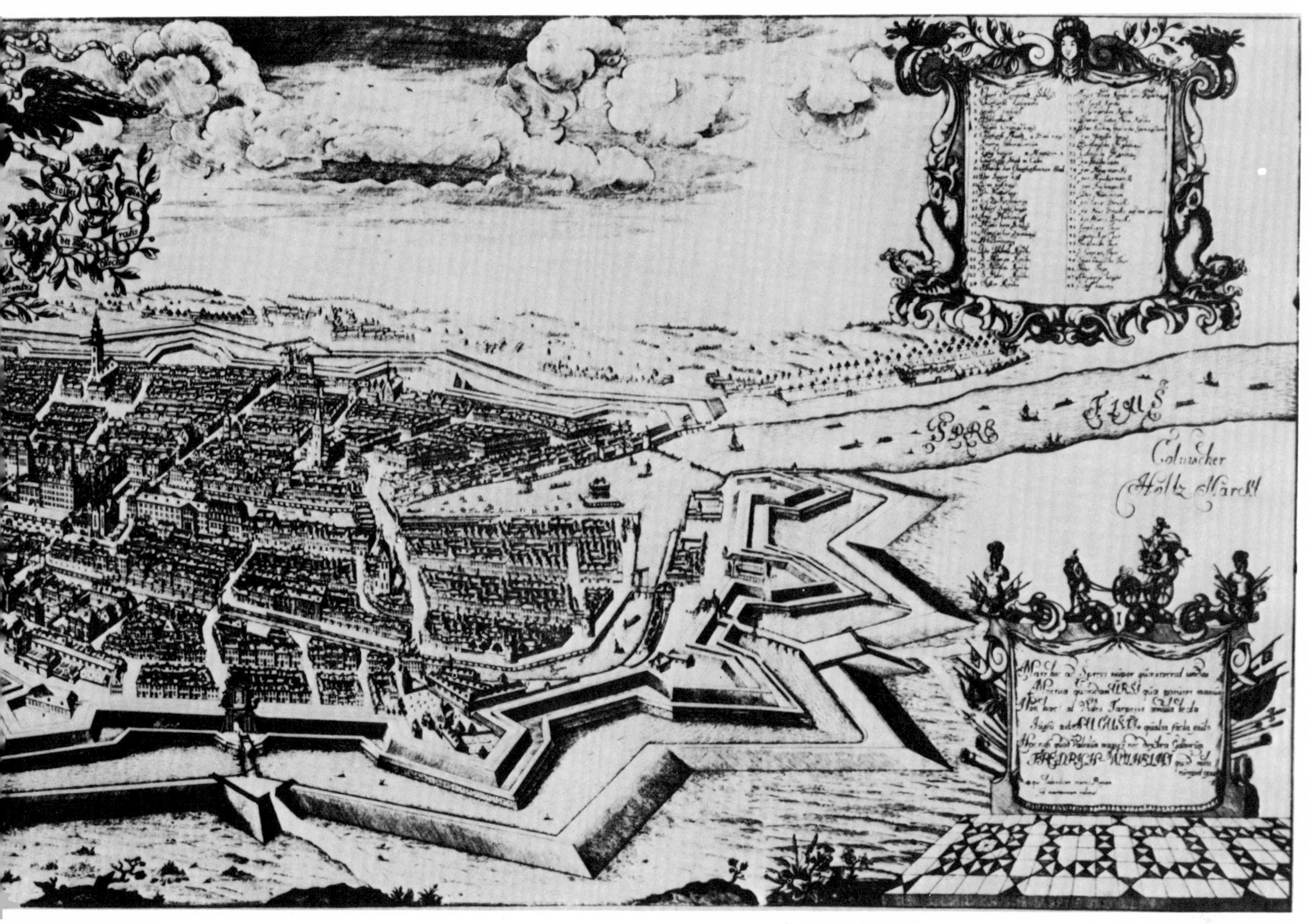

century. Following the devastations of the Thirty Years' War and the continued threat of Swedish, Turkish and French expansionist policies, lords, bishops, and kings from Elbing in East Prussia to Salzburg in Austria rivaled each other in the efficiency of their constructions. Often, as was the case in Berlin, the erection of such bastions would be accomplished by extraordinary expenditure of both manpower and funds. Their final success was questionable from several points of view.

Not only were the moats and bastions around Berlin considered inadequate, from a military standpoint, as early as fifty years after their completion, but the ramparts also quickly proved to be major obstructions to the development of the suburban periphery. Paradoxically, the very engineers who had surrounded the core of the established cities of Berlin, Cölln, and Friedrich-Werder with a tight ring of bastions and moats were themselves forced to recognize the need for urban expansion. In 1663, while the fortifications were still under construction, a new residential section was surveyed west of the old centers. Named Dorotheenstadt after its sponsor, Dorothea von Holstein-Glücksburg, second wife of the Great Elector, but also called Neustadt, it attracted those who desired and could afford to escape from the inner city; its new residents earned it the additional appellation, "Quartier des Nobles." Its limits are clearly defined in the view by Schultz: the river Spree forms the northern boundary, a moat and fortification wall the southern. The new section is connected with the old center by a narrow bridge at the east and with the forests of the ducal hunting grounds by the Potsdamer bridge at the west. The Tiergarten, parts of which had formerly occupied the site of Dorotheenstadt, is now a considerable distance from the palace.

Unlike the medieval centers of old Berlin and Cölln with their crooked streets and irregular intersections, Dorotheenstadt was laid out along the straight axes which surveyors and land speculators demanded. Three parallel east-west avenues, extending the entire length of the city, were created. The Letzte-Strasse (or Dorotheenstrasse), alongside a narrow waterway, formed the northern spine; the Mittel-Strasse separated the newly surveyed but still undeveloped areas from the built-up areas further south. The southern spine, and the most important of the three east-west axes since it was terminated at both ends by the two significant bridges, was an avenue which followed the center line of the old Linden.

The new Linden Allee, as it was called by Johann Stridbeckh in his ink sketch of 1691 (Figure 5), was an impressive successor to the original avenue, and residences of distinction as well as institutional buildings, such as the Akademie, soon rose along its borders. Its four rows of linden trees defined the two traffic lanes separated by a protected pedestrian promenade. According to Nicolai, its total width measured 14 *Ruten*, 2 *Fuss* (53.4 meters), which made it the widest street in all of Berlin.[8] This fact, coupled with its direct link to the fortified area of the Schloss via the Hundebrücke, made the new residential section seem less isolated and unprotected than may appear in Schultz' view. In 1736, after additional expansion toward the west, the Linden Allee terminated at a plaza called the Quarrée, but known after 1814 as the Pariser Platz. Between 1788 and 1791 the Brandenburger Tor, designed by Carl Gotthard Langhans, was erected there (Figure 6). This imposing monument was one of the first examples of civic architecture in the neo-Classical idiom to appear on the continent. It became Berlin's propylaeum, marking the western entrance

5. Johann Stridbeckh. The Linden Allee from the east, 1691.

6. Brandenburger Tor by Carl G. Langhans, 1788–1791.

to the Unter den Linden, Prussia's future *via triumphalis*, and facing east toward the palace in the heart of the city.[9]

At the founding of Dorotheenstadt, the Linden Allee became the major axis of the capital's expansion toward the west and south. Every surveyor's compass would be fixed upon its center line. A detail of the J. F. Schneider plan of 1802 demonstrates this fact clearly (Figure 7). All of Friedrichstadt, the large fan-shaped section toward the southwest, would be solidly keyed to the Linden Allee in the north.[10] Begun under Friedrich III as Elector of Brandenburg (1688–1701), later as Friedrich I, King *in* Prussia (1701–1713), the development of this section of the capital was substantially enlarged in additional building campaigns launched by Friedrich Wilhelm I (1713–1740) between 1721 and 1736.[11] This major addition to the urban framework of Berlin continued the city's programmatic expansion toward the west. In contrast to the undirected development to the east of old Cölln and Berlin, the new Friedrichstadt follows a rigid pattern in which city blocks and axes reflect the uncompromising authority of its builder-kings. Its streets are straight, its planning regular, its borders clearly defined. Many of its residents were forced to live there by royal decree.

In conception, this new quarter began as a systematic continuation of Dorotheenstadt toward the south. In the first years of construction, from 1688 to 1706, the axis of the Linden Allee was repeated in parallel east-west avenues established at regular intervals to the south, and Friedrichstrasse became the central north-south spine. The original section of this street had already been shown by Schultz in his aerial view of 1688 (see Figure 4). At that time, it bisected Dorotheenstadt, connecting it by bridges to the countryside north and south of the city. By 1736, this prominent artery had been extended to the Oranienburger Tor, some distance beyond the Spree, in the north and to the Hallesche Tor at the southern apex of Friedrichstadt. Its total length measured 3.5 kilometers, more than three times the length of the Linden Allee, its perpendicular base line.[12]

Cutting through the flat countryside, through swampy marshes and meadows, the uncompromising axiality of this street was underscored by its architectural composition. Dismar Dägen, a Dutch artist, may have been the painter of a contemporary canvas which depicts Friedrichstrasse in its monotonous, almost hypnotizing, regularity (Figure 8). Planned by the surveyors of the king's army, its uniform town houses designed by captain-architects and constructed under the supervision of military officers, Friedrichstrasse readily reveals the bureaucratic mentalities which created it.[13] Even the workmen depicted in the foreground, whether

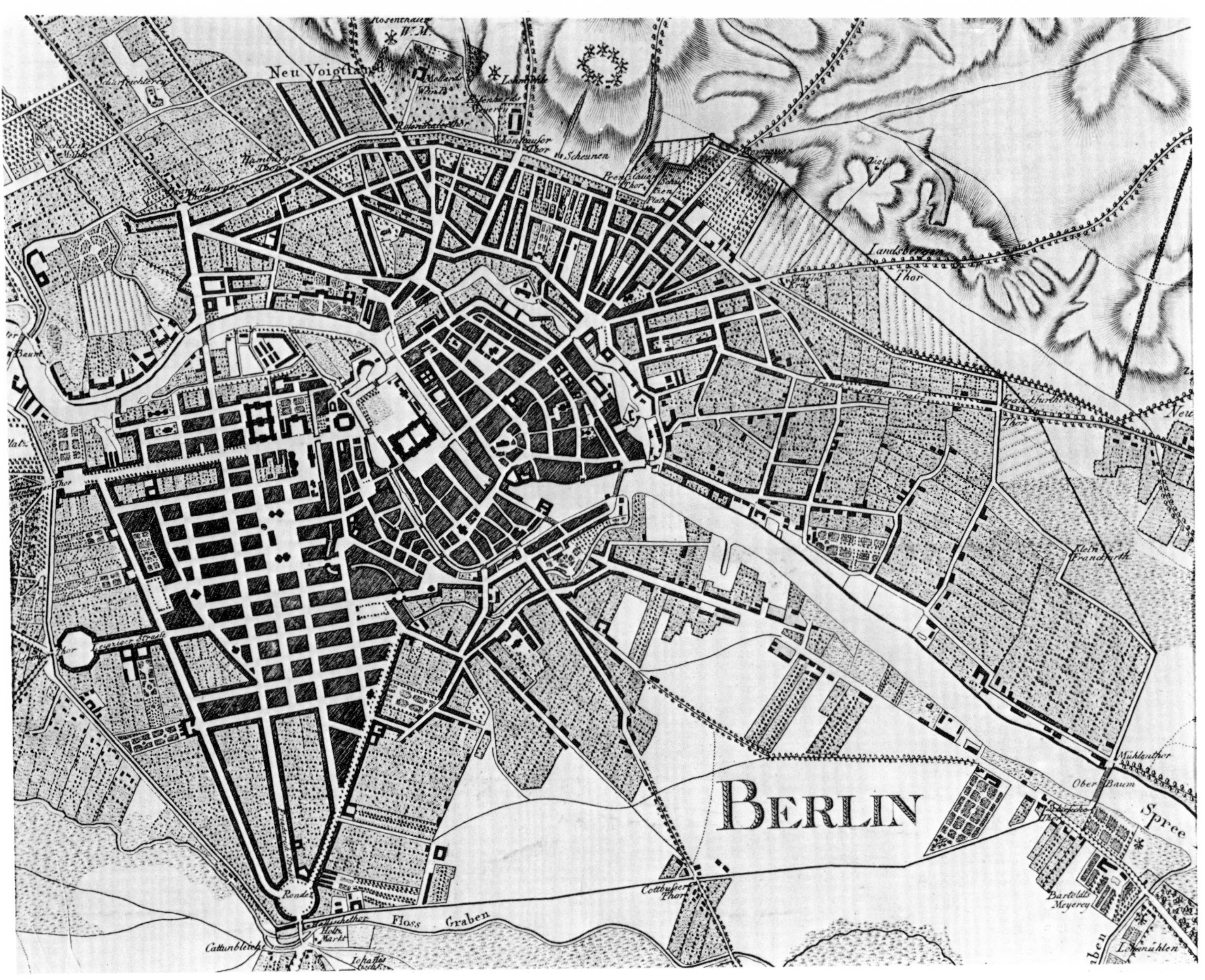

7. J. F. Schneider. Detail from map of Berlin and environs, 1802.

driving piles, pushing wheelbarrows, or directing the work, seem reduced to insignificance by the overwhelming presence of the relentlessly repeated facades.[14] Even the usually uncritical Nicolai could not refrain from commenting upon this character when he described this street in his record of Berlin's landmarks. In 1786 he wrote: "The houses along the streets which were built under King Friedrich Wilhelm are for the most part only two stories high and under a single continuous roof, which

8. Dismar Dägen (attributed). Construction of row houses along Friedrichstrasse; view from the south, 1732.

gives them a somewhat monotonous appearance."[15] Madame de Staël seemed somewhat more sympathetic, though not really enthusiastic, when she recorded her impressions of Berlin during a visit in 1804: "Berlin is a large city, the streets of which are very broad and perfectly straight, the houses handsome, and the general appearance regular; but as it is not long since it has been rebuilt, one sees there no traces of earlier times . . . Berlin, an entirely modern city, beautiful as it is, makes no serious impression; it reveals no marks of the history of the country, or the character of its inhabitants, and its magnificent newly built houses seem destined only for the convenient assemblage of pleasure and industry."[16]

The gridiron pattern of Friedrichstadt, with its uncompromising axes of streets lined with economy buildings modeled after Dutch prototypes, was only one aspect of its planning program. Another important aspect was the provision of several city squares, most of which were situated at the periphery of the new urban section toward the south and west between 1732 and 1736. At the southern terminus of the Friedrichstrasse, en route to Tempelhof where Friedrich Wilhelm I had his largest military drill field, a circular plaza was created, the so-called Rondeel (Bell'Alliance Platz after 1814). Its basic form appears to have been derived from the Place des Victoires in Paris, and, in its residential character, it resembles Parisian squares of the seventeenth century. Unlike the French example which is located near the heart of the city, however, Berlin's Rondeel is an outlying element, acting like a large vestibule to the new quarter of Friedrichstadt.[17] Its undisturbed central void could accommodate the incoming flow of military and other traffic from the Hallesche Tor, which would then be channeled into one of three major arteries converging at the Rondeel. In this respect it resembles the Piazza del Popolo in Rome, though it lacks a religious or civic monument typical of Italian examples.

The peculiarly Prussian character of the Rondeel, moreoever, is vividly demonstrated in a contemporary painting by an unknown artist (Figure 9). It shows the plaza and its surroundings, the strong spokes of the Wilhelmstrasse at the left, the Friedrichstrasse on axis and the Lindenstrasse at the right. The isolation of the plaza is emphasized by its enclosure: a continuous and uniform row of houses encircling it and extending the length of its connecting arteries. The planning of the area was clearly motivated by the same sense of economy and absolutist authority as the rest of Friedrichstadt. In fact, the only indications of human activity in the painting are restricted to Prussia's military: a guard detachment at the gate and a marching company within the plaza. Only the placement of a centrally located fountain shows some concern for enlivening the visual qualities of the site. These subsidized planning schemes of absolutist kings may have been the models for the barracks-like tenements of a later time condemned by Werner Hegemann in *Das steinerne Berlin: Geschichte der grössten Mietskasernenstadt der Welt*.[18]

Another square was located at the western terminus of the Leipziger Strasse, Berlin's second most important east-west axis, parallel to and south of the Unter den Linden. The form of this plaza may have been inspired by the polygonal outlines of the Place Vendôme. Again, unlike its famous Parisian counterpart, the so-called Achteck (Leipziger Platz after 1814) remained isolated from the fabric of the city. In Schneider's plan it appears as a large open space attached to a long axial channel, but it has no other connection with the city. Facing onto the Potsdamer Tor and the road leading to Friedrich II's favorite residence near Potsdam, the

9. Anonymous. The Rondeel with the Hallesche Tor, ca. 1735.

Achteck would be considered by Friedrich Gilly and later by Schinkel as the appropriate site for the projection of large-scale civic monuments.

The last of these peripheral squares of Friedrichstadt has already been mentioned. Located at the terminus of the Linden Allee and connected with the route to Charlottenburg, it was originally called the Quarrée. Until the erection of Langhans' Grecian propylaeum, this square had been treated as simply another checkpoint, one of several along Berlin's customs wall. Heavily guarded, as Wilhelm Chodowiecki's etching of 1764 shows (Figure 10), the old Brandenburg Gate, erected in 1734, was part of the continuous enclosure which controlled entry to the capital. The customs wall had been completed by 1736 and produced drastic planning limitations for Berlin until its demolition more than one hundred years later.[19] In the south and west it connected the outer edges of the three major peripheral squares and marked the furthest extension of Friedrichstadt.

In Schneider's plan the entire gridiron triangle of Friedrichstadt appears like a two-dimensional planning exercise (see Figure 7). Even the provision of several squares within the residential area, such as the dominant oblong of the Gendarmenmarkt with its theater and flanking

10. Wilhelm Chodowiecki. The Quarrée with customs wall and old Brandenburger Tor, 1764.

churches, cannot disguise the inherent monotony of the rectangular street plan. Furthermore, the royal engineers who served as surveyors to the kings did not succeed in integrating Friedrichstadt with the old urban core toward the east. Remnants of the outdated seventeenth-century fortifications still prevented communication between old and new parts of the capital. Not one major thoroughfare of the new project united these sections of the city; not one important east-west artery crossed the island and continued into old Berlin.

The Linden Allee remained the most important spine of modern development toward the west and the base line for Friedrichstadt toward the south. Yet, despite all of its power of direction, generous width, and dominant axiality, it was not effectively connected with the palace, the island, and the Spree. Goerd Peschken has suggested that Andreas Schlüter made a conscious attempt to correlate the axis of the Linden avenue with Portal V of the north or garden facade of his palace, which was erected between 1698 and 1703.[20] Yet, it appears that Schlüter was primarily concerned with a traditionally oriented scheme whose main axis would be keyed to the old sections of Berlin east of the river. Even though he had witnessed the expansion of the capital to the west and had worked toward the realization of the Zeughaus west of the island, other factors may have convinced him that an eastern orientation of the new palace was more appropriate.

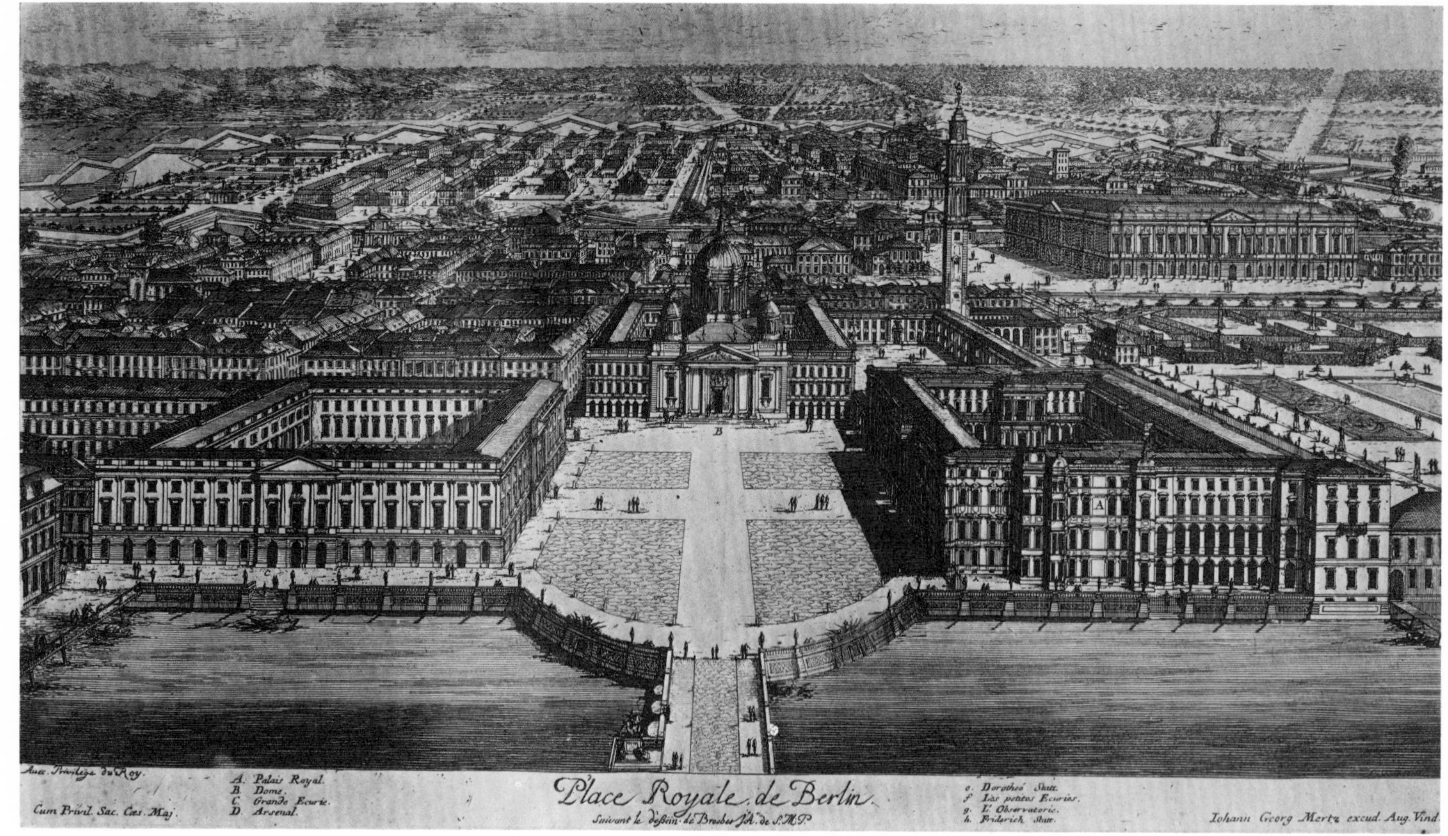

11. J. B. Broebes. Project for the expansion of the Königliche Residenzschloss, attributed to Andreas Schlüter, after 1700.

Berlin before Schinkel's Time

J. B. Broebes' aerial perspective (after 1700) of a project attributed to Schlüter supports this argument (Figure 11).[21] The palace complex is seen from the east; in the center foreground is the Lange Brücke (or Kurfürstenbrücke). A projection of its roadway was provided to receive Schlüter's famous equestrian statue of the Great Elector in 1703 (see Figure 12),[22] appropriately placed here since the bridge connected east of the river with the Königsstrasse leading to the St. Georgenthor (or Königsthor), one of Berlin's oldest city gates and the traditional entry point of its early Hohenzollern rulers to the capital.[23] The western end of the bridge opened onto a deep *cour d'honneur* leading to a dominant domed church and flanked by the palace on the right and stables on the left. While the palace retains remnants of the Renaissance château along the banks of the Spree, the church and royal stables were to be totally new. The latter, with its square plan, interior court, and the impressive articulation of its facades is similar to another building on which Schlüter worked, the Zeughaus, seen at the upper right.[24] Also clearly shown is Schlüter's project for a gigantic tower, the Münzturm, which would house not only the royal mint but also hydraulic equipment to serve the fountains in the palace gardens. Planned as the city's tallest structure, it would rise at the northwest corner of a hospital wing, west of the palace.

This superb engraving, outlining every major building in great detail, can even convince one of the validity of Peschken's reconstruction of the alignment of the center line of the Linden avenue with Portal V of the north facade of the palace. Yet, one cannot ignore the decisive orientation to the east, which is, after all, so strikingly demonstrated in Broebes' presentation.

Schlüter's intention to design for Prussia's provincial capital a palace as comprehensive as Inigo Jones's project for Whitehall and as stately as Louis XIV's Louvre was never realized. The partially completed Münzturm collapsed in 1706; the court chapel and stables were never begun. The magnificent southern facade of the palace faced onto a relatively narrow Schloss-Platz (Figure 12). Only the impressive monument to the Great Elector, together with the city palace of Graf von Wartenberg (1701–1702; later the Alte Post) on the east bank of the Spree, remained to give some indication of the intended scope of Schlüter's plans. His efforts produced only a limited coordination between the old quarters of Berlin and his new, incomplete palace block on the island. The outstanding architect of the Baroque in northern Germany was not able to unify the four major topographical components of Berlin: river, island, building, and street.

Even as late as the early nineteenth century, the eastern continuation of the Unter den Linden was awkwardly correlated with the palace.[25] East of the Platz am Zeughaus, an antiquated wooden bridge, the Hundebrücke, still served as the avenue's only link to the island. Moreover, the area immediately to the west, with its obstructive remnants of old fortifications, could hardly qualify as a coherent environmental unit. The otherwise unconcerned Friedrich Wilhelm III is reported to have demanded a renovation of this section shortly after he became king in 1797. A detail of a plan of 1804 by J. C. Selter (Figure 13) shows the physical condition of central Berlin at the beginning of the nineteenth century. The regularity of the grid pattern of Friedrichstadt in the west contrasts strikingly with the narrow streets, irregular blocks, and plazas of the eastern sections of Friedrich-Werder, Cölln, and old Berlin. Since the time of Schlüter, several large civic and religious structures had been added to the central area, some filling spaces formerly occupied by the seventeenth-century bastions. The palace block on the island, however, remains the most impressive form within the developing capital. With its substantial three-

12. Jean Rosenberg. The Königliche Residenzschloss; south facade with Lange Brücke and statue of Friedrich Wilhelm, the Great Elector, 1781.

and four-story wings completely enclosing two large open courts, the palace complex spans almost the entire width of the island, its main facade facing south onto the Schloss-Platz, its northern flank exposed to the vast expanse of the former Lustgarten. The ducal gardens of the seventeenth century had been transformed into a drill field for Prussian troops by 1713, the year in which Friedrich Wilhelm I, known as the Soldier King, succeeded to the throne. The large area of grass surrounded by a double row of poplar trees laid out by David Gilly in 1798 and shown on Selter's plan could hardly re-create the splendor of the original pleasure garden which had been conceived by more enlightened Renaissance princes. An additional environmental problem existed directly north of the replanted area. The Pomeranzengraben, an old moat retained after the destruction of the fortifications, forced the river traffic to make awkward turns around the island and also prevented easy access to the northern half of the island. The central area of Berlin, then, was still dis-

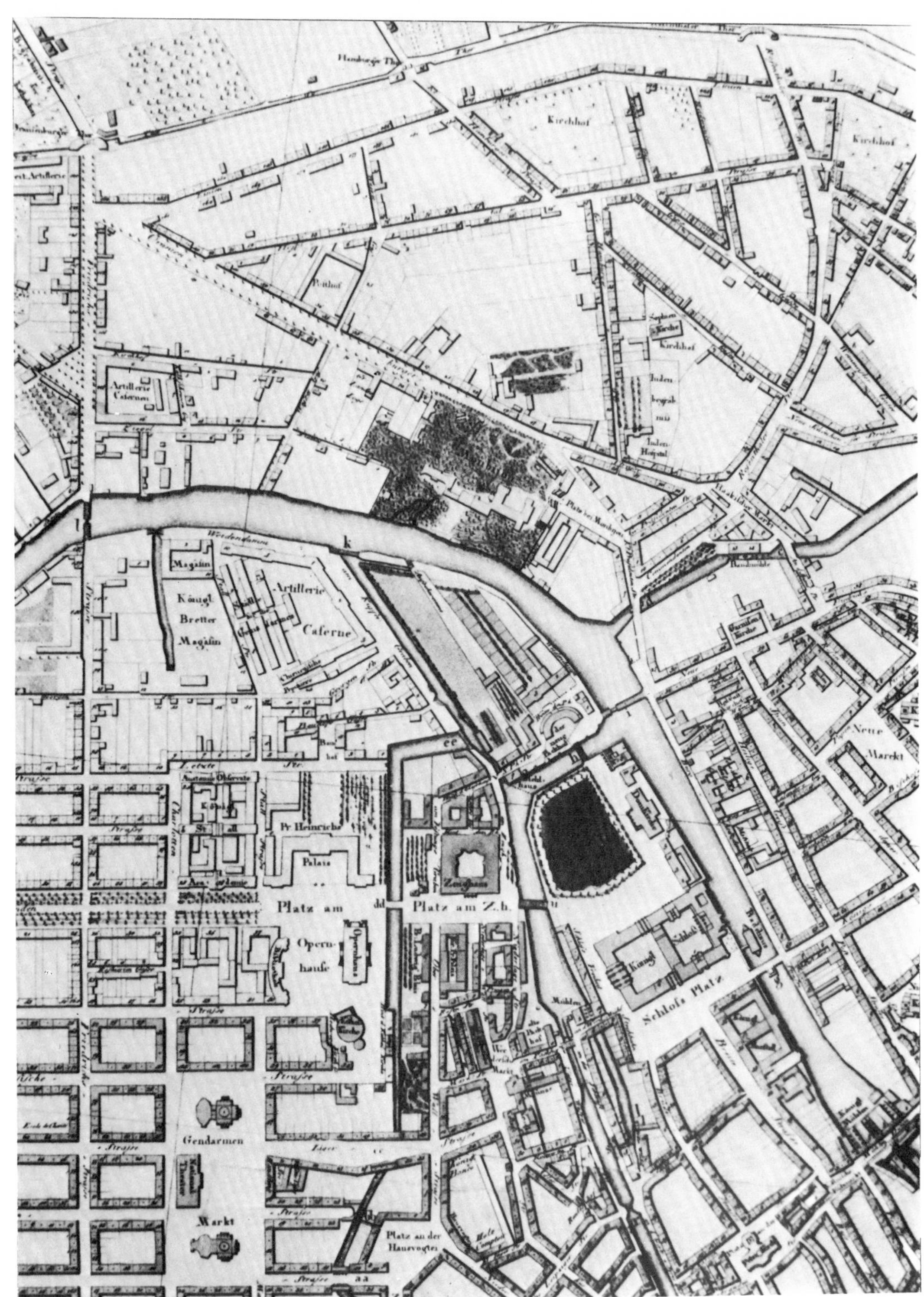

13. J. C. Selter. Detail from map of Berlin, 1804.

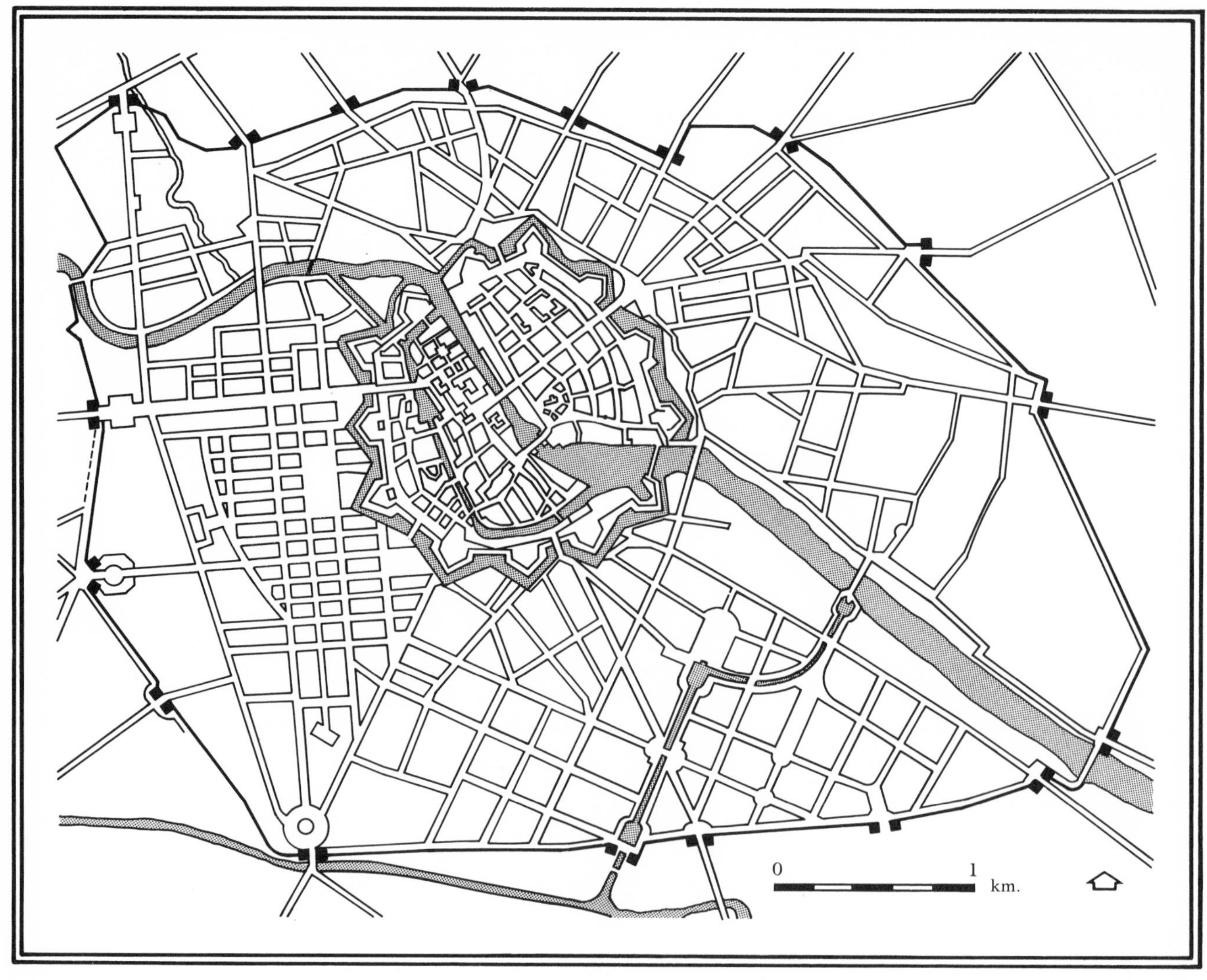

14. Map of Berlin showing expansion from the seventeenth to the nineteenth century.

organized: its civic structures unrelated; its land and water traffic hampered; its core only inconveniently accessible, while its suburbs continued to expand.

Berlin before Schinkel's Time

Figure 14 provides a visual summary of the growth of Berlin from its founding to its condition just prior to the elimination of its customs walls in the middle of the nineteenth century. One can easily appreciate the comment made by an anonymous visitor to the city near the end of the eighteenth century: "Berlin is a royal residence, a manufacturing, commercial and country town, a village and a dairy—all combined within a circular wall."[26] In 1786, the year of the death of Friedrich II and some 550 years after the founding of Berlin, Friedrich Nicolai had recorded the following facts: "Berlin has 15 city gates, 268 streets and plazas, 36 bridges . . . and 33 churches . . . The entire circumference (according to calculations by Major von Tempelhof) is 4,546 *rheinländische Ruthen* [17.138 km.] . . . and the total area of the city is 931,935 *rheinländische Quadratruthen* [ca. 3.5 qkm.]."[27] This thorough chronicler also tabulated the population of Prussia's capital as:

8,633	citizens
504	foreigners
102,498	other inhabitants
33,386	military garrison
145,021	total[28]

At first glance, these statistics appear impressive. They indicate, for instance, that Berlin had grown from a mere 6,000 inhabitants at the end of the Thirty Years' War to one of Germany's largest cities, despite the disastrous wars during the reign of Friedrich II. Yet many of the city's residents in 1786 were members of the military. The kingdom's largest garrison was stationed at Berlin, and Friedrich II is said to have looked upon the city primarily as a gigantic parade ground. Even more important is the backwardness of Berlin's social and cultural life both in relation to its impressive population figures and the physical presence of outstanding institutions and architectural projects that Friedrich II had bestowed upon the city during the early part of his reign. Although he had revived the Academy founded by Friedrich I and fostered both scientific and humanistic learning, not until 1810 was a university established in Berlin.

A partial explanation of the ambiguity of Berlin's position can be found in the military policies of Friedrich II's reign, which left even the noblest plans unrealized and the finest buildings empty. Another reason for Berlin's gradual decline from the "Spree-Athen" of Friedrich I might stem from the king's decision to transfer governmental and cultural activities to his private retreat at Schloss Sanssouci near Potsdam. In short, the official capital of Prussia was only a large and important city if measured by population statistics alone. Not until after the death of Prussia's best-known king in 1786 did the image of Berlin gradually change from that of a relatively isolated provincial city to that of a capital of progressive cultural standards. And not until after Napoleon's defeat at Waterloo in 1815 were the spirited and talented men who served Friedrich Wilhelm III able to realize the full potential of Berlin as a nucleus of humanism, scholarship, and art—a royal residence befitting a victorious monarch.

Friedrich Wilhelm III lived in and ruled from his small city palace in the heart of the capital. The building he chose as his residence was not the large Schlüter Schloss, but a less imposing structure that had been the first city residence of Friedrich II when he was crown prince.[29] Unlike his more famous eighteenth-century predecessor, Friedrich Wilhelm III was a man of simple habits and undistinguished tastes. Nevertheless, he possessed the ambition to assure a lasting legacy of his reign and a position of pre-eminence for Prussia through his personal sponsorship of ambitious building programs. Private travels had acquainted him with a greater number of impressive sites than Friedrich II had been able to see. Whereas the latter's strictly guarded youth and a subsequent war-dominated career had permitted only brief visits to Dresden and the Rhineland, Friedrich Wilhelm III found the leisure to venture as far as Rome and Naples. In addition, political circumstances and family relationships added opportunities to see Paris and London and to visit St. Petersburg, the generously planned capital of Russia.[30] Finally, he was intelligent enough to enlist the support and counsel of distinguished men of learning and the arts. Unlike Friedrich II, who failed to appreciate the native talents of Herder, Winckelmann, and Lessing, the younger monarch received and sponsored men like Alexander and Wilhelm von Humboldt, as well as Schadow, Schinkel, and Rauch. In many instances it was their creative efforts which transformed the monarch's tentative ideas into outstanding manifestations of science, architecture, and art. Though the king's name would be inscribed above the doors of the new university and the public museum, the men who served him deserve to be honored as the true source of Prussia's cultural eminence.

However, neither singly nor in combination could these men hope to create a physical context for this new spirit of Prussia's capital city to rival the grandeur of a Paris under Napoleon, the charm of a Nancy under Stanislaus, or the dimensions of the new Federal City in the United States of America. Continuing financial difficulties, bureaucratic codes, and the lack of determination on the part of the king forced the artists and architects of a modern Berlin to acknowledge certain limitations. Then, too, existing environmental situations that had resulted from adaptations of foreign models in the recent past would have to be considered before improvements and embellishments could begin.

Berlin before Schinkel's Time

In matters of city planning in particular, it appears that the Paris of Louis XIV (that is, the Paris of Colbert) was probably the single most important influence on Berlin after the end of the seventeenth century. Friedrich I's expansion of the royal Schloss in the center of the city, as well as the approach to it by way of a statue-adorned bridge, suggest that the Prussian king was certainly aware of the recently enlarged Louvre and that he might have tried to create an approach to his palace in Berlin reminiscent of the Pont-Neuf in Paris. The layout of Friedrichstadt appears, moreover, to have been inspired by Colbert's first master plan of Paris.[31] Broad, tree-lined boulevards surrounding most of Paris, giving easy accessibility to various city quarters and providing an environment of airiness and cleanliness, were a hallmark of his scheme. These additions were realized in Berlin if only to provide enough straight streets and open plazas to display the Prussian army. Friedrich Wilhelm I is said to have demanded a setting large enough to review all of his troops in a single parade. His son, Friedrich II, concentrated his efforts on building projects in Potsdam after renouncing his youthful plans for the embellishment of the capital. His initial enthusiasm and support for the creation of a Forum Fridericianum in the heart of the city dwindled after he dismissed its planner, Georg Wenzeslaus von Knobelsdorff, by 1745 and became involved in a series of wars. This forum had originally been envisioned as a Prussian version of the French *places royales*, typified by the competition in 1748 for a grand plaza dedicated to Louis XV. The combination of palace, academy, library, and opera house would have rivaled the best projects recorded in Pierre Patte's famous composite plan of Parisian squares of 1765. Unlike the French who were concerned with creating a setting for the display of the king's image, however, Friedrich heeded the critical words of Voltaire and requested a plaza without his statue but bearing his latinized name and surrounded by cultural institutions.

In the end, the forum consisted of little more than Knobelsdorff's Palladian Opernhaus and Boumann's city palace for the king's brother, Prince Heinrich. Across the vacant space created by the demolition of the fortifications would rise the undulating facade of the Königliche Bibliothek, which was modeled after a project from Baroque Vienna, Fischer von Erlach's Michaeler facade of the Wiener Hofburg. Thus, at the end of Friedrich II's reign in 1786, the central section of Berlin was essentially a loose assembly of impressive but unrelated buildings and spaces. Because of three disastrous wars, the king's lack of interest in the city, and the absence of men like Schlüter and Knobelsdorff, Berlin could boast of neither a city square as generous as the Place Louis XV in Paris nor a sequence of urban spaces as delightful as those of Nancy.

Berlin before Schinkel's Time

It remained for Friedrich Wilhelm III, then, to authorize the embellishment of Berlin beginning in 1815 and to see it transformed into an architecturally significant European capital in the course of the next twenty-five years. He was fortunate to find among his civil servants an artist and architect of outstanding ability and determination. Karl Friedrich Schinkel would utilize all of his talents to fulfill the wishes of his sovereign and, at the same time, try to realize his own principles of architecture and environmental planning. His task was to add a number of new civic and military

15. Eduard Gaertner. *Panorama von Berlin*, 1834: (*A*) View toward the south.

buildings to the panorama of central Berlin, but he also felt the need to effect order and harmony in an area of the city where existing components were isolated, unrelated, and often surrounded by vestiges of the provincial town which Berlin once was. There now seemed to be an opportunity to create a total and harmonious urban environment in the very heart of what was to become a major European city.

This task would become the major concern, spanning the entire professional career of an architect who never professed to be a city planner and who neither followed a specific theory nor copied existing schemes. He thought of architecture not as an individual expression, but as a means, subservient to human needs, within the framework of urban life. As an architect his primary concern would be directed toward the improvement of human life itself. His attention would focus on the totality of an environment in which architecture would aspire to a simple but noble goal: "The ideal in architecture is totally achieved only when a building complies completely with its purpose, in all parts and as a whole, spiritually and physically."[32]

Berlin before Schinkel's Time

In 1834, less than twenty years after Schinkel began his transformation of central Berlin, his achievement as an environmental planner was summarized in an impressive panorama by Eduard Gaertner (Figure 15). Using the roof of Schinkel's Friedrich-Werdersche Kirche (1824–1830) as a vantage point, Gaertner encompasses a 360 degree view in the six panels of his painting. The artist and members of his family are given a conspicuous place in the foreground. Closer to one of the short towers, Schinkel, with his friend Peter Christian Beuth, is shown pointing toward the almost completed Bauakademie (1832–1836), one of his last buildings and his favorite. It was erected on the site of the former Packhof, an unsightly assembly of antiquated warehouses opposite Schlüter's royal palace, which is partially visible at the extreme left. To the south, directly behind the towered main facade of the Werdersche Kirche, Schinkel had planned a broad street to be lined with shops and other commercial facilities. This street was to cut through a maze of old residential quarters and connect the Schloss-Platz south of the palace with the Gendarmenmarkt as a continuous and uninterrupted east-west artery from Fried-

(*B*) View toward the north.

richstadt to old Berlin. At the Gendarmenmarkt itself and clearly visible between its twin domed churches, stands the Schauspielhaus (1818–1821), Schinkel's first international triumph. Much further to the south, barely visible on the distant horizon, rises his Kreuzberg monument (1821), like the spire of a Gothic church cast in iron.

Berlin before Schinkel's Time

Continuing the panoramic sweep of Berlin's skyline toward the northwest, there emerges the dome of St. Hedwig's cathedral, designed in 1747 by Jean-Laurent Le Geay under the auspices of Friedrich II. For its plan he followed Serlio's drawing of the Pantheon in Rome since St. Hedwig's was meant to be Berlin's first "modern" Catholic church. The adjacent open plaza, envisioned by G. W. von Knobelsdorff to become the Forum Fridericianum, is bordered by Unger's Königliche Bibliothek (1775–1780) to the west and by Knobelsdorff's own Opernhaus (1741–1743) to the east. The recessed frontal court of Johann Boumann's palace for Prince Heinrich (1748–1766) faces onto the Opernplatz from the north. In 1810 the newly established Friedrich Wilhelm-Universität was installed in this

building and one of its prominent founders, Alexander von Humboldt, is seen in Gaertner's painting standing beside a telescope gesturing and explaining something to two friends. Immediately to the right of Boumann's building, set within a chestnut grove, stands Schinkel's Neue Wache (1816–1818), its flat roof and pediment just visible above the pitched roofs of nearer buildings. The first and the smallest of several buildings which Schinkel designed for the capital, the Neue Wache appears overshadowed by the stately Baroque block of the Zeughaus (1695–1706). Gaertner's thoughtful eye for composition and for an undisturbed sequence of the architectural scene prompted him to leave one pinnacle of the church incomplete. Beyond this point, to the northeast, we can see the simple geometric form of Schinkel's Museum (1823–1830), its long, colonnaded facade flanking one side of the redesigned Lustgarten. The brilliantly lighted Domkirche, its facade recently remodeled by Schinkel, and a corner of the royal palace at the extreme right complete the panorama of major structures in central Berlin.

From this enumeration alone one can sense the effect which so many important buildings designed by Schinkel must have had on the general character of central Berlin. Besides these structures, streets and plazas, bridges, waterways, and promenades were also created, changed, or enhanced by him. Although his efforts to transform the physical environment of central Berlin caught the attention of his contemporaries, our own century has remained largely unaware of this important aspect of his work. Despite the fact that Fritz Stahl had pointed out as early as 1912 that the total physical context was more important to Schinkel than the isolated building,[33] Sigfried Giedion and Werner Hegemann subscribed to a theory perhaps best summarized for our age by Emil Kaufmann. In *Von Ledoux bis Le Corbusier*, he dismisses early nineteenth-century planning in a single paragraph: "The new city planning can only be considered here in a few words; it can only be appreciated in its spirit of a system of individualistic pavilions. Thought of as totally heterogeneous, the buildings were to stand out splendidly. With such intentions, each one wears a cloak borrowed from the past; it presents itself as Greek, Gothic or as a creation of the Renaissance. But in this diversity the new is also revealed: a complete unconcern for the total effect. Each building remains in absolute isolation, none of them is part of the whole."[34]

Even if a cursory study of early nineteenth-century planning may have left Emil Kaufmann and others with the impression of a "complete unconcern for the total effect," it is now absolutely necessary that we begin to investigate the principles espoused by architects of that era. No longer is it possible to overlook the efforts of the men largely responsible for the shaping of the physical foundations upon which numerous modern cities have been built. It must be recognized that men like Schinkel did, in many instances, complete rather than originate urban settings. Certainly the problem of organizing an existing section within a city is far more demanding than creating an "ideal" city plan on virgin soil. And the study of a challenge of this sort would perhaps benefit modern urban planners more than late eighteenth-century schemes such as Washington, D.C., and Karlsruhe, where magnitude in planning and grandeur in building became the principal dictates of organization and expression.

Berlin before Schinkel's Time

Perhaps because current urban problems force architects and planners to concentrate once more on such totalities as environmental design rather than isolated and self-contained "monuments," it will be interesting and informative to see how men of the early nineteenth century solved similar, if not identical, problems. To finish or to correct what previous ages had left incomplete or neglected demanded not only technical skill and administrative foresight, but also flexibility, respect for the old, and the ability to meaningfully adjust old patterns to new needs.

As recent projects have aptly demonstrated, the planning of environments cannot depend on visual, formal, and spatial qualities alone. Final success must be judged on the basis of combined artistic and practical considerations or, better, on the total humanistic content which a given project embraces. Consequently, Schinkel's transformation of central Berlin cannot be judged solely as a statement of visual form; it is also a total work of art, a *Gesamtkunstwerk*, which Walter Gropius rightfully considers the architect's most challenging task.[35] Nor did Schinkel's efforts for central Berlin stand alone in history; they were contemporary with planning schemes being carried out by modern architects in other European cities. The names of John Nash, Leo von Klenze, Friedrich Weinbrenner, Giuseppi Valadier, and the French team of Percier and Fontaine come readily to mind. Schinkel knew most of them personally, and his comments and observations on their work, which will be referred to or quoted subsequently, are illuminating judgments of his contemporaries' abilities. Schinkel deserves to be counted among these traditionally accepted planners of the nineteenth century, even though his works were created within the context of a particular set of circumstances that distinguish both the problems confronting him and the solutions he proposed.

Before a final and critical conclusion regarding his achievements can be reached, two important aspects of his professional career must be investigated: first, his extensive and diversified training; second, the practical application of his developing principles. Only after a careful study of several forces which shaped his talents and skills will it be possible to trace the sequence of his planning projects and to evaluate their merits and faults.

Berlin before Schinkel's Time

II Schinkel's Training in Berlin

The most productive years of Schinkel's career did not begin until 1815—almost twenty years after his initial introduction to the profession of architecture. Historically speaking, he belonged to that "much tried generation" of artists whose careers were interrupted or delayed by revolution, political depression, and war and whose ranks included such men as the talented J. M. Gandy (1771–1843) of Britain and Benjamin Henry Latrobe (1764–1820) of the young Republic of America.[1] But, unlike the first and, to some extent, the second of these contemporaries, Schinkel was fortunate enough to be able to utilize his years of waiting in such a way that the experiences and activities of this period contributed greatly to his subsequent career as an architect.

Much like Le Corbusier of our own time, Schinkel grew and matured through his apprenticeship to some of the best masters in Europe and through his travels, which were undertaken in order to expand his study of both nature and architecture. Like Le Corbusier, he also turned to painting. This occupation taught him to extract the essence of visual experience, to record in his sketchbook conformations of natural and man-made environments and to construct in his paintings evocative scenes of a romantic world. Among the treasure of over four thousand of his extant graphic works are innumerable examples which can easily serve as guidelines to his growing artistic talents, interests, and vision. The development of his talents and the maturing of his vision occurred under circumstances which must be considered if we are to understand his unique contribution to the history of man's physical environment.

Schinkel was born in 1781, the second of five children of a prominent pastor in the town of Neuruppin in the Mark Brandenburg. Many years later the Prussian writer and poet Theodor Fontane assembled the few known significant facts of Schinkel's childhood and youth.[2] His inquiries revealed a father's sensitive response to his child's early artistic inclinations. Music, drawing, and theatrical plays were practiced in Schinkel's boyhood home. His father's guidance as a preacher and teacher and the warm and orderly home atmosphere provided by his mother became, in a sense, the foundation of his environmental and aesthetic awareness, qualities of his later life which have been noted by many writers. It was in the parsonage at Neuruppin that Schinkel participated in the design of puppet theater scenes, performed and listened to good music, and learned to appreciate the beauty and simplicity of everyday functional objects—all of which provided the seedbed from which so many of his future interests would spring.

More dramatic and possibly more important for his future career as an architect was young Schinkel's presence during the almost total destruction of his hometown by a devastating fire in 1787. The event was personally traumatic since his father suffered fatal injuries while attempting to rescue helpless families in the town. To a sensitive child of six, the fire, the death of his father, and the subsequent rebuilding of the town must have left indelible impressions. How greatly he was influenced by the total change of his physical environment from an erstwhile semimedieval town to a new gridiron-planned city must remain a matter of conjecture. Perhaps those whose childhood experiences were gained during and after World War II in the ravaged cities of Europe can judge the effects of these events in Schinkel's early life more effectively. Certainly the appearance of a new *Gymnasium* in which he would spend at least one year and a total change of building character along familiar streets and squares must have had a significant impact.

Schinkel's Training in Berlin

Five years after this dramatic event in his native town, Schinkel's mother moved the fatherless family to Berlin. The young boy entered the Gymnasium zum Grauen Kloster, but left in 1798 before completing his studies there in order "to devote his life to the fine arts and architecture." The previous summer he had seen the exhibition of competition entries for the memorial monument to Friedrich II, and at the age of sixteen he decided to become an architect. In March 1798 he entered the atelier of David and Friedrich Gilly as a full-time apprentice. The young Gilly returned from a prolonged study tour in December, and until his death in August 1800 Schinkel had the benefit of his inspiring direction. In addition, he joined the first class of Prussia's Bauakademie in 1799. After concluding his training there, he departed in 1803 for a two-year tour through Austria, Italy, and France.

At that brief moment in history, from 1797 to 1803, not another city in Europe—including Rome, Paris, or London—held more promise for an aspiring youth in the architectural profession than Prussia's capital, Berlin. Rome, the fountainhead of inspiration for Winckelmann and Goethe, had been blocked by Napoleon's military campaigns. Paris, Europe's traditional center of culture and taste, was experiencing turmoil following the Revolution. London, the largest European capital, was ruled by a sick king and undermined by financial depressions.

In contrast, Prussia enjoyed a few years of peace, prosperity, and cultural growth. From the death of Friedrich II in 1786 until Napoleon's victory at Jena in 1806, Prussia enjoyed the guidance of liberal kings. Friedrich Wilhelm II (1786–1796) and Friedrich Wilhelm III (1797–1840) did not dictate fashions of taste or principles of art. Though the latter frequently exhibited a lack of determination in matters of large-scale architectural projects, both monarchs fostered creative talents and supported artists and humanists in their conscientious attempt to change the image of Prussia and its capital from military emphasis to intellectual and artistic excellence. For the moment Berliners could again feel justified in speaking of their city as the "Spree-Athen."[3] A forum of distinguished artists, architects, and teachers gathered in Prussia's capital, contributing their energies to this renewed spirit.

Schinkel's Training in Berlin

In the two short years between 1786 and 1788 at least four architects or artists of established reputation arrived in Berlin. Friedrich Wilhelm von Erdmannsdorff (1736–1800) came to remodel the Königskammern in the royal palace. He became Berlin's foremost modern Classicist, having been a student of Clérisseau in Rome and an admirer of Palladio and Robert Adam. His design for Schloss Wörlitz (1769–1773) near Dessau, rightfully considered his masterpiece, was also the first statement of neo-Classicism in Germany. Gottfried Schadow (1764–1850), sculptor, writer, and teacher, returned to Berlin in November 1787, after a three-year stay in Rome to assume the directorship of all royal sculpture commissions and later of the Akademie der Künste. Carl Gotthard Langhans (1733–1808), former mathematician and historian and now architect, was called from Breslau. His former title of Geheimer Kriegsrath was duly changed to Direktor of the newly founded Oberhofbauamt. Perhaps the most consequential appointment to a Berlin post was that of David Gilly

(1748–1808), who had been a distinguished architect-engineer in the provinces since 1770 and who came to the capital in the capacity of a royal Oberbaurath to work as an architect and teacher.[4] As early as 1793 he founded the Bauschule and was later instrumental in establishing Berlin's well-known Bauakademie in 1799. This is the institution Schinkel attended during its first years of operation. In 1800, reports Rave, "Schinkel stands at the top of the best eighteen student-apprentices," selected from a student body of ninety-five.[5]

Men who inspire other men are rare. Moreover, an act of inspiration is an intangible force and, therefore, seldom recorded. It belongs to a vast realm of human experiences which all of us take for granted; perhaps this explains why history seldom takes it into account. And yet, despite its initial obscurity, an inspiring force sometimes manifests itself in the accomplishments of those who respond to its urge. A great teacher's noblest legacy, therefore, may be the superior life and achievement of his student. Such, it may be argued, was the case in the teacher-student relationship between David Gilly and Karl Friedrich Schinkel.[6]

An excellent recent study of Gilly's life and career makes clear that this Prussian civil servant was neither a fashionable designer nor a revolutionary architect.[7] He was a man of sound professional background, practical experience, and successful accomplishments. Before coming to Berlin he had spent most of his life in the eastern provinces of the kingdom where he had developed canals, supervised government-sponsored building and planning projects, and occasionally designed country estates for the landed aristocracy. Early in life he had learned that the services he rendered had to be fit for a young, war-plagued country and for people of limited means. When he designed Schloss Paretz, perhaps his best-known work, he did not have to be reminded by the future king "to think always that you are only building for a poor manor-house owner."[8]

In short, David Gilly brought to his Berlin post precisely what men like Langhans, Erdmannsdorff, and others lacked: a sense of simplicity, economy, and practicality. These were the maxims of his numerous publications and the underlying philosophy of his teaching at the Bauakademie.[9] His influence on the curriculum there tended to bring it closer to the practical engineering point of view of the École Polytechnique rather than the grandiose planning schemes of the traditional royal academies of art and architecture. His emphasis on construction acted as a tempering force on the young generation of Romanticists he taught in Berlin.

It is quite likely that the young Schinkel benefited from the lessons of

David Gilly much more than even the best of his biographers has implied.[10] It may be argued that it was not a spark of genius which raised Schinkel from obscurity to success, from a fatherless childhood in a parsonage to the front rank of European architects, but respect for practicality and economy in building, firmly developed professional skills, and tactfully exhibited acts of diplomacy and compromise—basic disciplines he owed to David Gilly. In addition, we should remember that Gilly possessed a keen awareness of history as well as a fondness for innovation. He owned a fine architectural library, which, in turn, inspired Schinkel's zest for travel in order to study famous monuments in their actual settings.[11] Only after all of these important but rarely documented influences are taken into account can one add that David Gilly also taught him the basic skill of draftsmanship.

While it is easy to understand how drawing techniques and practical methods of operation could be instilled in a receptive student by a competent master, it is more difficult to cite specific characteristics of planning which the young Schinkel might have learned from his first teacher. Gilly's work on the country estate and village of Paretz had been substantially completed when Schinkel began his apprenticeship in 1798. Its informal layout and the assembly of various building types and styles within the complex are not repeated in Schinkel's later planning schemes. During the following year, however, Gilly was concerned with a problem of environmental design which would later occupy Schinkel.

The area involved was Berlin's long-neglected former Lustgarten. It had been a large open space, a drill ground, since 1713, and it still appeared little more than this even after the erection of Boumann's Domkirche at the eastern flank of the square in 1747–1750. Two contemporary views by Jean Rosenberg illustrate the state of the local environment (Figures 16, 17). The first shows the square (or Place d'Armes) from the west, with a corner of the Zeughaus and its plaza in the foreground. The Domkirche is seen in the center across the empty expanse of the drill ground, while to the right stand the old apothecary wing and the north facade of the royal palace. This facade, in all of its Baroque splendor, is the most impressive form in Rosenberg's second view of the square, seen from the north. To the left is the Domkirche; behind it, the old stock exchange building. In the foreground the Pomeranzengraben is spanned by a typical Dutch drawbridge leading to the commercial area that had developed in the northern section of the island during the second half of the eighteenth century.[12] Both views of this important public space in the heart of Berlin reveal a disturbing incongruity between the permanent, sober qualities of royal, civic, and religious buildings and the temporary, non-

16. Jean Rosenberg. View from the Platz am Zeughaus onto the former Lustgarten, 1780.

17. Jean Rosenberg. The former Lustgarten from the north, 1777.

descript character of vendors' booths and shacks along the canals and wooden shelters for guards at the bridges; one can even see laundry hung out to dry in the open square. Foreign visitors who expressed their admiration for the grandiose scale and remarkable impressiveness of Berlin's Baroque monuments were equally critical of the ramshackle appearance of their immediate surroundings.[13]

This was the condition of the environment when David Gilly was asked to landscape a large part of the square in 1798. His work can best be described by referring to a later plan of the site drawn by Schinkel (Figure 18). Instead of the formal parterres, terraces, and fountains of Renaissance times, Friedrich Wilhelm III's taste demanded nothing but a simple field of grass and an orderly arrangement of bordering trees. Double rows of poplars were to screen the Kupfergraben at the west, continue along the Pomeranzengraben, and form a straight line at the east facing the church. The placement of the southern border line, however, presented some difficulty. Gilly had to take into consideration the unsatisfactory connection of the Hundebrücke with the island and the awkward relationship of its axis to the long facade of the palace. In solving the problem, he tried to accommodate both the practical and visual demands of the site. He explained his solution in these words: "I found it necessary to keep one part of this avenue in parallel alignment with the palace in order to avoid an awkward appearance [between the shape of this space and straight formations] of the soldiers during parade exercises. That is to say, if a continuous straight line had been drawn from the bridge to the [southern] end of the Domkirche, an acute angle would have resulted at that corner and the open space in front of the palace would have seemed rather oddly shaped."[14]

The resulting southern border line was not straight. Near the canal it was parallel to the old bridge (an extension of the center line of the Unter den Linden), but about halfway along its length it turned slightly in order to create a reasonable open space alongside the northern facade of the palace. In 1800 Schadow's statue of Leopold Fürst von Anhalt-Dessau, Prussia's drillmaster under Friedrich Wilhelm I, was placed where the border line changed direction. For the first time since the erection of Schlüter's equestrian statue of the Great Elector a century earlier, a freestanding sculpture played an effective role in the demarcation of vistas and the alignment of axes within Berlin's urban center.

The significance of this humble attempt to restore order and create a more meaningful environment at this site should not be underestimated. The plan Schinkel drew in 1819 delineating Gilly's solution for the Lustgarten area included Schinkel's own proposal for a new bridge to replace the

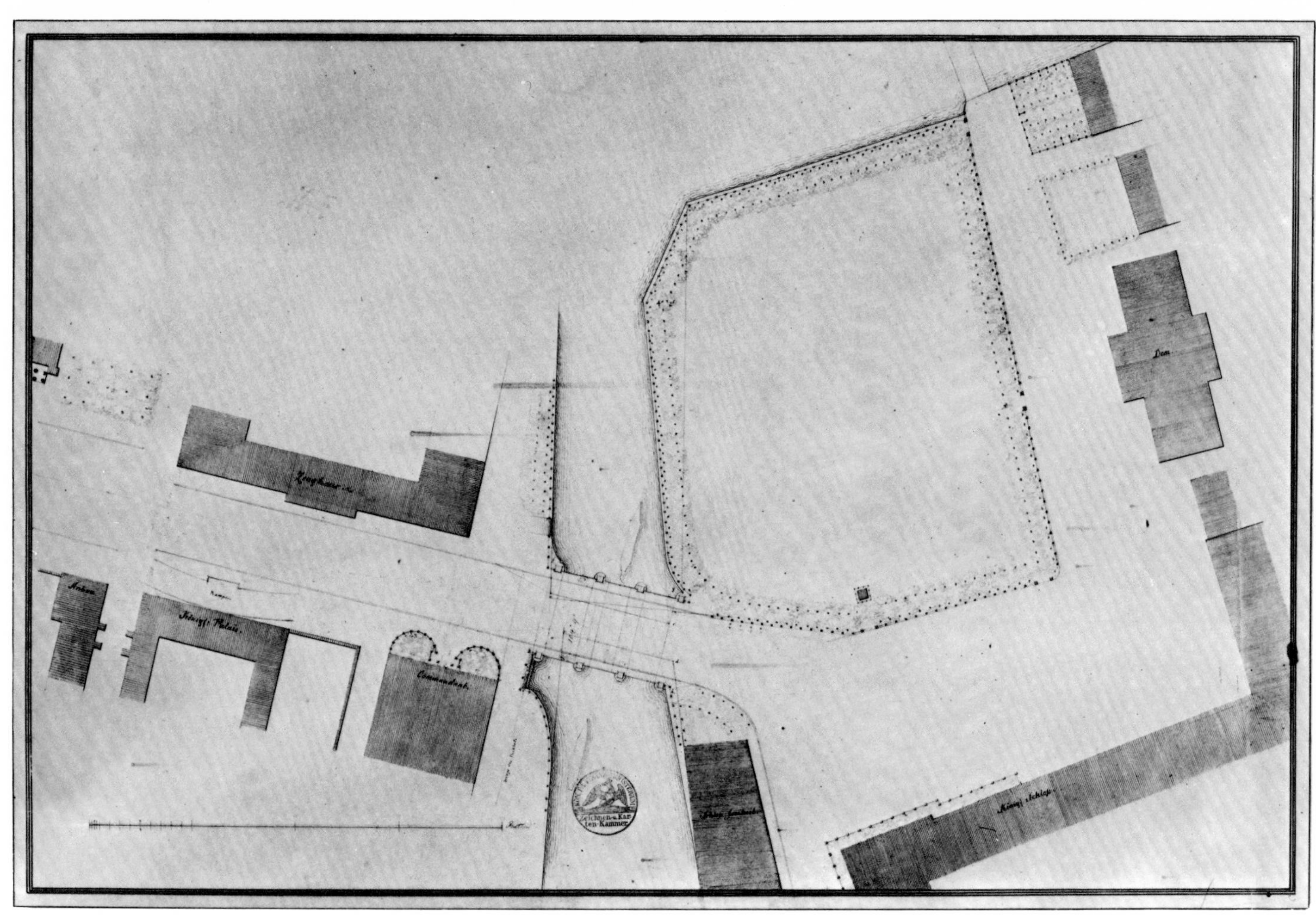

18. Site plan of a new bridge at the Lustgarten, 1819.

unsightly and inadequate Hundebrücke. He wanted to expand the scope of the redevelopment beyond the limits imposed on Gilly. This idea was not original with Schinkel, however; it had been conceived by David Gilly's talented son, Friedrich, probably shortly before his death in 1800 at the age of twenty-eight. His design for a new bridge ranks among the finest civic monuments of his short career (Figure 19). It combined his father's practical sense in the choice of iron for trusses and plates and his own inherent preference for simple, massive forms in the modeling of its stone piers and abutments.

Compared to bridge designs by other architects of the period, such as Soane's well-known scheme for a triumphal bridge in 1776 or projects of the same decade by Boullée and Ledoux, Friedrich Gilly's architectural treatment of this important, yet utilitarian, structure clearly reveals to what extent he was able to disregard fantasy and symbolism in favor of practicality, clarity, and simplicity of form.[15] For instance, the piers of Gilly's bridge are not modeled in imitation of ancient ships, as were those in the designs of Boullée and Ledoux. Instead, they are simple, half-rounded masses of plain ashlar masonry, strong enough to carry loads, withstand drifting ice, and repel river craft. Gilly also rejected the excessive application of superstructures that characterized Soane's elaborate scheme. Instead, he approached the clear-cut silhouette of the Pont Neuf in Paris, using only two pairs of obelisks as sober elements of decoration.[16]

This design was probably the young Gilly's last professional statement, and, like so many of his projects, it remained unrealized. Almost twenty years later Schinkel presented his own design for a new Hundebrücke and had the satisfaction of seeing it built between 1819 and 1823 (thereafter referred to as the Schlossbrücke; Figure 20). He rejected the powerful forms of Gilly's piers and chose a less massive series of supporting members joined by low arches of stone. The piers and abutments were emphasized by pedestals topped with sculpture and joined by an elegant iron balustrade with repeating panels that depicted confronting sea horses and tritons in curvilinear patterns. Distinctive differences between the two men in their treatment of architectural form is clear from this comparison. Their differences in treating the environment are less obvious, but upon examination it may be seen that the younger Gilly, too, influenced Schinkel's attitude toward planning.

To summarize Friedrich Gilly's character and artistic personality, one would have to say that he was among the best trained, most talented, and most promising architects of his time.[17] Guided by his competent father since childhood, trained under Erdmannsdorff, Chodowiecki, Schadow, and Schaub, widely read and traveled as a young adult, Gilly displayed

19. Friedrich Gilly. Project for a new bridge at the Lustgarten; view from the northeast, ca. 1800.

20. Schlossbrücke at the Lustgarten; view from the south, 1819–1823.

21. Friedrich Gilly. Travel companions on the way from Jena to Weimar, 1 May 1797.

both practical and theoretical knowledge as well as considerable talent and imagination. Added to this were serious application, a friendly personality, and daring, if not always revolutionary, vision. Wilhelm Wackenroder, upon meeting the twenty-one-year-old Gilly in 1793, wrote to a friend: "Any description would seem too weak. This is an artist! . . . Ein göttlicher Mensch!"[18]

Many of his graphic works betray to the fullest his youthful power and romantic individualism. His series of watercolor drawings of the Marienburg (1795), for instance, published as a portfolio of aquatints in 1799, was one of the first graphic recordings of a medieval complex by an architect of the late eighteenth century. His approach was not archaeological; he abstracted the historical monument, isolating specific parts in space and composing them into powerfully direct statements of form and volume. Gilly looked at architecture as he looked at men: as solid, monumental forces created to elevate the noble spirit of life and art and to contain it permanently (Figures 21, 22). Perhaps it was through the inspiration of Asmus Jakob Carstens (1754–1798), a distinguished painter and draftsman, and Friedrich Wilhelm Becherer (1747–1823), a successful

22. Friedrich Gilly. Schloss Friedensstein, Gotha, 1797.

architect, both teachers at the Berlin academy, that Friedrich Gilly acquired his characteristic linear shorthand drawing technique, which permitted him to summarize impressions rather than labor over details. Silhouettes, outlines, and sharply foreshortened perspectives would accent the volumetric quality of masses—the essence of his own architectural designs. The arcade at Schloss Friedensstein in Gotha (see Figure 22), for instance, is a dramatically contrived assembly of solids and voids and visual axes. It appears at once modern in its reduction to essentials and Baroque in its forcefully theatrical perspective, which drives the oblique vista to a distant point. It is obvious that Gilly's main concern was the almost Spartan purity of geometric shapes and the dominance of isolated architectonic elements in space.[19]

Schinkel's Training in Berlin

Despite his incredible inventiveness and instinct for abstraction, Gilly frequently displayed a typically eighteenth-century fascination for grandeur, variety, and Roman scale. Many of his favorite motifs resemble late Roman examples as illustrated in Robert Adam's celebrated work, *Ruins of the Palace of the Emperor Diocletian at Spalatro in Dalmatia*. His fascination with plain surfaces, battered walls, coffered tunnel vaults, and domes might also be traced to an unlimited number of neatly drawn or romantically contrived records of famous archaeological sites. The works of Piranesi, Le Roy, Robert Wood, Stuart and Revett were in the Gillys' extensive library.[20] In addition to these deluxe volumes, an endless list of less renowned illustrated sources remained to be exploited. For instance, no less than twelve books on the Greek treasures of Sicily alone appeared after Goethe visited the island in 1787. Although Gilly, as every creative man, would always try to transform historical models to make them conform to his personal artistic style, he conducted his research in a very systematic manner. Waagen reports that he had an extensive collection of views of buildings arranged according to country and also in the order of his personal preference.[21] These collections of books and drawings would ultimately become Schinkel's training ground, the first important stage in his development as an architect and a planner.

What effect did the exercises in drawing, the availability of famous illustrated publications, the scholarly yet practical character of the training under the Gillys have on Schinkel? Was Friedrich Gilly's method of analyzing, abstracting, and recording architectural form continued by his student? The answer could perhaps best be supplied by examining a previously unpublished page filled with a number of architectural, structural, and decorative details drawn by Schinkel in Paris in 1804 (Figure 23). Schinkel did not usually crowd a page with several impressions or concern himself with structural aspects and building plans at such an early stage. This particular example probably indicates that some of the construction details were included upon the request of the elder Gilly, who had asked Schinkel to investigate the *Bohlendach*, a structurally simple and economical type of wooden roof truss construction popularized in France by Delorme. Schinkel may have composed the sheet in this fashion since it accompanied a letter to David Gilly which contained specific references to his findings as well as his well-known tribute to the deceased Friedrich Gilly.[22] What is most important, however, is that part of the drawing demonstrates how Schinkel's approach had changed from that of his young master, whom he had so profoundly respected. One has only to compare Schinkel's view of a theater building at the bottom of the sheet with Gilly's drawing of the palace at Gotha to detect one of their basic differences in seeing the world around them.

Schinkel's Training in Berlin

Gilly idealized his world, abstracting it into a striking visual composition of architectonic forms and airless spaces. Schinkel, on the other hand, recorded the theater as a specific form and suggested its particular physical context. Because of the chosen vantage point, one senses the breadth of the plaza; curving ramps, a fountain, and neighboring buildings

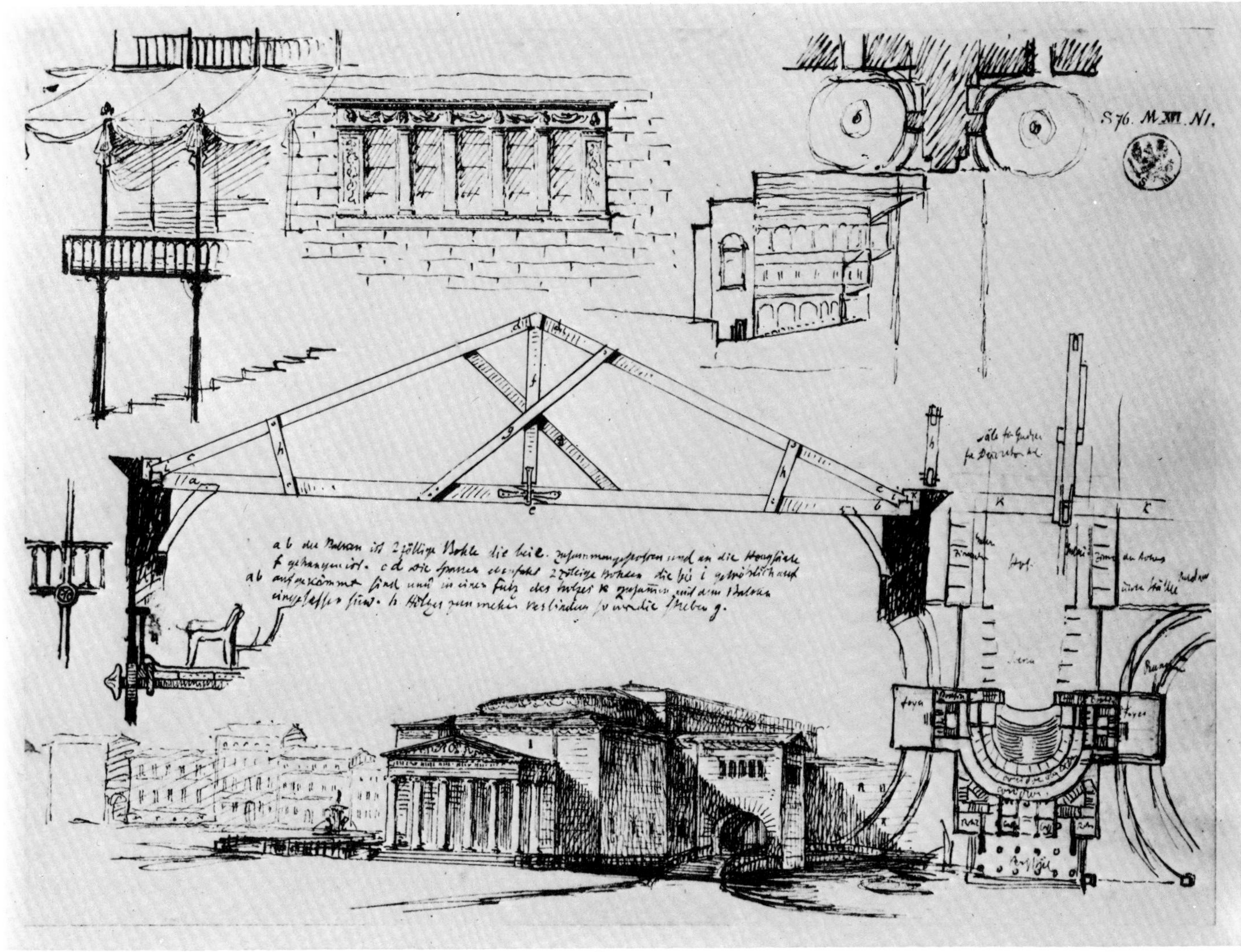

23. Studies of a theater in Paris, 1804.

convey a quick impression of the local environment. Schinkel's tendency to convey a picturesque or *malerische* quality through the use of shadow to define form and create atmosphere contrasts with Gilly's harshness in outlining solid masses. Both artists employed eye-level observation points, thus indicating their distance from the earlier eighteenth-century practice of bird's-eye views (see Figures 8, 9, 11). Schinkel's use of an oblique angle perspective, also found in drawings by Gilly, identifies his visual approach as "modern." The greatest difference between the two, however, remains in their respective attitudes toward buildings as reflections of human life. For Gilly, an existing structure was an object to be reduced to its essential forms and recorded as a striking composition. For Schinkel, a building was an operational organism to be seen and understood in the total context of its physical surroundings.

Whether Gilly influenced his student in the area of planning is a more pertinent question here. Beyond his distinctive manner of recording existing structures, what was Gilly's approach to the creation of a new environment? While he was never given the opportunity to realize any of his schemes, we can nevertheless form some conception of his methods and aims from his drawings and his plans for projects. Among these are an occasional quick sketch of a city plan, the layout for an ideal city, and numerous theoretical schemes for large-scale urban complexes, some of which Schinkel copied.[23] None of these rival his well-known design for a memorial monument to Friedrich II, which he entered in the competition of 1797.[24]

Seen in a broad historical context, Gilly's design manifests in architectural terms the age of German intellectual enlightenment embodied by Schiller, Herder, and Winckelmann. It also represents that rare and brief moment in the cultural history of Prussia and Berlin when artists, poets, and intellectuals proclaimed the greatness of Republican Rome and classical Greece and strove to rejuvenate their promise of beauty, permanence, and grandeur. As such, this monument stands as a cornerstone of the Romantic age. Moreover, Gilly's work cannot be understood unless it is recognized as the manifestation of a sincere patriotic sentiment—a necessary condition in an attempt to give formal substance to the concepts of grandeur and nobility in honor of the king whom Voltaire had acclaimed as one of the "greats" of history.

It is not necessary to duplicate previous studies which analyze the monument's stylistic heritage, but it is pertinent to weigh its merits as a statement of environmental design. Gilly reacted to the prescribed program for the competition characteristically; he broke all the rules, or, rather, he followed none. Unlike Langhans, who was probably responsible for the formulation of the specifications for the competition and who followed them to the letter, and won, Heinrich Gentz, Alois Hirt, and Gilly selected their own sites. In addition, they may have overestimated Friedrich Wilhelm II's enthusiasm for a large-scale monument to his predecessor and the resources of Prussia's ministry of finance. Gilly reasoned, perhaps justifiably, that the scope of a memorial monument to the late king could not be restricted to a small circular temple set within the narrow limits of the Unter den Linden. Instead, he demanded that the new memorial be one of the largest structures in the entire capital, visible from afar and isolated in its own majestic setting.

He selected the large octagonal plaza, the so-called Achteck, at the western periphery of Friedrichstadt. This square, although enclosed by private residences along its northern and southern boundaries by 1797, promised not only the required area for a grandiose monument, but also the proper framework for the memorial to the honored king. In addition, Gilly recognized the strategic symbolic connections between the plaza, the adjacent Potsdamer Tor, and the road to Friedrich's favorite residence at Potsdam, some fifteen miles to the west. All of these considerations contributed to a magnificent and strongly idealistic architectural concept that was graphically expressed in terms of a perspective view executed in gouache and a site plan (Figures 24, 25). His program is at once highly rational and deeply emotional, logical in its planning and overdramatized in its pictorial presentation.

A huge, barrel-vaulted gateway rises at the western border wall of the city and forms the entrance to the temenos. Its mass of solid stone and its plain, unadorned surfaces convey the spirit of Boullée, while the arrangement of its two intersecting barrel vaults recalls the Arch of Janus in Republican Rome.[25] To the right and left, as part of the triumphal arch and extending along the reinforced customs wall, are military guard rooms hidden behind screens of columns similar to Robert Adam's favorite Roman motif. Finally, crowning the arch and facing toward the cenotaph, Gilly envisioned a Roman quadriga. Unlike Schadow's vibrant, victorious team atop the Brandenburg Gate, Gilly demanded reverence, calm, and majesty: a chariot without its driver, the horses poised at a standstill before the monarch's shrine.

The gateway to the plaza can perhaps be considered as Gilly's counterpoint, in the Roman vaulted idiom, to Langhans' Brandenburg Gate, which recalls the Propylaea at Athens. As an introduction to the monument itself, however, it becomes part of a more complex environmental setting. Its main arched opening was calculated to create a frame for the monument beyond. The arched form was repeated and continued in the barrel vault

24. Friedrich Gilly. Project for a memorial monument to Friedrich II; view from the southeast, 1797.

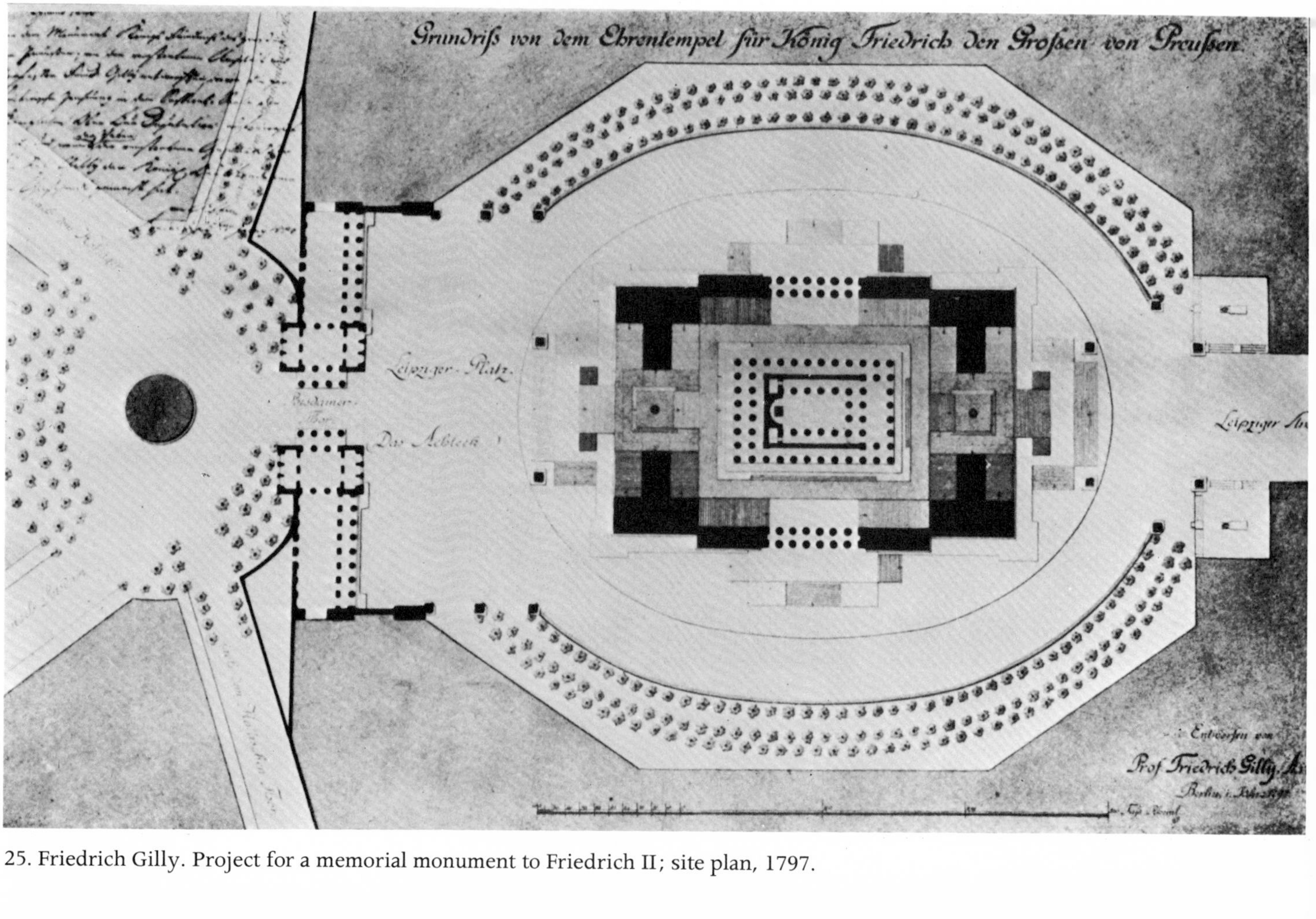

Grundriß von dem Ehrentempel für König Friedrich den Großen von Preußen

Leipziger Platz

Das Achteck

Entworfen von
Prof. Friedrich Gilly

25. Friedrich Gilly. Project for a memorial monument to Friedrich II; site plan, 1797.

which pierced the massive podium, extending the axial view from the gateway down the entire length of the Leipziger Strasse to the Spittelmarkt, a distance of about two kilometers. In addition to this controlled vista of amazing magnitude, there was also a complex arrangement of staircases and platforms around and atop the podium from which people could view the entire horizon of the city of their king. It can be argued that, though seemingly a monument of isolated grandeur, Gilly's memorial did relate, in its own way, to the greater environment of the city. However, just as it acknowledged the presence of the city on its own terms, it dominated the local setting into which it was placed. Traffic entering by the Potsdamer Tor would be channeled around the base of the monument, whose outermost edge formed a large oval. Rows of trees following the same curvature would provide shaded pedestrian walks as well as mask the existing angled facades of the octagonal plaza. New buildings in the Tiergarten area were to follow prescribed limits of height and uniformity of style. The roads entering the Potsdamer Platz, immediately west of the gateway, were to be partially relocated in order to conform to this symmetrical pattern. Thus, Gilly's conception of site development extended beyond the physical limits of his project and may be considered the basis of a master plan for a total environmental unit within the context of a larger urban setting.

In the past, the significance of Gilly's monument to Friedrich II has been seen in the distinctive pictorial qualities of the large perspective rendering. The strictly axial scheme is shown in a strikingly theatrical oblique view. By using this device he was able not only to strengthen the three-dimensional solidity of his volumes, but also to suggest the sweeping movement of the curvilinear elements of his design. Using the low wall separating the pedestrian paths from the roadway as a foreground silhouette, he created an expansive, almost panoramic, stage for the display of his monumental forms. The entire scene is brilliantly lit. Every plane, every edge is clearly defined. Nothing is faulty, weak, or incomplete. The dark, massive shapes and battered profile of the base intensify by contrast the pristine form of the Doric temple above. Not a single person is depicted. No one stands on the platform and gazes over the skyline of the city; no carriage enlivens the broad roadway. Gilly's palette of icy blues and grays underscores the solemnity of the setting—an environment of reverence and awesome stillness.

Though praised as an artist, Gilly has been criticized as a designer. His mixture of forms and styles, such as the Roman or Assyrian base supporting a Grecian temple, has long been considered an element of incongruity in this grandiose scheme. But eclecticism, if employed as a means of reconciling the values of past and present, can be justified as a valid aesthetic position. In the hands of less talented and less sensitive men Gilly's concept of a gigantic, man-made acropolis would become a formal cliché. The Walhalla (1830–1842) by Leo von Klenze and numerous projects by Haller von Hallerstein are typical, not to mention the National-Galerie (1865–1875) in Berlin, which was designed by August Stüler in accord with the initial conception of Friedrich Wilhelm IV. In addition, it has been pointed out that "the monument is not an ornament which is integrated with the space of the plaza. Instead, the plaza plays an exclusively subordinate, supporting role; it surrounds the monumental building mass like a courtyard."[26] Certainly it is clear from Gilly's own writings that he had no intention of relegating his cenotaph to a subordinate role. The monument, not the space around it, was his principal concern. Yet, he would have transformed a huge octagonal void at the periphery of Friedrichstadt into a magnificent architectural showplace and related it to the fabric of dull, monotonous urban patterns.

The true legacy of Gilly's monument must be sought in its merits as a work of environmental design, and only incidentally was it a source of inspiration. Upon seeing the magnificent presentation drawing exhibited at the Berlin Akademie der Künste, Schinkel decided to become an architect, and, although he never imitated specific plans or details, he did perpetuate and broaden certain of Gilly's principles. To better understand the relationship between master and student, an informative comparison can be made of Gilly's memorial monument of 1797 and Schinkel's design of 1814 for a church in commemoration of the War of Liberation (Dom als Denkmal für den Freiheitskrieg) for the same site in Berlin (Figure 26).[27]

At first glance, nothing seems further removed from Gilly's classical cenotaph than Schinkel's medieval church. Two worlds of thought and style appear to clash head-on, and the polarities of the Romantic age are clearly represented. If Gilly's work can be characterized as an architectural manifestation of the age of German intellectual enlightenment, Schinkel's constitutes an exuberant expression of German nationalist sentiment in Prussia. But how could he reconcile the conflicting forces within this movement? Could any architectural style at once embrace the idealism of Johann Gottlieb Fichte's "Reden an die Deutsche Nation," the realism of the costly victories of the allies against Napoleon on Europe's battlefields, and the sentimentalism of the personal taste of a Prussian monarch? Seen in retrospect, the answer is no. On the other hand, Schinkel could not have known then that the forms which had appeared "German" to a young Goethe at Strassburg and "Prussian" to himself in medieval monuments of provincial Berlin, were actually French in origin.[28]

26. Project for a memorial church in Berlin; view from the west, 1814.

Schinkel could scarcely have drawn his inspiration for a projected national memorial church in Prussia's capital from the cultural heritage of the very land whose feared and despised emperor had finally been defeated. Nor could he have found approval for such an interpretation of a "vaterländischen Styl" from a Prussian king who, unlike Friedrich II, spoke German to diplomats, generals, and servants alike.

Schinkel's design for a memorial church resulted from a conscious effort to transform Goethe's rediscovery of a Germanic medieval past into a national and modern architectural statement. Although certain Italianate forms and details are noticeable, the young Prussian architect tried to emulate Goethe's favorite Münster in Strassburg. In the nature of its style, in its enormous size, and especially in the spirited message of Schinkel's accompanying writings, one can easily discern artistic and symbolic qualities that link Berlin with Strassburg. It appears to be no coincidence that a large rendering of the west facade of the Strassburger Münster had recently been completed by Schinkel and would later be displayed in the royal palace in Berlin (Figure 27).[29] However, the major

27. Rendering of the west façade of Strassburger Münster, with second tower added, ca. 1812.

components of the west facade of Schinkel's church in Berlin were probably drawn from Prussian models. Its octagonal towers might have derived from the *Westwerk* of the old Hohenzollern Thumb-Kirche as recorded by Caspar Merian in his view of Berlin of 1650 (see Figure 3). This relationship seems logical since the new church was to house the sarcophagi of the Prussian kings. The dominant triple niches can be traced to the still extant facade of old Berlin's Heiligegeist-Kapelle of 1288 or to the west front of Chorin, one of the best-known Cistercian abbey churches near Berlin.[30] In addition, Schinkel suggested the use of foundation stone and facing brick, a vernacular method of construction and finish common throughout the Prussian provinces during late medieval times. He had learned to appreciate the practicality and economy of this method from David Gilly. Also, his interest in and professional efforts directed toward the preservation and restoration of numerous historic monuments had taught him that the plaster coating used during the previous century had been imported and was alien to building methods in northern Germany during the late Middle Ages. One of Schinkel's lifetime efforts was directed toward the revival of this brick, or *Backstein*, architecture and culminated in his well-known Bauakademie of 1832–1836.

Beyond the Germanic or Prussian building forms and techniques, Schinkel incorporated a measure of classical formality and some Italianate details. The church stands on axis in the center of an arcaded enclosure, and it is elevated above the pavement of the plaza in order to enhance its dominant placement. An Italianate cupola marks the crossing—a silhouette that may have been derived from the lantern of Pisa cathedral, one of his favorite forms.[31]

In his design of the Dom Schinkel, the Prussian Romanticist, attempted to create an idealistic architectural statement which may appear as florid and sentimental as a contemporary novel by Clemens von Brentano. Even as early as 1817, Johann Heinrich Meyer criticized the current Romantic trend: "Greatly, even effusively, one honored the external appearances of a past which one deemed superior; one attempted to force a return to the old Germanic spirit."[32] Rave, however, was more sympathetic, calling Schinkel's attempts to formulate a neo-Gothic idiom as "a trying, a groping and a struggling, a romantic hoping and longing, and through it all something totally new."[33] In time Schinkel himself would conclude that the fusion of Gothic and antique elements was futile and that the classical style of the Greeks was the only historical expression which could inspire excellence and ensure lasting value.

This early attempt by Schinkel to build in the "ergreifenden Styl altdeutscher Bauart" produced a more serious conflict in the evolution

28. Friedrich Freiherr von Schmidt. Maria im Siege von Fünfhaus, Vienna, 1868–1875.

of nineteenth-century eclecticism than is commonly acknowledged. His design of 1814 exerted a powerful influence on Friedrich von Schmidt and his student, Imre Steindl, who transformed Schinkel's search for a modern Germanic style into formal maxims which ultimately constituted the hard-core idiom of Europe's academic neo-Gothicism during the latter part of the century. A glance at von Schmidt's west facade of the Fünfhaus church in Vienna, 1868–1875 (Figure 28), and Steindl's exuberant river facade and dome for Hungary's Parliament in Budapest, 1883–1902 (Figures 29, 30), leaves no doubt that both architects had been well acquainted with Schinkel's project for Berlin. Schmidt reduced the longitudinal scheme of the memorial church to a centralized, domed structure, but retained many features of Schinkel's original composition for the west facade.[34] Steindl's impressive neo-Gothic structure with its crowning dome evokes the spirit of Schinkel's church and even borrows certain details from a drawing of the side elevation of a somewhat modified final version.

29. Imre Steindl. The Parliament House, Budapest, 1883–1902.

30. The Parliament House, Budapest; detail of dome.

The importance of the purely formal qualities of Schinkel's design for the memorial church in the context of nineteenth-century architecture is probably much greater than has been previously recognized.[35] Its value as an example of environmental design may also prove to be of critical significance for this study. In comparing the church and its plaza to Gilly's monument to Friedrich II, it is necessary to realize that both men, master and student, attempted to create a total physical environment and not merely an isolated, self-contained monument.

Schinkel's site plan for the Dom (Figure 31) echoes Gilly's characteristics of dominance, axiality, and symmetry; in other respects it appears more realistic in approach and presentation. Both the written specifications and the graphic documentation of the site communicate Schinkel's concern for the nature of an actual situation. He first surveyed the entire area and recorded its correct topographical conditions. While Gilly had ignored the true size and shape of the Achteck in his site plan, showing it as a large elongated octagon, Schinkel accurately recorded the existing plaza and indicated the changes necessary to accommodate his proposed monument. He also noted that the plaza was surrounded by private property, which had to be respected in the process of enlarging the site. In his specifications he emphasized the necessity of purchasing land, changing roads, and extending the customs wall in order to guarantee the professional legality of his proposals. In this plan, the arcade shown in the sketch of the west facade was replaced by a screen of natural foliage. Whether for visual or economic reasons, Schinkel must have felt that Berlin's unsightly customs wall should be obscured, rather than strengthened as Gilly had proposed.

His "Neues Potsdamer Thor" is a much less significant element within the total complex than was Gilly's grand gateway. And yet Schinkel realized that the entrance from the west was a controlling factor in the visual comprehension of his monument. His sketch shows the view a visitor would see upon passing through the gateway: the elaborate west facade of the church seen on axis. Gilly's temple was also placed on axis with his entrance arch, but in rendering the scene he chose an unusual viewpoint showing the monument at an oblique angle from the southeast and thus breaking with the traditional practice of focusing on the major axial elevation.[36] Schinkel adopted this pictorial device in other schemes and expanded its potential to incorporate peripheral features of an existing environment that would affect his own addition. Though Gilly's fertile imagination first conceived a modern visual approach to architectural form in space, Schinkel's more rational direction made this new vision useful for practical, functional purposes.

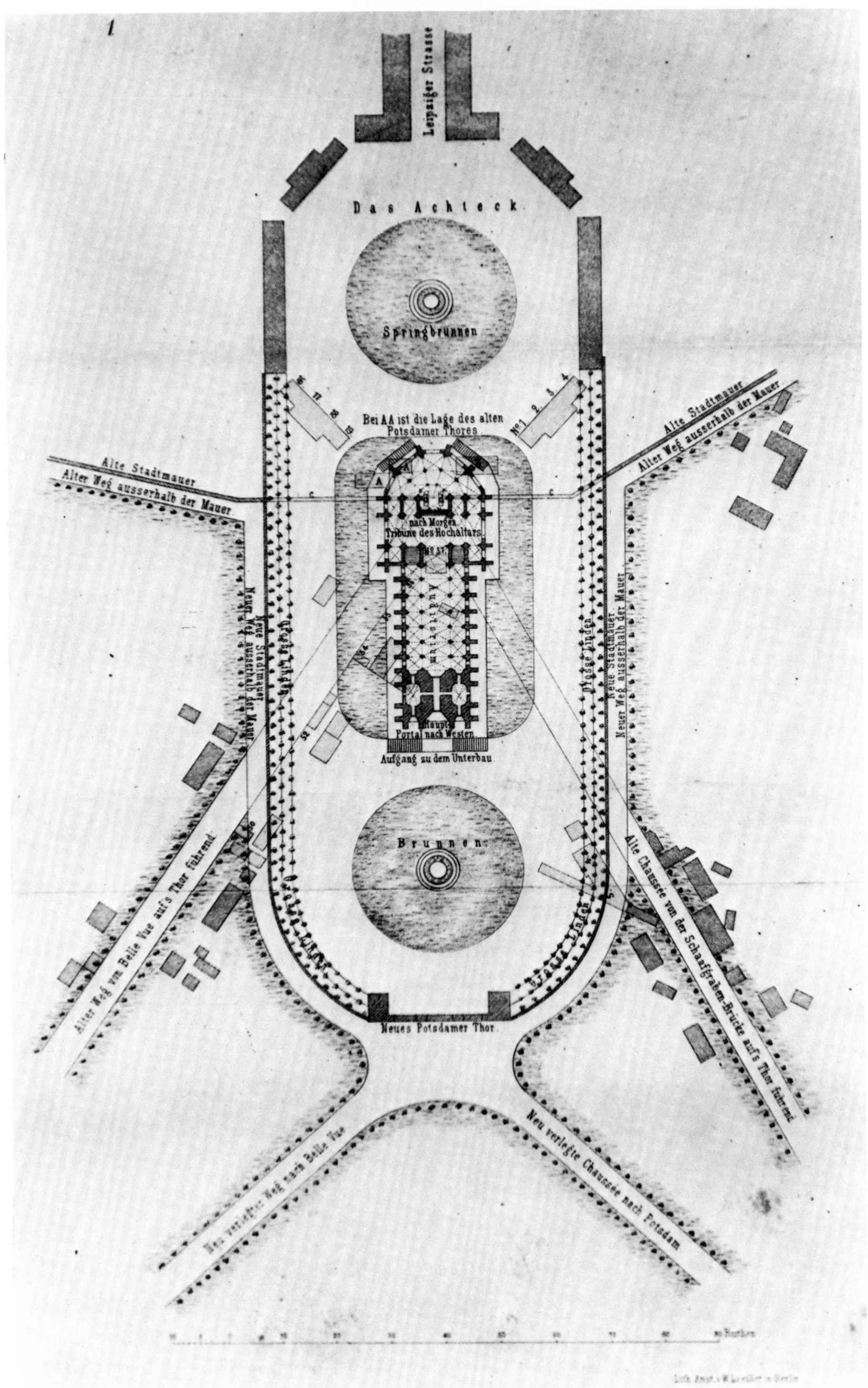

31. Project for a memorial church in Berlin; site plan at the Achteck.

Even during the early part of his career, a characteristic trait in Schinkel's professional attitude—the recognition of the existing physical conditions as a prerequisite for the implementation of his own programs—stands in contrast to that of Gilly. However flamboyant Schinkel's church design may appear and however demanding he may seem in his requests for large public spaces surrounding his structure, his written and graphic documentation concerning site utilization, purpose of program, and projected solutions is presented in a realistic and professional manner. One quickly detects a personal inclination toward the orderly and the logical. For instance, his first act in approaching the problem of a great religious monument was to study the existing conditions of the site. His survey of the Achteck and surrounding area resulted in a topographical record which was more accurate than the best previous one by J. C. Selter of 1804 (see Figure 13).[37]

Schinkel, the professional architect and civil servant to the crown, would always be conscious of the realistic nature of his work and duties. Careful investigations, such as site studies and budget calculations, would precede his involvement as architect or planner, and often entire introductory passages of his specifications or *Begleitschreiben* were headed *Vortheile* (advantages) in order to stress the practicality or necessity of his professional judgment or choice. Similar arguments would be used whether choosing a museum site or appealing for the preservation of a sculpture by Andreas Schlüter. Financial matters were treated in an equally professional manner, as his extant estimates for the Museum am Lustgarten clearly reveal.

Friedrich Gilly, on the other hand, had seldom been forced to recognize limitations or make concessions. Although his project for the Friedrich II memorial is an example of his artistic genius and visionary approach, the impressive design would lose much of its impact if judged on strictly realistic terms. As he neglected to record the correct conditions of his chosen site, he made no attempt to correlate his plans with the requirements of the competition. Compromise, even for the sake of seeing his design realized, was not one of his professional traits. For the young Gilly, it was the expressed sentiment and the grandiose scale of a monument which superseded his father's credo of simplicity and restraint.

Although Schinkel did not accept compromise in matters of principle, he certainly learned to be flexible and adaptable in dealing with the problems and limitations of his official position.[38] For instance, his willingness to provide alternate stylistic schemes, as in the case of the Friedrich-Werdersche Kirche, may have been looked upon by him as an inevitable consequence of working for a king with limited aesthetic

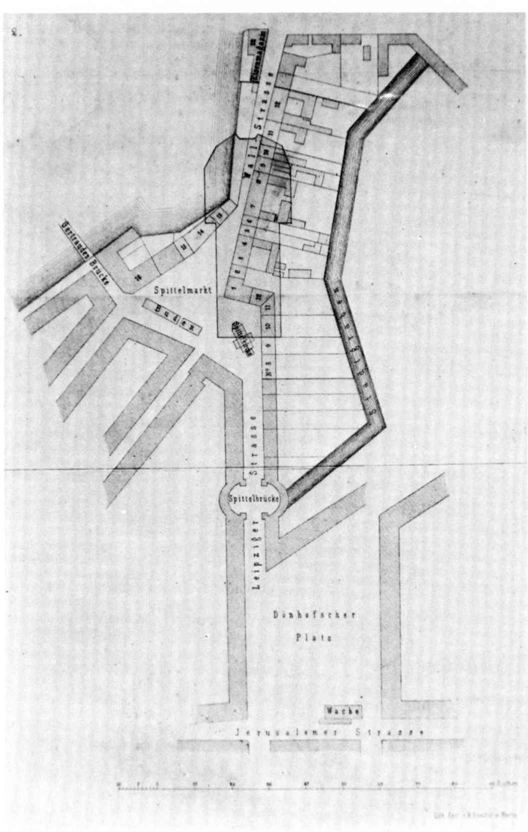

32. Project for a memorial church in Berlin; alternate site at the Spittelmarkt.

judgment, imagination, and taste. Even Rulemann Eylert, perhaps the most flattering of the monarch's biographers, would occasionally acknowledge the king's severely simple manner in confronting life, politics, and art.[39] Known to his intimates as a man of "three-word conversations," Friedrich Wilhelm III would often limit his approval of works of art on exhibit to the sounding of a nasal "Hm!" High praise, according to Schadow, would be expressed by a short "Hm, hm!" sometimes followed by "that's all right."

In regard to Schinkel's project for the memorial Dom, the architect himself may have sensed that all of his efforts could have been in vain had he not tried to gain the fullest support of his royal patron. Consequently, he was ready to provide whatever was necessary to pursuade the king to commission his design. The monarch had apparently expressed interest in seeing a structure of such size and symbolic importance in closer proximity to the royal palace, and the Spittelmarkt at the eastern terminus of the long Leipziger Strasse might have been suggested. Schinkel realized the dilemma of his position: if he refused to anticipate this change, his chances to build would surely have been lost; if, on the other hand, he complied unquestioningly, the scope of his envisioned environmental program would have been curtailed. Reacting diplomatically, he prepared an alternate site plan which complied with the king's suggestion (Figure 32). However, he refused to go beyond a diagrammatic scheme and pointed out that this arrangement would minimize the symbolic and civic values that were to be manifested in the great church. A shrine to the nation adorned with the sculptured portraits of Prussia's kings could hardly fit into a congested commercial section of the old city. It needed open spaces around it, and these could only be provided with great expense and effort at the Spittelmarkt. Schinkel carefully reiterated the advantages of the Achteck as the more appropriate setting. There he not only found the opportunity to expand freely, but he also recognized, as had Gilly before him, the strategic importance of the site. Not only did major highways from the west converge there, but the erection of a large-scale monument also presented a challenge to mold an entire environmental unit within the expanding urban quarters of the capital. The total complex would become at once a part of the city and a nucleus of attention, befitting its patron, its nation, and its people.

In contrast to Gilly's concept of a sanctuary dedicated to the spirit of a dead king, Schinkel's written statements about his complex display a concern for living human beings. Even during construction he envisioned that the project could be a workshop and training ground for a young generation of native craftsmen, artists, and even engineers. The practical experience thus gained, he noted, would be more valuable to the arts and trades of Prussia than theoretical instruction at an art academy. This urgent call for practical training voiced by Schinkel in 1814 anticipated similar demands of John Ruskin and William Morris by nearly a generation.[40] Could this serious concern for the improvement of quality and professional standards in the face of a coming industrial age qualify Schinkel to be named among the "Pioneers of Modern Design"? His demand for the good design of items produced by mechanized processes and for quality of craftsmanship in the building trades and his promotion of the arts as an integral part of life ranked high among his pioneering efforts and formed the framework for his own architectural thought. "The beautiful," he wrote in later years, "appears to be one of the bases of existence upon which rational life is built. Without this foundation one struggles with barbarism."[41]

Schinkel's predilection for economy, practicality, and quality had been fostered by David Gilly, his first and mostly underrated teacher. To

Friedrich Gilly, alternatively, he owed some of his basic and lasting principles as artist, architect, and planner. Schadow once called Schinkel "the reincarnation of the young Gilly" and, like Gilly, he was to learn that conditions in Prussia remained unsympathetic to daring artistic concepts and especially to the realization of monuments conceived in the spirit of idealism rather than in adherence to standards of economic feasibility and pragmatic purpose. He soon realized that no matter how valuable and noble the idea or how promising the project, he could only succeed if he were willing to recognize the inevitable consequence of his position as a civil servant: he must abide by the conditions prescribed by the law and by the taste of his king. The dismissal of his project for the church near the Potsdamer Tor would be only one of many instances which proved that the final success in executing a building or in promoting an extensive environmental plan did not depend on the foresight, labor, and talent of the architect, but primarily on the support of the king.

Though the memorial church was never built, Schinkel was given a royal commission for the same site in 1823. Much less grandiose in scale and less dramatic in concept, his design for the new Potsdamer Tor reflected the desires of the king and the resources of the state (Figures 33, 34).[42] Two small guardhouses flanking the opening in the city wall were all that was demanded. Although Kugler's brief analysis of Schinkel's design in 1842 focused exclusively on a criticism of its style, more recent historians have recognized that this project embraced a much broader context than Kugler realized or, for that matter, than the royal commission required.[43]

Schinkel did not confine himself to unappealing requests to copy the king's favorite city gates in Frankfurt and to incorporate the second-rate sculpture groups by Wilhelm Christian Meyers which had been recently salvaged from the old Opernbrücke near the Zeughaus (see Figure 54). His intention was to use the new gateway as a catalyst for improving the surrounding environment. Consequently, his perspective does not focus on the two guardhouses alone, but on their critical position within a larger context. He visually reverses the roles of these military and customs checkpoints, which he looked upon as "heitere Barrieren," into scenic architectural gateposts which control and direct an unobstructed vista into the heart of the city. He invites the eye of the visitor to travel the same route and distance which Gilly may have envisioned in channeling an axis through his gate and monument and continuing along the Leipziger Strasse. Schinkel's position and the nature of the commission would not allow him to propose so grandiose a scheme as a sequence of dramatic tunnel vaults to accentuate this vista, but, true to the principles of

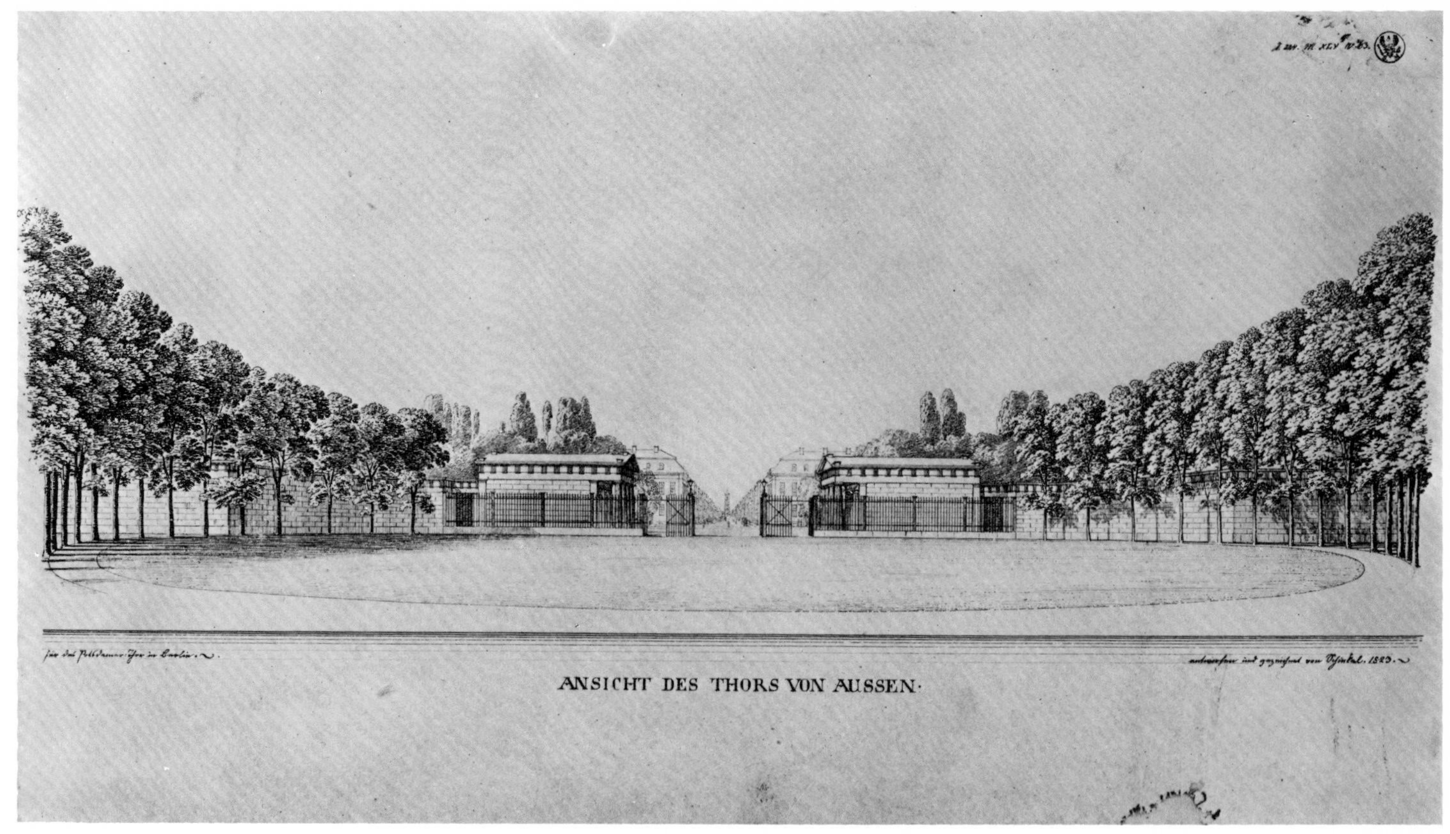

33. Design for the Potsdamer Tor; view from the west, 1823.

Baroque planning, he calculated and drew his one-point perspective as a dominant and uninterrupted axis. Moreover, he represented his overall scheme in a most realistic manner, looking directly onto the gates from the west and projecting a properly scaled termination at the far end of the street. An Italianate campanile was to rise adjacent to the old church at the Spittelmarkt, acting as the visual focal point of the long vista from the Potsdamer Tor.[44]

Schinkel also envisioned the improvement and embellishment of adjacent squares. Unlike Gilly, who had stipulated that additions west of the gate were to follow patterns of classical architecture, he had to depend on landscaping to control the uniformity of the plaza. Perhaps in recognition of the close proximity of the Tiergarten to the west as well as his desire to hide the customs wall and provide shade for pedestrians, he proposed a continuous row of trees to define the perimeter of the circular Potsdamer Platz. Schinkel did, however, rely on Gilly's earlier scheme

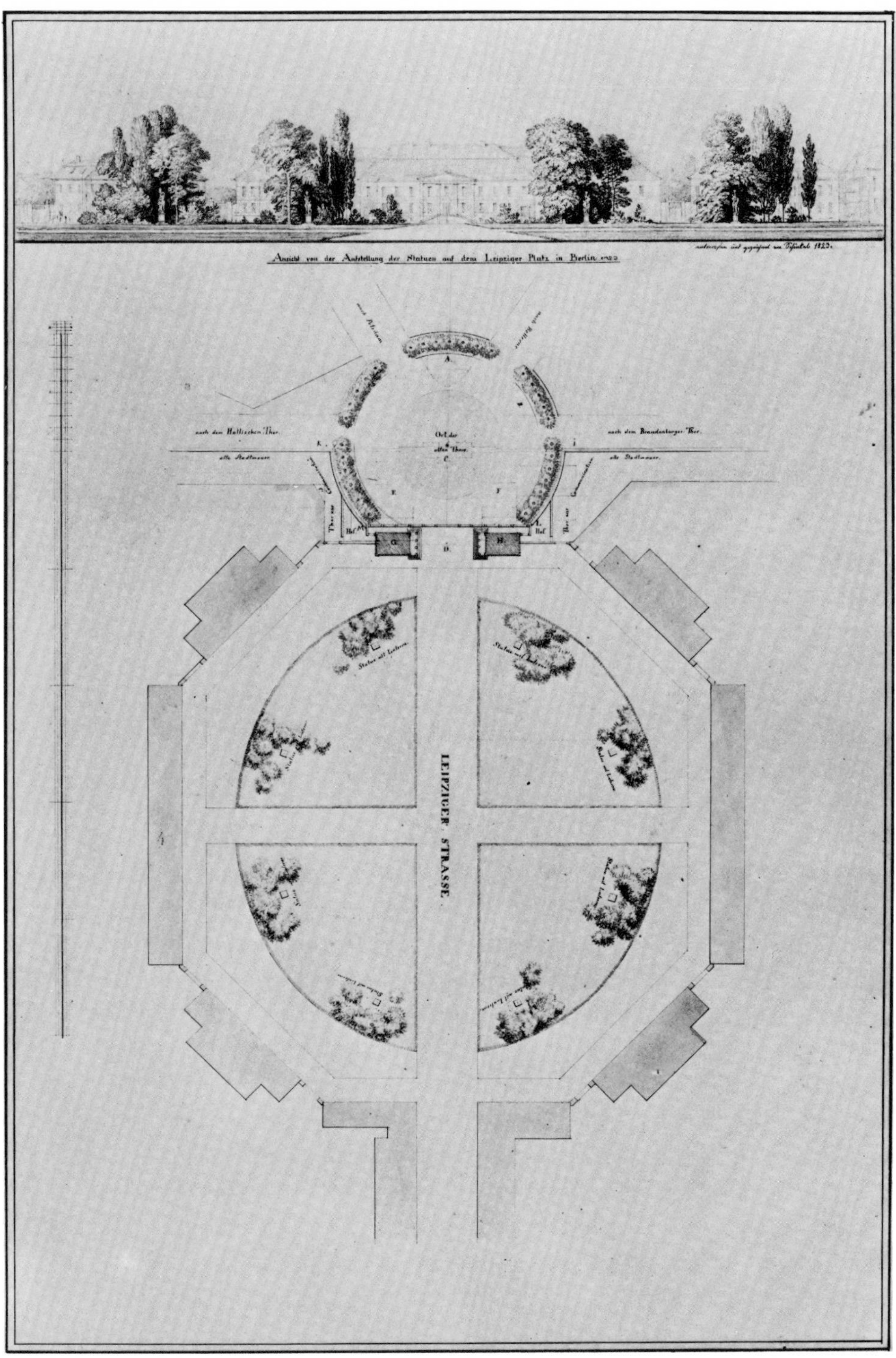

34. Design for the Potsdamer Tor; site plan and longitudinal section of Leipziger Platz, 1823.

in providing a setback of the gatehouses. This may have been done, as Rave suggested, to provide a curved frontal court for carriages and wagons waiting to be channeled through the checkpoint. Since the position of the opening was thus improved, the new gatehouses could relate in a more meaningful way not only to the vestibule-like space outside the wall, but to the larger Leipziger Platz (the former Achteck) east of the Tor as well.

This residential plaza was divided by two intersecting streets, the major thoroughfare corresponding in width to the Leipziger Strasse in the east and the space between the guardhouses in the west. A roadway to service the surrounding residences followed the edges of the octagon. The transverse axis contributed to the organization of the large open space and provided minor vistas onto the two attractive, porticoed entrances of the town houses on opposite sides of the plaza. The remarkably long vista to a distant vertical tower (see Figure 33) was thus balanced by shorter views onto larger residential blocks within the plaza itself. Schinkel's drawing of this cross-axial view, on the same sheet as the plan (see Figure 34), also indicates the character of the landscaping in the central oval. In order to incorporate the works of sculputure which the king wished to have included, Schinkel set them against large masses of bushes and trees. This picturesque arrangement prevented the undistinguished statues from dominating the large open plaza. Indeed, by several subtle means—the new position of the guardhouses, the varied width of the two intersecting streets, the slightly irregular placement of the sculpture and foliage groups—Schinkel was able to organize the formerly undeveloped area of the plaza, to disguise the irregular shape of the octagon, and also, through landscaping, to create formal patterns which would relate the space outside the gates to that within. Thus, by the most economical means and even under the restrictions imposed by the willful king, Schinkel conceived an environmental unit which grew out of but far surpassed the original nucleus of the design.

Even this limited scheme of environmental coordination was not realized according to Schinkel's program. Although the two guardhouses were successfully executed, the campanile at the Spittelmarkt was not built, and the final execution of the landscaping of the Leipziger Platz was entrusted to Peter Joseph Lenné, the Generaldirektor of the royal gardens.[45] Once more, Schinkel's plans were curtailed. His original design for this project shows, nevertheless, that his tendency in planning for a given site was always to include more of the surrounding environment than the program as commissioned encompassed. In this instance he wished to effect a visual coordination between a gateway into the city and a point within the urban center. In trying to achieve this relationship he employed Gilly's Baroque axis without imitating or attempting to rival his master's scale or forms. The project for the gatehouses at the Potsdamer Platz thus constitutes an extremely important step in Schinkel's development as an environmental planner. It is at once tangible proof of his indebtedness to Baroque planning lessons which he inherited through Friedrich Gilly and evidence of his own ability to transform principles of the past into a new vision of meaningful order.

There can be no doubt that Friedrich Gilly was a decisive influence on the young Schinkel and that his legacy can be detected in projects as late as the Potsdamer Tor of 1823. But opportunities for Schinkel to broaden his vision and thus to grow as an artistic personality were not extinguished with Gilly's untimely death in August 1800. On the contrary, his activities became more diversified, temporarily combining practical application with continued theoretical studies. In a brief autobiographical sketch written in 1825, Schinkel recalled that during the interim years prior to his Italian sojourn the scope of his artistic and professional work was enlarged and he learned a number of important lessons. It seems almost certain that he continued his training at the Bauakademie. Although still a young apprentice, he was entrusted with the task of completing Friedrich Gilly's unfinished projects.

He was also engaged in the design of several structures for a number of manors throughout the Mark Brandenburg. In most instances it was a matter of remodeling an existing building or adding a minor one, such as a garden belvedere, stable, or dairy, and it was especially in the context of these early, little-known service units for country estates that the young Schinkel continued David Gilly's tradition of economical and sound building without even vaguely imitating his specific forms. More important, perhaps, these early commissions acquainted him with the interrelationships of function and form in nature and architecture. A manor house complex in the Mark Brandenburg was not comparable to a Palladian country villa. It lacked sophistication, regularity, and poise. But it was precisely that lack of order in general arrangements among the serving and the served units which proved so appealing in Schinkel's later sketches of vernacular architecture in Italy. And should it be surprising that a young apprentice who involved himself early in his career with remodeling and expanding country estates should later become a master in composing almost poetic form and space themes for princely retreats along the Havel River? Neither the aloof crown prince, Friedrich Wilhelm, nor proponents of taste, refinement, and learning such as Wilhelm von Humboldt and Hermann Fürst von Pückler-Muskau would have asked an architect to design their country villas if his knowledge had been limited to the academic models expounded by Durand.

Perhaps the final and most consequential aspect of young Schinkel's activities after Gilly's death was not so much employment of his practical skills, but contact with Prussia's elite, the culturally and socially superior landed aristocracy. Throughout his life reflections of aristocratic bearing and diplomatic ease were evident in Schinkel's relations with the king and nobility. Whether it was the almost paternal solicitude shown him by Heinrich Graf von Reuss-Schleiz-Köstritz,[46] the favorable recommendation to the brothers Boisserée which he earned from Goethe, or the respectful praise which the king accorded his architect-servant at his death, Schinkel seems always to have been treated as an acceptable aspirant to the higher circles of Prussian society. It is possible that he not only valued his contact with and service for counts, princes, and men of learning, but that he might conscientiously have exploited them. Eager to prove to his critical relatives and to the members of the older generation of Prussia's professional elite, such as his later rival Heinrich Gentz, that he could rise from a humble background to a position of eminence, he nevertheless realized that such acceptance could only be attained by efforts which reached far beyond the acquisition of superior technical skills. Consequently, his final years of apprenticeship included not only a broadening of artistic versatility (which would include work as a designer of chinaware) and the saving of every *Thaler* to finance his anticipated trip to Italy, but, possibly, many an undocumented instance of learning the subtle lessons of how to become a cultured gentleman. The age of Goethe did not accept an architect by mere measure of academic knowledge and technical skill. A student of David and Friedrich Gilly would be expected to become a man of culture as well as an artist of totality.

Among the many men with whom Schinkel became acquainted during these early years before his departure for Italy was Heinrich Gentz, one of the leading state architects in Berlin at the turn of the century.[47] Gentz, like Gilly, had received a royal stipend for travel which permitted him to spend nearly four years abroad (1790–1794).[48] Unlike Gilly, who saw neither Rome, the city of his dreams, nor the Greek antiquities in southern Italy, Gentz was able to spend nearly two years in the Eternal City and to retrace Goethe's journey through Sicily before Napoleon's army invaded the Italian peninsula. In addition, he spent some time in Paris, Amsterdam, and London—cities which had traditionally been the goals of traveling Prussian architects since the days of Knobelsdorff. Schinkel would be privileged to repeat Gentz's itinerary within a few years; his tour of Sicily during the summer of 1804 would follow Gentz's previous route almost precisely.[49] Even more conclusive for the establishment of a close relationship between Gentz and Schinkel, however, is the similarity of their reactions to specific ancient sites. Their respective written descriptions of the theater at Taormina, for instance, unmistakably resemble one another in both style and sentiment.[50] These passages should be read by every student of architecture today as outstanding examples of descriptive and analytic writing by professional men of the past. However, the messages contained therein should be understood as tributes to Goethe, who had literally led them through this distant land of classical antiquity. He had taught Germans to be humble in the face of nature and respectful in the presence of man-made works of excellence.[51]

The professional relationship between Gentz and Schinkel cannot, however, be judged by mutually shared sentiments alone. It must be seen in the context of strictly realistic affairs, which ranged in varying degrees of intensity over a period of more than a decade, from about 1797 until Gentz's death in 1811. Their first acquaintance was probably the result of Gentz's participation in the competition of 1797 for the memorial monument to Friedrich II. Although his original presentation renderings have long since been lost, an incomplete preliminary perspective drawing of his design (Figure 35*B*) and parts of his description have survived. These documents, amplified by Doebber's reconstruction drawing (Figure 35*A*), can provide a sufficient basis for analyzing Gentz's principles of environmental planning.

An illuminating comparison can be made between Gentz's design and Gilly's entry in the same competition (see Figure 24), and, in general, there is a definite affinity in formal and stylistic content. Both men expressed their concepts of a monument to the late king in what may be vaguely described as the contemporary French ideal: massive forms, simple surfaces, and striking silhouettes. Upon closer investigation, however, both Gilly and Gentz appear to have been equally indebted to Robert Adam. Many of their decorative devices—the hunching lions on pedestals, the conspicuous obelisks, and the sarcophagus-like details—could have been assembled from the frontispiece of Adam's famous pictorial volume on the *Ruins of the Palace of the Emperor Diocletian at Spalatro in Dalmatia*, published in 1764. Nikolaus Pevsner has rightfully called this work a "hall-mark of the Classical Revival."[52] Adam's colonnade screening a deep vaulted niche in the library of Syon House might have inspired the use of this Roman motif in the two projects, though similar compositions can also be found in the later works of Ledoux, such as the Temple of Terpsichore, 1770. The broad, angular staircases and dominant barrel vaults are hallmarks of contemporary French designs by Boullée and his followers. In short, however different the form of their temples may appear (Gentz obviously complied with the competition rules calling for a tholos), the major compositional elements of both designs are indicative of their authors' mutual appreciation of neo-Classical forms and their equally successful promotion of a creative eclecticism.

In the present context, however, a far more consequential difference lies in the choice and utilization of their respective sites. Gilly envisioned a semi-isolated sanctuary at a peripheral square of Friedrichstadt. Gentz, on the other hand, chose a location much closer to Berlin's civic and cultural center. He selected a site between the Opernhaus and the Zeughaus and proposed to continue the principal axis of the Unter den Linden directly through the center of his monument. Although he abstained from the effective use of a tunnel vault to dramatize this axis, he did emphasize it by the placement of staircases and landings, the alignment of two obelisks, and, of course, the dominant form of the circular temple crowning the upper platform. However, it is immediately apparent from the perspective view as well as from the site plan (Figure 35C) that Gentz's scheme did not rely solely on the dominance of a single axis, as Gilly's proposal had, but on a balance of directional forces as well as a counterpoint of spatial and volumetric components. A cross-axis, marked by a coffered barrel vault through the base of the monument, enhanced the raised position of the temple by the subordination of the low colonnades and open spaces to the north and south, while four corner pavilions defined and stabilized the edges of the site. The statue of Friedrich II was placed, significantly, at the intersection of the major and minor axes of the composition. It was sheltered by the domed temple, but easily viewed through its peripteral colonnade.

Beyond the formal and symbolic aspects of the monument, however, there are practical features which indicate Gentz's interest in environmental functionalism. His choice of site would have necessitated the removal of the antiquated Opernbrücke. His monument would have spanned the old moat and served as a magnificent replacement for the bridge. Thus, Gentz's design was not limited to the special requirements of a memorial; it would also have improved a specific situation and the environmental control of a significant area of the city. Gilly's concern for the broader context of his design had been limited to the suggestion that Friedrich II's French library should be installed in the cavernous base of the monument. He made no mention of the possible uses of auxiliary buildings, which are shown in his rendering but do not appear in the site plan. The supplementary structures in Gentz's design, on the other hand,

A

B

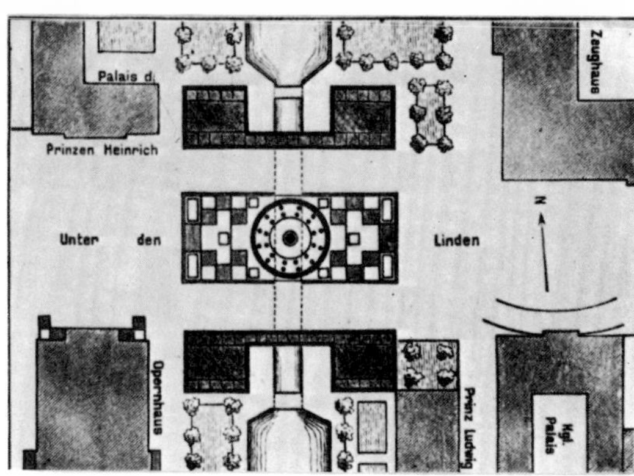

C

35. Heinrich Gentz. Project for a memorial monument to Friedrich II, 1797 (B). Reconstruction view (A) and site plan (C) by Doebber, 1915.

are not only significant components of the composition, but they are also essential members in the functional program of the complex. Each of the four pavilions was to serve a specific purpose. The one adjacent to the palace of Prince Heinrich was designated as a market hall—a structure, as Gentz explained, "which is very much needed in this area."[53] The decision to include such a utilitarian building in the civic heart of Berlin certainly reflects Gentz's awareness of the need for permanent commercial structures and his thorough acquaintance with the problems of his specific site. The unsightly *Buden*, as Berliners called the flimsy temporary vendors' booths, were everywhere in evidence (see Figures 16, 17) and, though obviously filling a necessary public need, were singularly unattractive. Their presence in the vicinity of such impressive civic structures as the

Opernhaus and Zeughaus was annoying and visually incongruous.[54] Gentz's solution was to replace these impermanent installations by a substantial structure of architectural beauty in the tradition of the Greek stoa. Though he considered the erection of a permanent commercial structure urgent in 1797, Schinkel would have to repeat the suggestion in 1817 and again in 1827. In fact, his well-known Kaufhaus design was planned for a site on the Unter den Linden within a block of the spot which Gentz had proposed for a market hall thirty years earlier.

The second pavilion, near the Zeughaus, was to accommodate a new guardhouse, replacing an old nondescript building which had served this purpose for many years. Schinkel would ultimately succeed in erecting such a structure on the same site in 1816, thereby making his debut as Berlin's official architect and planner. The third pavilion, next to the Prinzessinnen (or Prinz Ludwig) Palais, was meant to function as an extension of this small city palace. In 1793 Friedrich Wilhelm III, while still crown prince, had taken up residence in the adjacent Kronprinzen Palais. He would later ask both Gentz and Schinkel to design a connecting passage between the two palaces and a frontal extension for the smaller one. The so-called *Kopfbau* and the bridge over the Oberwallstrasse were completed in 1811 after designs by Gentz. Finally, the fourth pavilion, east of Knobelsdorff's Opernhaus, had been designated as "a café and restaurant for the convenience of the public, especially those who attend the opera during the carnival season." In the 1960's the East German government restored the Prinzessinnen Palais, converting it into a café and restaurant—the location being ideal for both the general public visiting the cultural center of the city as well as those attending performances of the renowned East Berlin opera.[55]

Gentz's entry did not win the competition, and his proposal remained an imaginative exercise in environmental planning. Yet the principles which it displayed would be assimilated by Schinkel and serve as points of departure for his own efforts to improve the environment of central Berlin. In sum, what were these principles? First, Gentz used a dual-axial scheme, a typical Roman and Palladian planning device, which permitted visual and architectural coordination between individual components and provided a tightly knit unity of parts. Second, he integrated components of varied character and function into a cohesive whole by means of a careful interplay of forms, spaces, and axes. Third, by consciously recognizing the needs of the existing site and allowing his own work to act as a compatible addition and not as a disrupting intrusion, he created an organized and, at the same time, pleasurable human environment.

As an architect Gentz respected contemporary tenets of design without falling victim to a blind obedience to academic formulas. Unlike Langhans, who would readily draw on forms, symbols, and details from Stuart and Revett, Gentz searched for a new and creative synthesis of ancient principles and permanent values in design. He also recognized and provided for human needs as an integral part of his solutions. Protection from sun and rain in urban centers may have been the concern of good planners since the days of Hippodamus in ancient Greece, and the perpetuation of this concern in modern times probably belongs as much to Palladio and to Percier and Fontaine as to Gentz. The arcades at Vicenza's Basilica, at the rue de Rivoli in Paris and the colonnades at the Unter den Linden in Berlin are their respective creative utilizations of an ancient principle. In Gentz's case, however, the functional use of colonnades as both a formal unifying link between parts of his composition and a necessary passage to protect pedestrians from the inclement weather and from the muddy thoroughfare, was quite different from the prevailing decorative use of colonnades in the parks and gardens of royal estates in Prussia as, for example, at Schloss Sanssouci.[56] Gentz also tried to respect and complement the historical buildings which surrounded his site. The total environment of Knobelsdorff's Opernhaus, Boumann's palace of Prince Heinrich, and the Zeughaus by Nering would have been enhanced by the presence of his new monument. In scale, format, and classical expression, Gentz's project did not appear as a grandiose statement in its own right. And yet the design embodied a distinct character and individuality. Its temple form could have provided a befitting counterpiece to Langhans' Brandenburger Tor at the opposite end of the Unter den Linden and served as a transition to Schlüter's palace on the island toward the east.

The true merit of Gentz's project must be found in its qualities as a comprehensive statement of environmental design. Originality for its own sake had certainly not been his aim; rather, he emphasized higher values. For future students of his work he best summarized his philosophy as an architect and planner in the following words: "In our day and age we seek to be Original. We equate the concept of beauty with the invention of new forms and fashions of decoration, indeed, with any kind of variety. And if it is not 'beauty' we seek, then it is surely our desire for glory. It is certainly true that an architect of our time considers it a greater shame to emulate a good building that has been done by another master than to invent a bad one on his own. It seems clear to me that, according to the ideal of the Greeks, it was the idea of art which prevailed and, according to the 'moderns,' it is the artist, because he has the opportunity to show ingenuity and inventiveness."[57]

Schinkel was a youth of sixteen when he witnessed the exhibition of entries in the competition for Friedrich II's monument at Berlin's Akademie der bildenden Künste in 1797. Three years later he prepared a presentation sheet which was his first extant planning scheme (Figure 36). Known as *"Villa bei den Zelten" im Berliner Tiergarten,* this conceptual design documented the lessons he learned during the earliest years of his training. A frequently published work, it has most often been used to illustrate Schinkel's dependence on Friedrich Gilly. However, the drawing reveals certain aspects which have little in common with Gilly's work. The mixture of stylistic elements, the awkward massing of the pavilions, and the incongruity of surface articulation show a greater degree of eclecticism and probably reflect the professional immaturity of the youthful, aspiring architect. Yet, the rather loosely arranged components seem to indicate a conscious rejection of a grand axial scheme in the Baroque tradition. Hesitant though the design may appear, it nevertheless reflects Schinkel's search for a more flexible method of organizing and relating forms in space.

Two pavilions at the edge of a large basin present symmetrical facades to a viewer on the opposite bank (lower section). Between them in the distance one sees two truncated obelisks flanking a roadway. A large open courtyard separates the buildings and extends from the road to the water. From a vantage point between the two obelisks (upper section), one sees the irregular disposition of the rear facades of the pavilions and at the opposite edge of the pool, on axis with the obelisks, a small temple-like building raised on a high podium. Although symmetry, axial alignment and grouping in pairs are all used as planning devices, it is interesting to note that all of the architectural components appear at the edge of the site. The center remains free and is only characterized by the flat planes of the courtyard and water basin. There are several focuses, and no single element dominates. The organization of the site depends on strict relationships which are more reminiscent of Gentz's manner of environmental control than of Gilly's schemes. Schinkel's design can be seen as a variation on Gentz's dual-axes theme—an application of the principle to a program which does not include a single dominant monument. There is still a question as to why Schinkel chose to exploit this theme in what is presumably his first attempt at environmental planning. What relationship did he have with Gentz at this time which would have encouraged his adaptation of this principle in his conceptual design?

Since 1796, even prior to his participation in the competition for Friedrich II's monument, Gentz had been an active supporter of the professional training of young architects in Berlin. For three years he taught

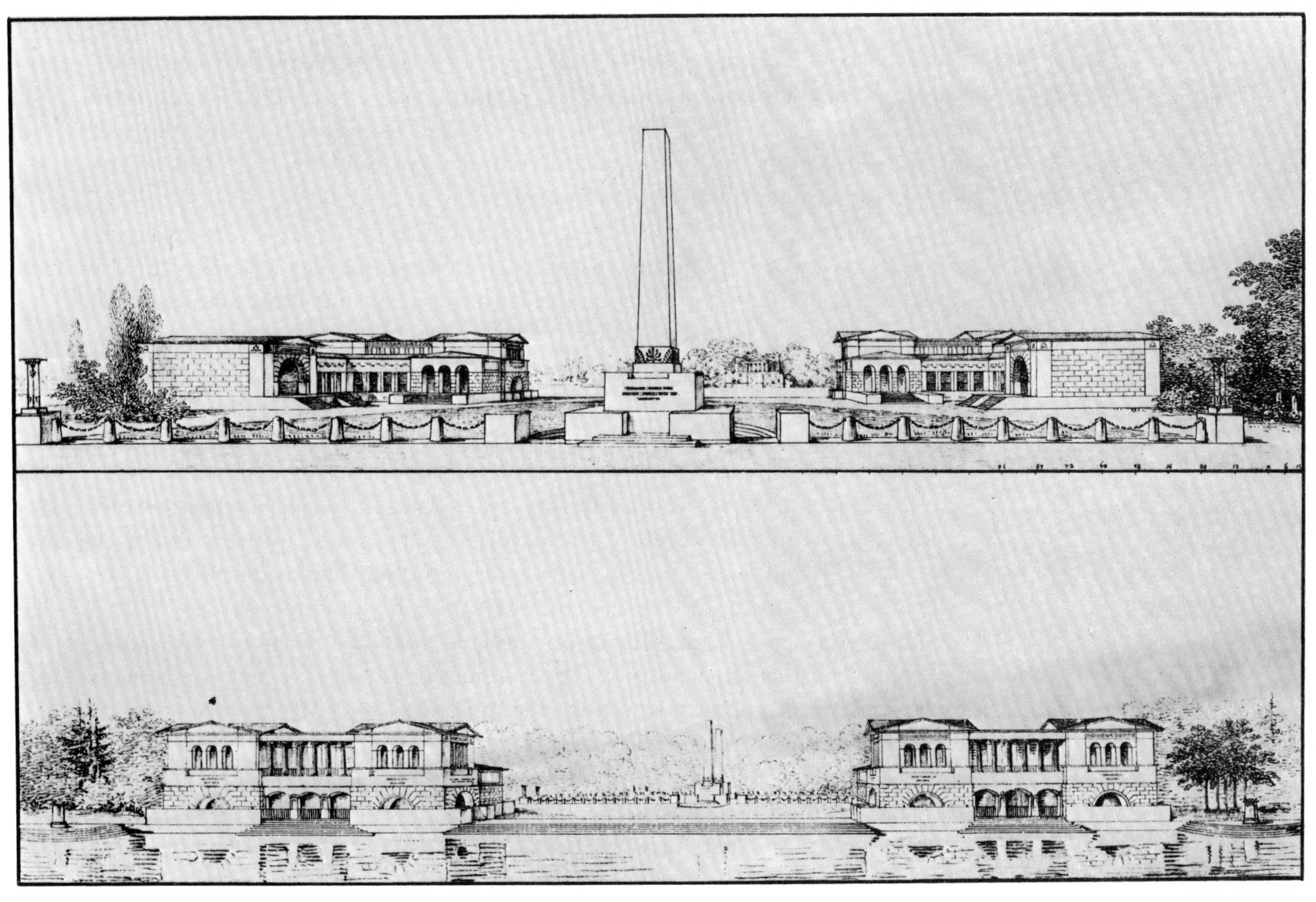

36. "Villa bei den Zelten" im Berliner Tiergarten, 1800.

at the "Akademie der bildenden Künste und mechanischen Wissenschaften etablierten architektonischen Schule," and in 1799 he joined Friedrich Gilly as an instructor at the recently founded Bauakademie. According to records in the former Berliner Geheime Staatsarchiv, Gentz began his lectures there in June 1799 and continued until the summer of 1800, when he departed on his first visit to Weimar. He taught "Stadt-Baukunst," or the art of city planning.

According to his *Studienplan* for the two consecutive terms during which he taught, Gentz seems to have emphasized a combination of artistic and practical training in the projection and siting of various building types. A second-term student (Spring 1800) was trained in design, cost estimation, and proper siting of civic, religious, and military buildings, ranging in scope, complexity, and consequence from a Spritzenhaus (fire station) to a Schauspielhaus (theater). The physical coordination of these structures with their respective environments appears to have been given special consideration, though the planning of entire cities was only mentioned in a single clause. The student had to present his solutions in *Exempel-Zeichnungen* (presentation renderings), which were used in the atelier for discussion and criticism by the instructor.

If Schinkel's *Villa im Tiergarten* was one of these *Exempel-Zeichnungen*, since its date corresponds with the period when he was a student at the Bauakademie, then several aspects of its nature become clear. The drawing technique which he used—thin, precise lines carefully defining surface patterns—imitates Gentz's manner of rendering (see Figure 35*B*). The perspective view from a slightly oblique angle is not used for dramatic effect but for clarity, and the two complementary views presented on the same sheet also indicate a desire for completeness and easy comprehension. These characteristics, along with the understandable awkwardnesses of a student effort in the design of the pavilions, also point to the possibility that this was indeed an *Exempel-Zeichnung* by Schinkel, composed as an exercise in planning for Gentz's course at the Bauakademie.

Schinkel's work must have impressed Gentz. It was a reasonably academic performance: clear in its statement of concept, articulate in its own measure of spontaneity, and disciplined in graphic presentation. It was perhaps for these reasons that Schinkel retained this sheet in his private files and Gentz would later recall its competence and promise. In 1806 he asked Schinkel to assist him in the preparation of final presentation drawings for another project in the vicinity of the Opernhaus and Zeughaus. From then until Gentz's death in 1811 a period of professional rivalry divided the two men. The former student was now prepared to challenge his teacher in proposals for the expansion of the Prinzessinnen Palais, 1809, and the mausoleum for Prussia's Queen Luise, 1810. In both instances, it has been assumed that Gentz's designs were chosen, but it still remains a matter of scholarly dispute to what extent Schinkel may have been an instrumental force in the final solution for both projects.[58] In any case, perhaps the circumstances surrounding their relationship during this period caused these two men of promise and talent to drift apart. In 1825, when Schinkel wrote a short autobiographical sketch, he omitted Gentz's name in listing his former teachers. As a matter of fact, the name of this deserving architect never appears in Schinkel's extensive writings. How can such an omission be explained?

Like sources of inspiration, causes of neglect are seldom documented. In Schinkel's case, I would ascribe his neglect of Gentz to a typically human failing: lack of appreciation of a fellow artist whose character and sentiment might have been too similar to his own to permit continued mutual inspiration. Nevertheless, it should be acknowledged that Heinrich Gentz probably had a more profound influence on Schinkel's development as an architect and planner than has previously been recognized.

When Schinkel left Berlin on 1 May 1803 to study the life, art, and architecture of foreign lands, he was already equipped with the inspirations and lessons of some of the finest teachers available in Germany around 1800. He was, therefore, more than just another journeyman artist from the North, bent on seeing and drinking in the fascinating sites of Italy, but a young man capable of understanding what Goethe meant when he wrote: "I consider the day I entered Rome as my second day of birth, as true revelation, the beginning of a new life."[59]

III The Lessons of Italy

Schinkel's diaries, letters, and graphic records of his first sojourn in foreign lands are extensive in scope and informative in the variety of their content. For a young adult, the total of his penetrating observations and independent studies is impressive and indicates a maturity beyond his years. It appears that nothing escaped his interest. His curiosity was constantly aroused, and his desire to learn was continually strengthened. He described, analyzed, and drew anything from a simple farmyard on the island of Capri to the complex majesty of the Capitoline Hill in Rome. Moreover, his literary and graphic styles seem to be of equal virtuosity, spontaneity, and depth. His writing reflects the observant and critical style of Goethe—without being mannered or affected. At times one is also reminded of the charm and lightheartedness of Joseph von Eichendorff's classic novel of the age of German Romanticism, *Aus dem Leben eines Taugenichts*. Like this contemporary Prussian poet and writer, Schinkel described both natural and man-made scenes and, in observing men, never failed to mention the humble or arrogant, the learned or ignorant who crossed his path. He purposely avoided crowds. In Dresden and Paris he spent most of his time in the "sacred halls" of museums. In Rome, the philologist and diplomat, Wilhelm von Humboldt, whose intelligence and temperament matched his own, became his patron. Rome and Sicily became his sources of inspiration.

Schinkel's innumerable sketches, paintings, and conceptual designs are invaluable for the study of his character and artistic development. Like his writings, these graphic works are an integral part of his Romantic world, vivid records of his observations, and sensitive reflections of his attitude toward nature. In the variety of their content and media they combine expressions of youthful enthusiasm and sincere humility in the face of natural grandeur. They also document the creative response of a positive and searching mind to new aesthetic experiences.

It is not surprising that the drawings and writings of his first tour through Austria and Italy also reflect a certain degree of bias, neglect, and controversy. Schinkel's general outlook and appreciation of life, nature, and art could be as broad or as restricted as that most generous age of our modern world permitted. While he was most enthusiastic in his appreciation of simple medieval brick buildings in Tuscany and elaborate Gothic cathedrals in Prague, Vienna, Milan, and Strassburg, he refused to recognize any value in creations of the Baroque period. Without realizing to what extent his master, Friedrich Gilly, and, indeed, he himself had been indebted to Baroque planning principles and stage designs, the young artist would join Winckelmann and Mengs in their rejection of the style. Consequently, Schinkel, like Goethe before him, found Dresden's splendid Zwinger to be "in the most wretched style."[1] On the other hand, he noted the "positive" aspects of the planning organization of this complex: a simple rectangular space surrounded by unifying facades resulting in an impressive civic plaza.

Following the current intellectual bias against Baroque pomposity, he wrote that "without doubt, the best style of architecture ended with Bramante,"[2] but he drew Michelangelo's Campidoglio with the same emphasis on its picturesque qualities as Piranesi had shown in his etching of 1756. This conflict of attitude toward the art and architecture of the post-Renaissance era during Schinkel's early years would be partially resolved at a later time, and by 1824, during a second extensive visit to Italy, the mature Schinkel would, in fact, extol Giulio Romano as one of the world's greatest geniuses.[3] Even during his first travels abroad, however, his antagonisms toward the work of the Mannerist and Baroque periods probably do not fully reveal his own personal inclinations. In Schinkel's refusal to find merit in Francesco de Santis' Spanish Stairs in Rome, which he must have descended frequently from his quarters on the Pincian Hill, he may have been echoing the currently popular artistic and intellectual sentiment.

Schinkel journeyed to Austria, Italy and France to see, to study, and to record as many impressions as possible. He had been prepared by the magnificent volumes in the Gillys' library and was quick to note when certain publications were proved inaccurate by his own observations.[4] His interest in landscape painting drew him to the works of Nicolas and Caspar Poussin and, eventually, to the painter Joseph Anton Koch. From these artists he would learn an even greater freedom in the manipulation of forms and spaces than Heinrich Gentz had been able to convey. Like such neglected contemporaries as J. M. Gandy, he quickly sensed that the vernacular architecture of Italy had a potential appeal in its picturesqueness and practicality and in the simple logic of its planning. Numerous references throughout his diaries and letters show that he was constantly aware of architectural totalities, of urban patterns, or large-scale planning schemes, and, like Camillo Sitte some eighty years later, Schinkel would climb church steeples, campanili, or hilltops to study the patterns of streets, plazas, and urban scenes below. Upon his arrival in Prague in June 1803, his most important single impression other than the great cathedral was the totality of the magnificent urban panorama. "One has to climb many hundreds of steps along numerous streets before reaching the castle atop the Hradčin, whence one has a magnificent view of the city."[5]

Unlike Alois Hirt, his history professor in Berlin, or Leo von Klenze, or even at times Heinrich Gentz, he was not interested in archaeological discoveries or in experiencing a grandiose and isolated monument. In a letter to David Gilly from Paris, dated 5 December 1804, Schinkel made the following characteristic observation of ancient temple sites in Sicily: "For the most part, the monuments of antiquity do not offer anything new for an architect, because one has been acquainted with them since one's youth. But the sight of these works in their natural setting holds a surprise which comes not only from their size, but also from their picturesque grouping."[6]

Because of this attitude, he did not usually record dimensions, details, or even elevations of buildings. He never concerned himself with the "very tiresome studies of floor plans and of all the strictly architectural components," wrote Hittorff in a belated eulogy to his Prussian colleague in 1857.[7] Therefore, deduced the Parisian architect and critic, young Schinkel could not have had a proper (that is, academic) training prior to his first exposure to the architecture of classical lands. Indeed, Schinkel, former apprentice of the Gillys in Berlin, had not been trained to conceive of architecture as a sum total of details. Nor was he concerned with sketching the quaint decaying ruins which had been such a popular preoccupation of previous generations of artists. If buildings he visited were in a semi-ruined or altered state, he often drew them as if complete and according to what he felt were their original conditions. It was also typical

37. Veduta di Roma, 1803/04.

of him to see as well as to draw with great breadth and precision and thus to create panoramas of total environmental contexts—complete and expansive records of life, nature, and architecture.

Schinkel's drawing of Rome, which he entitled *Veduta di Roma da mia l'ocanda in Monte Pinso presso la chiesa di St. Trinita dell'Monte* (Figure 37), is a splendid example of his artistic appreciation of the city's environmental totality. At first glance, it appears to be a perfect graphic pendant to his written description of the view which he enjoyed from his quarters on the Pincian Hill, Rome's traditional German artists' colony since the time of Mengs and Carstens. He recorded in his diary in October 1803: "My window commands a view which spans from the top of the Pincian Hill all the way across the western part of the city. Thousands of palaces, topped by towers and domes, are spread out below me. The distance is closed by St. Peter's and the Vatican, and beyond stretches the Janiculum in a low line, crowned with the pine groves of the Villa Pamphili."[8]

Both his words and his drawings reveal an attitude which would become typical of the nineteenth century—the idea of a *Weltbühne*, an outgrowth of the Romantic spirit most logically expressed in the creation of panoramas. Schinkel's view of Rome is indeed panoramic in character if not in scope. His scene encompasses an arc of some eighty degrees and a depth of several miles to the distant horizon. Yet this impressive expanse of the city is displayed before us like a skillfully arranged stage set. Even the fashionable ladies overlooking the scene from their balcony resemble patrons in their loge at the opera.[9]

The multitude of tile-roofed cubic structures, the shaft-like medieval campanili, and dominating domed churches are drawn with the crisp, precise lines becoming characteristic of Schinkel's style. The denseness of the urban concentration is made less overwhelming by the generous amount of white in sky and buildings, the thinness and clarity of the lines, and the almost complete absence of shadow. Implicit in Schinkel's rendering is the notion that the city, or at least a great part of it, can be viewed, encompassed, comprehended and, if need be, modified. Man's self-confidence has reached the point where he no longer need stand in awe of (therefore intimidated by) the great monuments of the past; he can visually and aesthetically cope with their magnitude by seeing them within the context of a larger world—yet one still to be comprehended in defined terms. Schinkel's *Weltbühne* embraces much, yet it is apparently still controllable. Here, as an artist, he set the scene for us, leaving an open stage-like foreground and emphasizing depth by the counterpoint between the heavily drawn repoussoir of the balcony at the left front and the strong lines and dominant height of the church of San Carlo al Corso in the right middleground, with an echo provided by the fainter form of St. Peter's in the distance. Later, as an architect in Berlin, he tried to manage and manipulate the forms of his buildings in space in order to create environments for the drama of daily life.

More than thirty years after Schinkel sketched his view of Rome, another German artist residing in the city painted his version of Rome from the Via Malta toward St. Peter's (Figure 38). Johann C. Reinhart's view is virtually the same as Schinkel's, though somewhat wider, reaching as far as the Pantheon and Column of Marcus Aurelius to the south and the towers of S. Trinità dell' Monte to the north. In contrast to Schinkel's deliberate rendering, Reinhart's painting indicates a conscious manipulation of light for effect. The conspicuous church of San Carlo al Corso is literally overshadowed in order to give prominence to the more famous basilica of St. Peter's. The use of chiaroscuro in the manner of Joseph Anton Koch, the acknowledged master among German painters in Rome,

38. Johann C. Reinhart. *Rom von der via Malta auf St. Peter,* 1835.

places Reinhart within the tradition of landscape painters going back to Poussin. Schinkel, though considered by his colleagues in Rome to be a landscape painter, was less interested in the pictorial qualities of urban or rural scenes than in their architectonic and environmental characteristics.[10] He never thought of himself as anything but an architect and all of the graphic works of his early career should be viewed in light of his own intentions. The directness and clarity of his drawing of Rome were qualities inherent in his concept of art. He was undeniably following the judgment of Winckelmann when he wrote: "The attempt to create a vulgar delusion of the senses is an unworthy effort in the context of art. This explains why a sketch is often more effective and impressive than the finished painting. The latter contains a great deal which one could easily do without. On the other hand, only the most essential is captured in a sketch, only that which stirs the imagination."[11] It was characteristic of him that he continued to prefer the crisp and economical linear strokes of

39. San Lorenzo fuori le Mura, via Tiburtina, Rome, 1803.

a pen and eschew the bold washes of Gilly and Boullée. Most of his sketches and finished drawings were classic delineations, capable of being easily transformed into exquisite engravings for his later publications.

When Schinkel did turn to the recording of individual monuments or complexes, he did so with the awareness of an architect discovering formal and spatial interrelationships, rather than a painter seeking pictorial effects. A revealing example of such a study from his early days in Rome is the drawing of San Lorenzo fuori le Mura of about November 1803 (Figure 39). Ignoring details which would have attracted a more archaeologically oriented student, Schinkel concentrated on the planes and volumes of the component parts of the complex. We sense the balance of tensions between the tall narrow vertical of the campanile and the lower broader blocks surrounding it. Any rigidity caused by the underlying organization of rectilinear elements arranged at right angles is mitigated by the picturesqueness of the varied shapes which make up the silhouette. Schinkel's understanding of this principle of asymmetrical variations growing out of a rational and ordered foundation would be added to Gentz's lesson of dual-axial arrangements, enriching his knowledge of planning possibilities and contributing an essential factor to his own later creation of imaginative and *malerische* compositions.

40. Farmyard on the island of Capri, 1804.

Reinforcing the positive qualities of picturesque grouping of simple structures were the many vernacular buildings which Schinkel found along his way. Of those he sketched, an interesting example is the watercolor drawing of a farmyard which he came upon while on the island of Capri in the summer of 1804 (Figure 40). He recorded his reaction to the directness and simplicity of this anonymous architecture: "On the section of the island known as Anacapri, one stands high above on a fertile plateau filled with neat little houses. In picturesque form and simplicity they surpass anything that I have seen of rural building groups."[12]

This drawing, one of the few watercolor sketches of his trip, reflects his feelings in a very personal way. His medium of expression enhances the "picturesque form," and creates an atmosphere of bright sunshine and warm shadows, of primeval forms existing in a timeless world. Even the massive walls of the fortress on the hazy hilltop seem no more advanced or articulated than the simple shapes of farm buildings below. Though the cubic blocks, their planes defined by light and corresponding shadow, may be reminiscent of the works of Nicolas Poussin, the interest in three-dimensional form, especially the bold contours of simple staircases, and the attention to the flow of space around and within the groups of buildings indicate the observant eye and sensitive brush of an architect.[13]

The lessons Schinkel learned and the multiplicity of impressions he gathered in Italy, made explicit by his sketches of such complexes as San Lorenzo or vernacular buildings, would be apparent in his sophisticated planning schemes of later years. His designs for villas and country retreats near Potsdam evoked memories of these Italian models, though their individual compositions were strictly Schinkel's own inventions.

The most important example of this villa group is the Hofgärtnerei (now officially known as the Römische Bäder) in the gardens of Charlottenhof, executed with the help of Ludwig Persius, his most talented student, and built in 1833–1834 (Figures 41, 42). Here Schinkel is at his most masterful in creating a rational and very strictly organized rectilinear grid as the basis for an ingenious juxtaposition of rudimentary shapes and classicizing temple forms, resulting in a picturesque total composition apparently wholly Romantic in character. As in his drawing of San Lorenzo, the tower plays a pivotal role; all other elements seem to radiate from its central position. But in the Gärtnerhaus the component parts are so varied in size and function, so well integrated with the open areas and manipulated natural growth, that the complexity of the total composition far surpasses the simple cluster in Rome. Plain open staircases connecting the various levels and trellised arbors richly laden with vines recall the bucolic scene on Capri, but the masterful manner in which these semi-enclosed elements are related to and interlocked with closed volumes and open spaces within the grid pattern is certainly the work of a mature and experienced architect.[14]

In speaking of the large sunken court with its varied asymmetrical borders, Philip Johnson noted its uniqueness in "the creation of emotional space, by such casual and eclectic means."[15] Certainly the special qualities of the Hofgärtnerei are those which appeal to our senses: the visual delight of unexpected vistas, the tactile sensations derived from the abundance of natural vegetation, and the simple physical pleasure of experiencing a succession of small or large enclosures, bright open courts, confined corners, shaded pathways, sudden openings, passages up, down, into, and onto terraces, gardens, tea houses, and temples. There is richness

41. Hofgärtnerei (now called Römische Bäder) in the Schlosspark Sanssouci, Potsdam; view from the west and site plan, 1834.

42. Hofgärtnerei; view from the south, 1834.

beyond description, "casual" only in the mind of the beholder. Every element, whether bearing wall, trellis post, or footpath edge, is keyed to the underlying rectilinear grid. Major axes are avoided, but there is an abundance of minor vistas, each with its special character, many with unexpected focal points or even none at all. The eye is enchanted, the mind intrigued, the spirit refreshed. One can well understand Johnson's comment that "it has haunted me ever since I first saw it thirty-two years ago."

Beyond the beauty of its environmental organization and the superiority of its interpretation of the Italian villa mode, the Hofgärtnerei has significance in the context of Schinkel's single most important planning statement of the latter part of his career: the project for a royal residence on the Acropolis in Athens. It appears to me that the small villa in Prussia which he designed in 1833 could be considered as a miniature version of and, in several respects, a plausible prototype for the complex in Greece of 1834.

Schinkel's unfailing skill in fusing logic and charm, order and variety is evident in his plan for this new royal palace (Figure 43). His design was heralded by Hittorff in Paris and by Leo von Klenze in Munich as one of the finest works of his entire career.[16] At first glance, it is apparent that

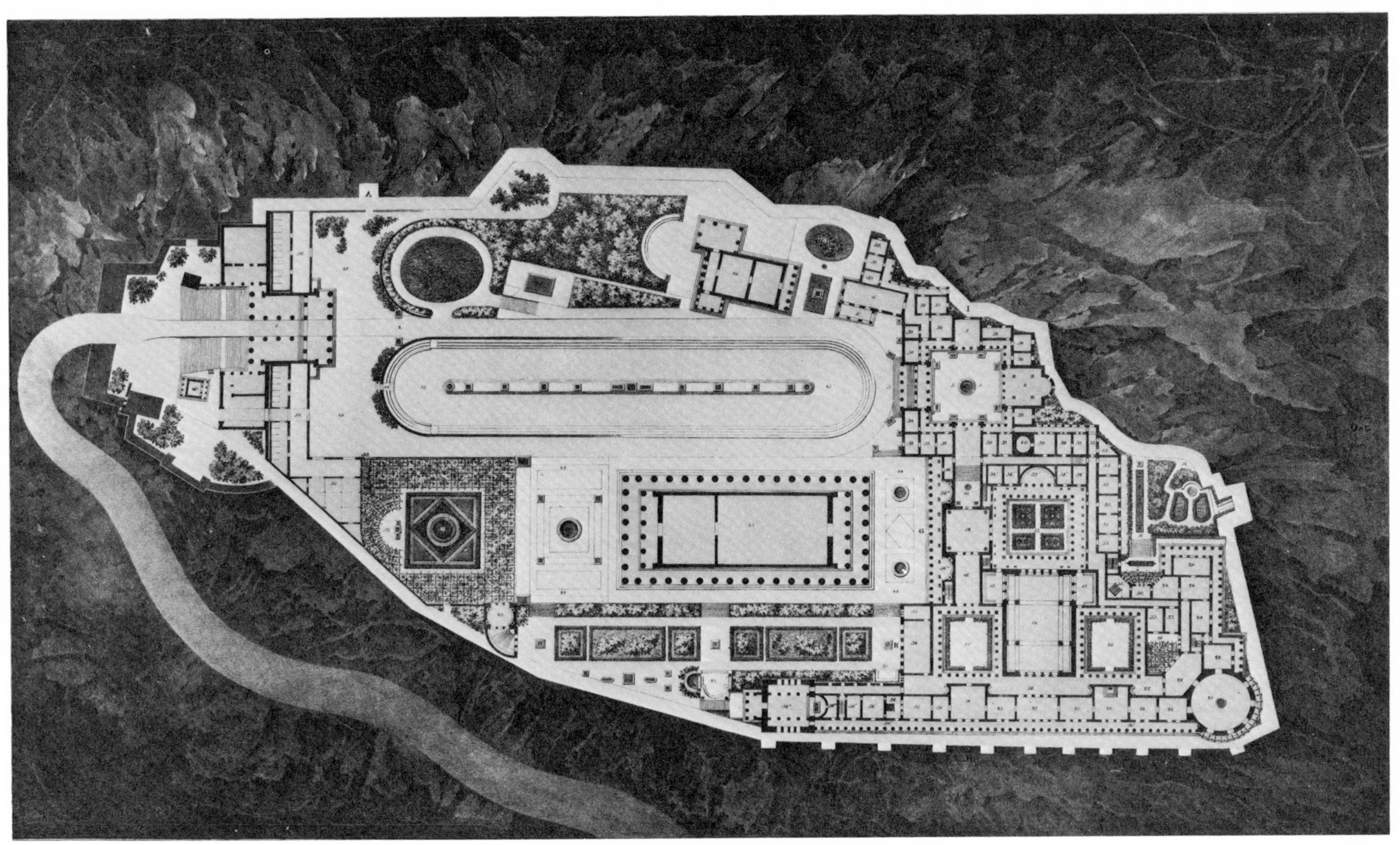

43. Project for a royal palace on the Acropolis in Athens; site plan, 1834.

Schinkel composed the layout of the palace with respect to existing Periclean masterworks.[17] Halls, apartments, courtyards, and galleries are separated from the ancient structures and carefully conform to their major alignments. In no instance would the height of the new buildings challenge the dominance of treasured archaeological remains. Schinkel's reverence for classical Greece was sincere, and the self-confidence of his age permitted what would later be considered a sacrilege. In the 1830's, however, his only concern was the formulation of aesthetic and practical means to express his conception of a modern Hellenic style. Characteristically, he composed an important letter to the crown prince of Bavaria, brother of King Otto I of Greece, in which he outlined some of the basic principles under which his project was conceived.[18] In addition, he illustrated his ideas in several perspective views, of which a rendering of the interior of the great Reception Hall is perhaps the best known. In a fanciful combination of colossal freestanding columns, open-web trusses, and decorative details and color schemes reminiscent of Robert Adam's

Pompeiian style, Schinkel fused lightness and strength, clarity and elaboration into a rarely matched synthesis of structure, space, and ornament. This final statement of his Grecian style had little in common with the "white Hellenism" of his concert hall at the Schauspielhaus or the serene expression of the peristyle at the Museum. It must be seen, as Leo von Klenze so pointedly said, as "the magnificent and charming midsummer night's dream of a great architect."[19]

In regard to the disposition or arrangement of the plan, Schinkel had to consider not only the requirements of function and convenience, but also the special climatic conditions and the restricted site. His earlier excursions in southern Italy and Sicily had taught him that these lands required solutions quite different from those of the more hostile north.[20] The numerous courtyards, open galleries, and outdoor gathering places of the Athens palace reflect Schinkel's conscious attempt to create an environment suited to the Mediterranean climate. The conditions of the site also challenged him to produce a distinctive composition. As had Mnescicles many centuries earlier, Schinkel responded positively to the demands of the irregular terrain. Sunken gardens, staircases, and terraces could overcome changes of elevation, and sections of natural irregularity could thus be utilized to their best advantage. A large depressed area to the north of the Parthenon, in the form of a Roman hippodrome, provided a spacious outdoor arena for courtly ceremonies and public gatherings in front of the palace entrance without interfering with the visual relationships between the ancient temples and Propylaea. In a subtle way it actually helped to unify the new palace complex at the eastern end of the plateau and the older structures which bordered it on the north, south, and west.

The plan of the palace itself reveals the underlying rationale which characterized the Hofgärtnerei. However, because of the more elevated purpose and grander scale of the project, the major areas display a formality and dependence on axes not found in the small villa. Although oval, circular, and semicircular forms are used effectively to relate certain elements to the whole or to create transitions in awkward areas, the dominant theme remains the ordered rhythm of interlocking cross-axes and the often symmetrical arrangement of rectilinear units. Despite the dependence on axes frequently emphasized as vistas, it is difficult to determine a definite center or focus of attention. Although the great audience hall stands out in size and is the logical formal culmination, a traditional axial entrance is avoided in favor of a more complex series of open and enclosed spaces along the path of approach. It is perhaps even more significant that he rejected the current academic concept of a city palace as a uniform and symmetrical foursquare block. Of this decision, he wrote: "A work such as this could hardly derive from the timeworn maxims of the neo-Italian and neo-French schools, in which especially a misunderstanding of the concept of symmetry has produced so much hypocrisy and boredom and reached such a stifling position of sovereignty."[21]

Schinkel's conception of the Athens palace was in keeping with his concern for a Mediterranean solution as well as his interest in complex, multiunit planning. This design also afforded the flexibility to allow a desirable connection with the ancient monuments of the Acropolis without impinging on their venerability or visual dominance. One wonders whether Schinkel was convinced that the Bavarian king of Greece would be content to live in a modern version of a Roman villa on the Acropolis. Even his suggestion that the juxtaposition of the dwellings of the ancient gods and the residence of the monarch was in the tradition of Mycenaean kings could not sway the court to accept his plan.[22] His project remained a "midsummer night's dream." Never again would a modern European architect display more idealism and innocence and, at the same time, more confidence and mastery of planning in a direct confrontation with one of history's noblest sites.

Though Schinkel had never visited Greece, his stay in Rome afforded him many opportunities to experience the particular power of monuments of the past—both those of ancient and more recent times. He recorded his reaction upon entering the city for the first time in October 1803: "Bare hills hide the view of a more distant, more beautiful horizon; the traveler's spirit loses the elasticity with which it eagerly seized the new objects that changed at every step, and it sinks into lethargy. But suddenly the sight of the first temple of the world, the Basilica of St. Peter's, enters the heart like a thunderbolt, the first view to appear from behind the hills; and then in the richest plain, distant Rome with its innumerable treasures spreads out little by little on its seven hills beneath the marveling traveler. A thousand attempts have been made to describe what one feels at this spot, and they have amassed sterile, empty sounds. It is wise to remain silent, for any word about the most sublime sounds common."[23]

Rome was not only the young traveler's headquarters during his Italian sojourn, but also his main source of knowledge, a school of the past, as Goethe had called it, where every day teaches so much that one needs a long time to digest it all. After a brief visit to Naples and to the remains along the pirate-infested Sicilian coast during the early summer of 1804, Schinkel returned to Rome and remained there until almost the end of that year. His studies continued and were expanded. He established contact with Joseph Anton Koch and several other resident painters. It is possible that during this time he also prepared some of his more important drawings for possible publication.[24] Among these was a perspective view of the Capitoline Hill, Schinkel's finest tribute to Rome (Figure 44).

The essence of Michelangelo's design for the Campidoglio is manifest in the totality and unity of its forms and spaces.[25] Each unit has been molded into a single, all-embracing concert of environmentalist art. Seldom before and never again has western man succeeded in casting civic nobility and pride into a more comprehensive, symbolic, and formal unity. Though the trapezoidal plaza with its surrounding magnificent facades and focal equestrian statue is a distinct environmental unit, Schinkel's sketch does not concentrate on it alone; it appears as an ordered element within the context of a picturesque urban setting. From his vantage point below in the Piazza Aracoeli Schinkel presents the Renaissance plaza as the crowning feature of his composition, though his modern eye insists on an oblique angle and avoids the required axial view.[26] The plain facade of Santa Maria in Aracoeli and its mountainous staircase command almost as much attention as the finely articulated planes of Michelangelo's facades and the gentle slope of the cordonata. Schinkel's amazing range of observation extends from the humble beggar woman in the foreground to the crisp lines of a benevolent Marcus Aurelius and beyond the hill to the barely visible cupola of SS. Martina-e-Luca. It is the broad physical and human context which concerns the nineteenth-century architect and not the limitations of a contrived outdoor salon, however artfully devised.

Just as Schinkel avoided a view of the Campidoglio alone, he did not sketch innumerable details of the buildings or sculpture. Yet certain elements could not have escaped his trained eye, and the precision with which the Castor and Pollux groups and the end bays of the lateral palaces were rendered indicate his keen awareness of significant features. Though Schinkel never copied any of Michelangelo's forms, the boldness of the colossal pilasters and the masterful interplay of horizontals and verticals within the trabeated system found distinct, though purified, echoes in some of his masterworks in Berlin. The integration of sculpture and architecture, whether as part of the formal substance or as freestanding works relating to a larger spatial unit, would also become a characteristic of his later projects for the Prussian capital. The second version of his design for the Museum at the Lustgarten (summer 1823) called for two equestrian statues atop the spur walls flanking the frontal stairway and four groups of horse trainers at the corners of the parapet above the central rotunda (see Figure 77). Explaining their importance to the building and

44. View of the Capitoline Hill and Sta. Maria d'Aracoeli, Rome, 1803/04.

its environment, he wrote that "these crowning groups of sculpture must be seen as a final component absolutely essential for the effect of this building in the context of its site, if it is not to be devoid of character."[27]

Schinkel was never given an opportunity to design his own Campidoglio. The flat topography of the Mark Brandenburg and the absence of aspiring patrons prevented him from realizing any project which included a stimulating site, antique remains, and totally integrated surrounding facades. However, as architects are prone to do anytime, anywhere, he exercised his imagination by creating fantasies—designs responsive to hypothetical situations unhampered by practical or functional requirements. Three conceptual designs by Schinkel, which were probably executed after his return to Berlin in 1805, are of special significance in revealing his reaction to the lessons of Italy. None of the three were titled, dated, or signed by Schinkel, and their purpose remains obscure.[28]

The first is usually referred to as *Dom auf einer Anhöhe* (Basilica on a Hill; Figure 45). The dramatic variations in topography, marked by terraces, multilevel buildings, and stairways, including a grand ascent to the classical temple-church, indicate Schinkel's enthusiasm for sites with complex terrain. Both the awkward mixture of stylistic features and the unclear relationships of many parts also indicate that he has not yet reached the state of maturity so evident in the Hofgärtnerei. The Italianate character of the architecture is unmistakable, and the legacy of Michelangelo is revealed especially in the major crowning structure. A more direct reference can be seen in the second fantasy scene, generally called *Stadtplatz am Meer* (City Square by the Sea; Figure 46). The horse trainers of the Campidoglio stand atop monumental pedestals flanking a stairway at the left. If one were able to turn the corner and mount the steps, one would naturally expect to find Marcus Aurelius and the Senators' Palace. Instead, the composition opens on axis to reveal the re-created and rearranged Piazzetta of Venice. The campanili with their gaily flying banners and the statue-topped columns emphasize the perspective toward the distant lagoon while the entire foreground is left free for the stage-like space into which three wide stairways descend. Ephemeral figures populate most of the open area, adding an indication of human activity lacking in the first scene.

The third fantasy design was given a typically complex mid-nineteenth-century Germanic title by Schinkel's son-in-law and compiler-editor of his literary *oeuvre*, Alfred Freiherr von Wolzogen. He listed it as *Grosse Komposition wie der Mailänder Dom gestellt sein müsste* (Large Composition Showing How Milan Cathedral Should Be Sited; Figure 47). Although Schinkel did study the cathedral of Milan during his trip to Italy, the

45. Basilica on a Hill, after 1804.

church depicted here is not a faithful rendering of any specific structure, but a compilation of Gothic forms and features with perhaps Milan and Prague contributing the dominant components.[29] It has also been suggested that the port city which the cathedral overlooks is meant to be Trieste, though it is reminiscent of a number of studies of such scenes, including a beautiful sketch of the harbor of Genoa. The conclusion, then, is that this, too, is a hypothetical scene, a creation of fantasy based upon known components, but arranged and united into a totally new and imaginary composition.

Besides being distinguished from Schinkel's studies of existing sites by their imaginary nature, the three drawings also have certain mannered and illusive qualities in common which make one consider them as a

46. City Square by the Sea, after 1804.

group though each has its own distinctive character. Though different historical styles are employed and different environments suggested, the essential distinctions are primarily of mood: the silent, somewhat aloof, and noble classical world; the more public, civic spaces of the spirited Venetian scene; the idyllic atmosphere of a romanticized Gothic cathedral removed from its customary urban setting. The definition of these moods roughly corresponds to the categories of Renaissance *scene* as outlined by Serlio: tragedy, comedy and pastoral (*Tragedie, Comedie, Satire*).[30]

The first scene depicts the private palatial world of a highborn protagonist dominated by the overwhelming presence of a structure embodying superhuman force. It fulfills the requirements of a setting for tragedy by its severely classical forms. Schinkel is careful to employ the orders in correct hierarchy, reserving colossal Corinthian columns and pilasters for the great domed basilica. The presence of statues in deep niches con-

47. Cathedral on a Height Overlooking the Sea, after 1804.

forms to Serlio's rules, and the general severity is in keeping with the lofty tone of tragic drama. Quite a different spirit pervades the second scene, intended for comedy. One can easily imagine the "cittadini, avocati, mercanti, parasiti, & altre simili persone" acting out their human drama in the public plaza, which is a mixture of Venetian, Roman, and Pisan motifs. The lighter, less serious atmosphere is conveyed by pennants flying from tall masts atop the campanili and radiating lines emanating from the horizon, perhaps suggesting special lighting effects. The lyric sentiments of the pastoral can be discerned in the third scene, elevated by the infusion of Romantic concepts. The rustic and densely wooded setting prescribed by Serlio is transformed into a benign vision of nature fused with the newly appreciated creations of illiterate men of the Dark Ages.

It is apparent that, though the three designs may be exercises in the presentation of scenes for the three dramatic modes, they merely take Serlio's program as a point of departure. They obviously reflect the changes in drama and stage design which had taken place since the sixteenth century. After August Wilhelm von Schlegel had translated the plays of Shakespeare at the end of the eighteenth century, the great actor, Friedrich Ludwig Schröder, successfully introduced them to the German stage, thus paving the way for the development of Romantic drama. One can easily imagine the design for comedy as a setting for *The Merchant of Venice*. Of the three, it most closely imitates the Renaissance form of a flat forestage and raised rear, a squared floor and an emphasis on perspective. Yet, the implied scope and spatial expanse of the set removes it from the conceivable dimensions of the Renaissance stage. The setting for tragedy is even further removed. The placement of the architectural volumes follows the *veder le scene per angolo* system developed by Ferdinando Galli da Bibiena in the eighteenth century.[31] The complexity of levels and spatial configurations and especially the lack of sufficient stage space seem, however, to indicate that the design was not intended for an actual production. The same may be said of the scene with the Gothic cathedral. Just as the Romantic playwrights of the period were breaking the bonds of convention and conceiving dramas too vast to be contained in the theater,[32] Schinkel could envision theatrical settings beyond the scope of any stage. The vast crowds and grandiose movements of contemporary drama and opera, which tried to encompass all of life, could only be accommodated on the spacious platforms and broad stairways of Schinkel's imaginary medieval acropolis. Schiller could dream of such a setting for his *Die Jungfrau von Orleans*, but he would have to be content with more conventional painted scenery.

While Schinkel was awaiting the opportunity to design actual scenery for the stages of Berlin, he found that the imagination he displayed in the three conceptual designs could be turned to the creation of landscape paintings. His most famous work in this genre is the *Mittelalterliche Stadt am Wasser* (Medieval City by the Sea) of 1813 (Figure 48),[33] which can justifiably be considered as an outgrowth of his exercises in Romantic theatrical settings. The very composition, with human activity centered on a landing in the foreground where men are unloading small boats, is reminiscent of a scene in Giuseppe Galli Bibiena's *Architetture e prospettive*.[34] As in the case of the three drawings, there was no need for the *Mittelalterliche Stadt* to be transformed into an actual stage set. It could exist solely as a fantasy, creating in color and light a Romantic vision of an idyllic world.

A preliminary study for the painting reveals Schinkel's careful construction of the plan and siting of the monumental cathedral (Figure 49). The angle perspective and the method for determining it are the same as

48. *Medieval City by the Sea*, 1813.

in the system advocated by Ferdinando Bibiena. The perspective is calculated, and the elevation projected from corresponding points on the plan. We can begin to appreciate Theodor Fontane's remark that Schinkel "painted like an architect and built like a painter."[35] The church is composed of faceted volumes which appear to be as solid as the reinforced promontory on which it stands. Only in the finished painting are the surface planes replaced by an iron-like network of brittle tracery. A neo-Gothic pseudolinearism has been grafted onto a structure conceived essentially in terms of mass. Schinkel could create in oils on canvas a Gothic fantasy of great power and Romantic daring, but his architectural

49. Preliminary study for *Medieval City by the Sea*.

masterworks would necessarily take the form of solid, though finely articulated, volumes of classical proportions. The *malerische* character of his architecture would come not from decorative surfaces or other coloristic effects, but from an approach to the total environment of a building, the essential features of which he was assimilating and developing during his years as a painter. His interest in the interrelationship between nature and architecture, for instance, was stimulated by his observations in Italy, sustained by exercises in fantasy landscapes such as the *Mailänder Dom* and the *Mittelalterliche Stadt*, and it found its ultimate success in the Hofgärtnerei.

Schinkel's preparation for his role in helping to shape the environment of central Berlin was not complete, however, until he had learned to simulate the final dimension in urban planning—the movement of men through the spaces created. His early and continued interest in the theater finally culminated in the opportunity to design stage scenery for actual productions, thereby enabling him to view his own works in a re-creation of reality before he ever erected a major building. Beginning in 1815 he enjoyed the active support of Karl Graf von Brühl, the Generalintendant of the royal theaters.[36] When fire destroyed the Nationaltheater in 1817, Schinkel was commissioned to design a new Schauspielhaus. Although many of his own sets were lost in the same fire, some of his original designs for plays and operas have survived, among them a scene for E. T. A. Hoffmann's *Undine*, 1816 (Figure 50). Schinkel's setting for this Romantic opera is a medieval marketplace, resembling in its general character the Hauptmarkt in Nürnberg. A Gothicizing fountain is placed emphatically in the center foreground, a three-dimensional prop around which the action can take place. The backdrop is composed of buildings in the medieval style of northern Europe, including two Gothic churches viewed at an angle from the east, like the cathedral in *Mittelalterliche Stadt*.

Certain aspects of the design of scenery for the stage—the manipulation of forms in illusionistic space, the control of scale, the effect of perspective diminution—were lessons that Schinkel had already mastered in his landscape drawings and studies of fantasy scenes. They continued to sharpen his awareness of the visual qualities of man-made environments. In addition, the design of actual settings for the theater necessitated the creation of a workable space for human action defined by a physical framework of essentially architectural elements. The performers, gathered around the Gothic fountain or moving about the stage it dominated, could simulate the interaction of human movement and static form within a restricted spatial perspective. Dramatic performances in temporary and

50. Design for the stage setting for the opera *Undine* by E. T. A. Hoffmann, 1816.

necessarily artificial settings could thus provide a kind of testing ground for the exploration of the dynamics of public environments. A more tangible advantage derived from the design of scenery was the crystallization of stylistic experiments in the form of props, such as the Gothic fountain. Two years after the production of *Undine*, Schinkel reinterpreted and refined the form of the fountain in more permanent cast iron for the monument to the Freiheitskriege on the Kreuzberg. His work for the theater, then, should not be considered as a secondary and less consequential activity, but, rather, as an integral part of his development as an architect and a professional designer deeply concerned with the quality of man's environment.

A final word must be said about another aspect of Schinkel's early productive period, one which is closely related to his work for the theater. Soon after his return from his journeys in Italy and France, he became interested in the new phenomenon of panoramas and, later, dioramas. Supported by Wilhelm and Carl Gropius, he held his first public exhibition of so-called optical-perspective paintings in 1807 and continued these presentations with growing success until 1815.[37] His panoramas were displayed in either the royal stables, in a specially constructed enclosure near St. Hedwig's cathedral or in spaces provided by Wilhelm Gropius during the annual Christmas fairs. With a keen sense for the taste of his mixed audience in entertainment-hungry Berlin, he depicted remote and exotic places and romanticized timely events. At the opening of his panorama show entitled *The Burning of Moscow* in 1813 the streets were crowded hours in advance, and people risked their lives trying to enter the overfilled showroom. His success with the public was largely because of his imaginative skills in intensifying the visual and psychological impact of his presentation with music and special lighting effects. He was able to arouse religious feeling, bordering on sentimentality, by providing a choir backstage, or to enliven scenes of nature by simulating Alpine sunsets with cleverly manipulated lights hidden behind transparent screens. Though this kind of entertainment for the masses was criticized by more sensitive observers, from a strictly public relations point of view Schinkel's quasi-theatrical productions proved to be a tremendous success. As a matter of fact, it has been commonly acknowledged that his appointment as a civil architect in 1810 was in part a result of the personal interest which Queen Luise took in his early panorama presentations.

More important than the entertainment value of his shows, however, were the perceptions which the creation of these panoramas contributed to his understanding of large public environments. The only extant example of his work in this genre, a copy in the form of a small etching of his *Panorama of Palermo* of 1808 (Figure 51),[38] can hardly convey an impression of the scale of the original painting. While the etching measures less than fifteen inches in diameter, the original panorama was about fifteen feet in height and ninety feet in length. The execution of this enormous oil painting occupied Schinkel for some four months; when finished, it had to be exhibited in a specially designed temporary building. A copy of the original was produced for exhibition in St. Petersburg as late as 1844 and assumed the even more ambitious proportions of thirty feet in height and seventy feet in diameter. These dimensions are significant because they convey some idea of the proportional relationship between the observer and the represented scene. Unlike the traditional

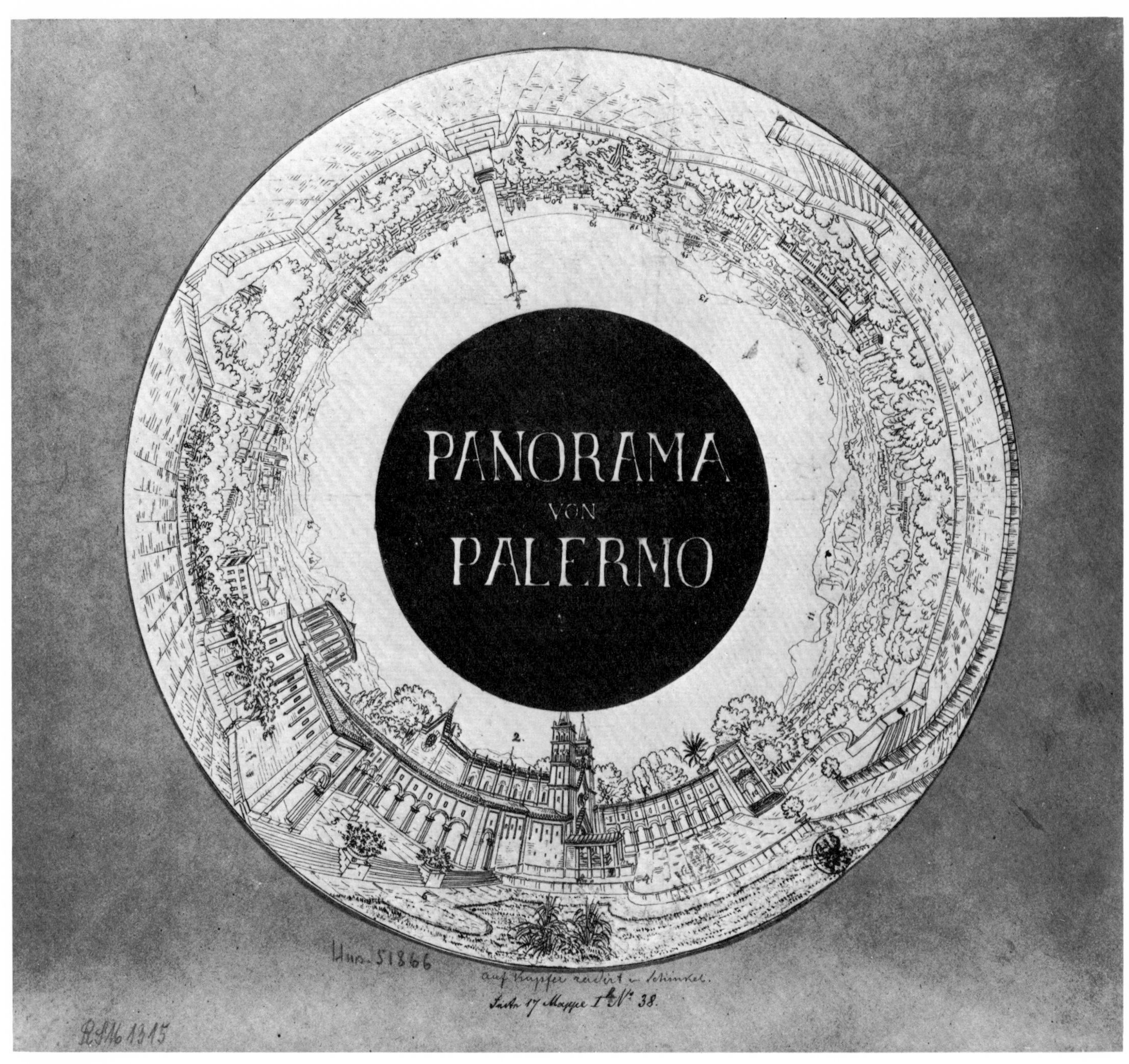

51. Etching by Schinkel of the large *Panorama von Palermo* of 1808.

eighteenth-century *Guck-Kasten*, a miniature stage set viewed by only one person at a time, a panorama of such size would surround a group of observers like a modern expanded cinema screen. Thus, the combination of painting, music, light, and sound effects did not merely enhance the entertainment value of such a showing; it anticipated, in a sense, the modern concept of environmentalist art.[39] The enormous size of Schinkel's panoramas would certainly have contributed to the spectator's total involvement. In contrast to his experience in a theater, his contact with the panorama was direct and personal. He was audience and actor alike. He was enclosed by and became part of an artistically created total environment.

It is, therefore, the scale of these panoramas which should be recognized as the most consequential aspect of the relationship between these painted environments and the three-dimensional world of actual buildings and spaces. By encircling the spectators with an ever-changing perspective, Schinkel realized that the architect's organizing of physical environment could not be restricted to a single building, street, or space. Man's vision was broad—even the layman was becoming aware of this through the popularity of panoramas—and his involvement was dynamic, not static. The relationship of building, space, and man was constantly changing and, to avoid chaos, some harmony of spirit would have to infuse the whole. The environmental unity which Schinkel sought to achieve often had to be created out of disparate components. While a Baroque architect could rely on unity of form and an ordered progression to a definable climax, the problems presented to a nineteenth-century planner were neither so comprehensive nor so well defined. It is perhaps for this reason that the environmental planning which Schinkel carried out in central Berlin has been overlooked or, at best, underestimated. Yet his contemporaries must have understood and appreciated his impact on the city, as evidenced by Eduard Gaertner's panorama (see Figure 15). It is, in a sense, a tribute to the untiring efforts of one man to modify, improve, and enhance the physical environment which was the stage on which the citizens of Berlin assembled. Schinkel's conception of the role of the architect in society reflects his breadth of awareness and his essentially humanistic approach to the act of creation: "To be an architect means to be a man who ennobles all human conditions. Within his sphere of creative effort he must embrace all branches of the fine arts. He fuses sculpture, painting and architecture into a single expression of art, according to the demands of man's moral and rational life."[40]

IV The Transformation of Central Berlin

Karl Friedrich Schinkel commenced the second phase of his career as an architect in 1815. This important point in his life coincided with the conclusion of the Napoleonic wars and the resultant revival of building activity in Prussia's capital city.

However enlightened Berlin's intellectual life may have appeared during the years of war and occupation, its architectural promise remained unfulfilled.[1] Friedrich Gilly had died in 1800 without leaving a single significant building executed. Nothing had come of the plans for a memorial monument to Friedrich II, a proposal which had once rallied the aspirations of an entire generation of idealistic and creative minds in trying to give visual and formal substance to the idea of a new "Spree-Athen." As a result of increasing inactivity, Heinrich Gentz in 1801 sought the patronage of the court at Weimar, where Goethe became his mentor and friend. David Gilly, the teacher of a generation of modern Prussian civil architects and the founder of the Bauakademie, died a pauper's death during the French occupation in 1808. Upon his return from exile in Memel and Königsberg in 1809, the king requested Gentz to add an annex to his city residence and, in the following year, to design a mausoleum for the recently deceased Queen Luise. Except for these projects, there was no building activity of consequence in Berlin from the moment a victorious Napoleon entered the city in 1806 until the conclusion of the war.

In 1815 the population of Berlin stood at about 200,000, in contrast to London which was soon to reach 1,000,000. This was the beginning of a new era, however, and Prussia would be challenged to rise to the stature of a major European state. For those who had urged political and social reform, the Congress of Vienna signaled an end to their hopes and the beginning of a reactionary period. For an architect like Schinkel, however, this year brought the promise of a real beginning of professional activity, for which he had waited in patience, frustration, and hope for nearly ten years. He was promoted to the rank of Geheimer Oberbaurath, in charge of the Berlin bureau of the Prussian Oberbaudeputation.[2] Friedrich Wilhelm III, shortly after his return from the signing of the peace treaty in Paris, ordered Schinkel to prepare designs for a new royal guardhouse to be constructed opposite his city residence in Berlin.

Today, some 150 years after its completion, the Neue Wache remains as one of Berlin's most renowned buildings and a tribute to its creator.[3] Expertly restored after World War II, it now serves a memorial function.[4] Seen from a public garden across the street (Figure 52), the building looks like a massive piece of sculpture, as if cast from a single mold. Its plain

52. Neue Wache, 1816–1818; south facade after restoration.

surface, crisp outline, and masterful balance of open and closed components are confidently contained within its firmly drawn silhouette. The deep recesses of the frontal portico create emphatic areas of shadow, which contrast with the solid forms of the sunlit stone and yet seem as palpable as the dense foliage of the chestnut trees framing the cubic structure. One could hardly find a more appropriate example in the history of modern architecture to bear witness to Le Corbusier's statement that "contour and profile are the touchstone of the architect."[5]

In its present state, Schinkel's Neue Wache is presented to us as a building of classic proportions, elemental shapes, and carefully balanced lines. It seems to be a self-contained monument of serene independence and solidarity. However, such a judgment may prove to be oversimplified and in part misleading. In order to understand the importance of this work and to appreciate its intrinsic values, it would be necessary to investigate the several intermediate stages of its design and attempt to discover the architect's approach to the planning of the total environment, of which the building as such is the most crucial part.

Perhaps the overriding importance of this commission was the fact that it confronted Schinkel with a realistic situation. Unlike many of his previous activities, such as sketching, painting, and the layout of conceptual designs, this one forced him to accept the stringent limits of an actual professional program. These limits concerned not only the purpose, size, and budget of a specific building, but especially the fact that the new guardhouse was to stand within a predetermined physical context. Although it will become evident through a study of various preliminary designs that he attempted to expand the environmental scope beyond the given limits, the original program clearly outlined a complex and challenging site. Consequently, it is best to begin by looking at the nature and conditions of this site at the time when he received the commission.

The general area into which the guardhouse would be placed was skillfully recorded by Jean Rosenberg in an engraving of 1780 (Figure 53). From the large plaza in the foreground, the perspective view extends west down the tree-lined promenade of the Unter den Linden. On either side stand important royal and public buildings: on the left, the Kronprinzen Palais and the Opernhaus; on the right, the Zeughaus and the palace of Prince Heinrich (which became the Friedrich Wilhelm-Universität in 1810). Between these last two impressive structures there is a small, low building, the Kanonierwache, which housed the guard attached to the Zeughaus. This outdated shelter was to be removed, and a new building for the royal honor guard, which could not be accommodated in the small Palais, was to be erected in its place.

53. Jean Rosenberg. Platz am Zeughaus; view from the east, 1780.

54. J. C. Krüger. View of Opernbrücke from the northeast, 1776.

The designated site between the Zeughaus and the university was complicated by the presence of an old moat, the Grüne Graben, which cut through it from north to south. The Unter den Linden spanned this ditch by means of a bridge adorned with statuary, vaguely discernable in Rosenberg's engraving and seen more clearly in a view drawn by J. C. Krüger in 1776 (Figure 54), drawn from approximately the spot where the old guardhouse stood and looking toward the Opernhaus. Rave suggests that the desire to remove this unsightly and hygienically undesirable watercourse might have provided the original impetus for renovation of the area.[6] The site, then, was rather restricted, surrounded by important buildings of irregular forms and various styles and characteristically isolated in space. The strong directional force of the Unter den Linden flowed into the large open plaza, but found no focal point. A juxtaposition of diverse architectonic elements existed, but no unified environment.

Schinkel's preliminary sketch of the area (Figure 55) already indicates his general approach to the problem of siting the new guardhouse. With a few rough strokes he indicates existing buildings and quickly establishes the essential configurations of the physical environment. His concern goes beyond the narrow limits of the projected individual building and encompasses surrounding structures and the significant spaces that

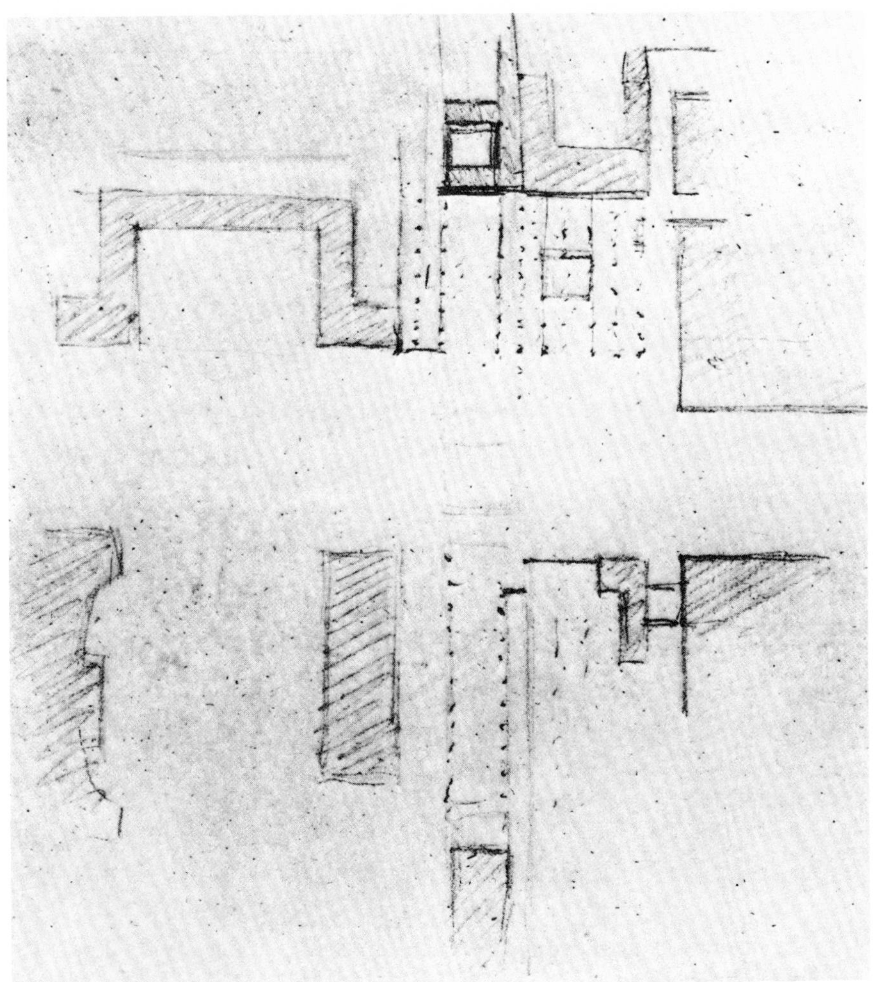

55. Neue Wache; preliminary site plan, 1816.

separate them. Important changes are immediately apparent. The bridge across the old moat has been eliminated and the Platz am Opernhaus and the Platz am Zeughaus have become part of a broad continuation of the Unter den Linden. Thus, for the first time since the days of Andreas Schlüter, a Berlin architect recognized the intrinsic power of the city's most dominant axis and sought to strengthen its uninterrupted vista.

The new guardhouse is placed at some distance from the avenue, beyond the rear facades of the university and the Zeughaus and adjacent to the office of the finance minister.[7] A broad, deep path to the building is cut through the grove of chestnut trees which covered the plot and a similar tree-lined path is suggested on axis south of the avenue. The major directional force of the Unter den Linden is slowed first by the

56. Neue Wache; first design; view from the south, 1816.

broad expanse of the university court and the open space opposite it, and then by the transverse axis of the narrower tree-lined vistas to the north and south. There is an attempt to balance the spaciousness of the major artery by the visual tension of a constricted intersecting path.

A certain ambiguity in the relationship between the guardhouse and the avenue becomes apparent in Schinkel's perspective drawing of the site (Figure 56). Within a public area of monumental buildings, a feeling of intimacy is created by the dense foliage which isolates the small structure and seems to shelter it from its powerful neighbors. Such a Romantic setting hardly seems appropriate for the soldiers of the royal guard and, indeed, the arrangement appears to have been an adaptation of the siting of the mausoleum of Queen Luise in the park of Schloss Charlottenburg (Figure 57). The small memorial temple with its simple Grecian portico had been executed by Gentz, after a design by Schinkel,[8] and erected in a secluded area of the palace grounds in 1810. It is approached by a very long path through a silent wood and its serene isolation complements the quiet dignity of its simple forms. Perhaps the existing chestnut grove at the guardhouse site inspired Schinkel to repeat the Romantic emphasis on nature of the mausoleum setting. The facade of his cubic structure with its three dark openings is locked into the converging lines of its guardian trees in the same manner as the funerary temple. Indeed, the only alteration in the design is the Egyptian rather than Grecian character of the guardhouse created by its battered walls and covetto cornice.[9]

Though the positive aspects of Schinkel's first scheme, mainly relating

57. Mausoleum of Queen Luise, Schlosspark Charlottenburg, 1810.

to improvements of the Unter den Linden, can be praised, his solution for the Neue Wache itself was not in keeping with the character of a military guardpost, nor with the wishes of the king. Friedrich Wilhelm III, as Krieger vividly relates, was primarily interested in watching his soldiers parade.[10] Consequently, he insisted that the guardhouse be close to the street, within viewing distance of his residence, the Kronprinzen Palais (henceforth referred to as the Königliche Palais).

After a careful restudy of the entire situation, Schinkel submitted a new site plan for the area, several drawings for a modified building design, and a document (*Denkschrift*) which explained his concept and the reasons for his revised solution. The first and last items are of foremost significance here. They express his will to succeed and serve as a measure of his growth as a professional architect. The site plan in particular demonstrates that his principal aim in designing his first major building was the improvement of the larger urban context. He looked upon the guardhouse as a catalyst, a force which could tie together those formal and spatial, visual and functional properties of the area and discipline it into a single and coherent statement of environmental design.

Unlike the previous sketch of the site, this second plan (Figure 58) is executed with utmost precision and topographical accuracy. Existing buildings and spaces are correctly drawn, scaled, and identified.[11] Additions to or alterations of existing parts are explicitly expressed in graphic and descriptive terms. Previous suggestions to eliminate the bridge and the old moat are retained, but the plan is expanded to include

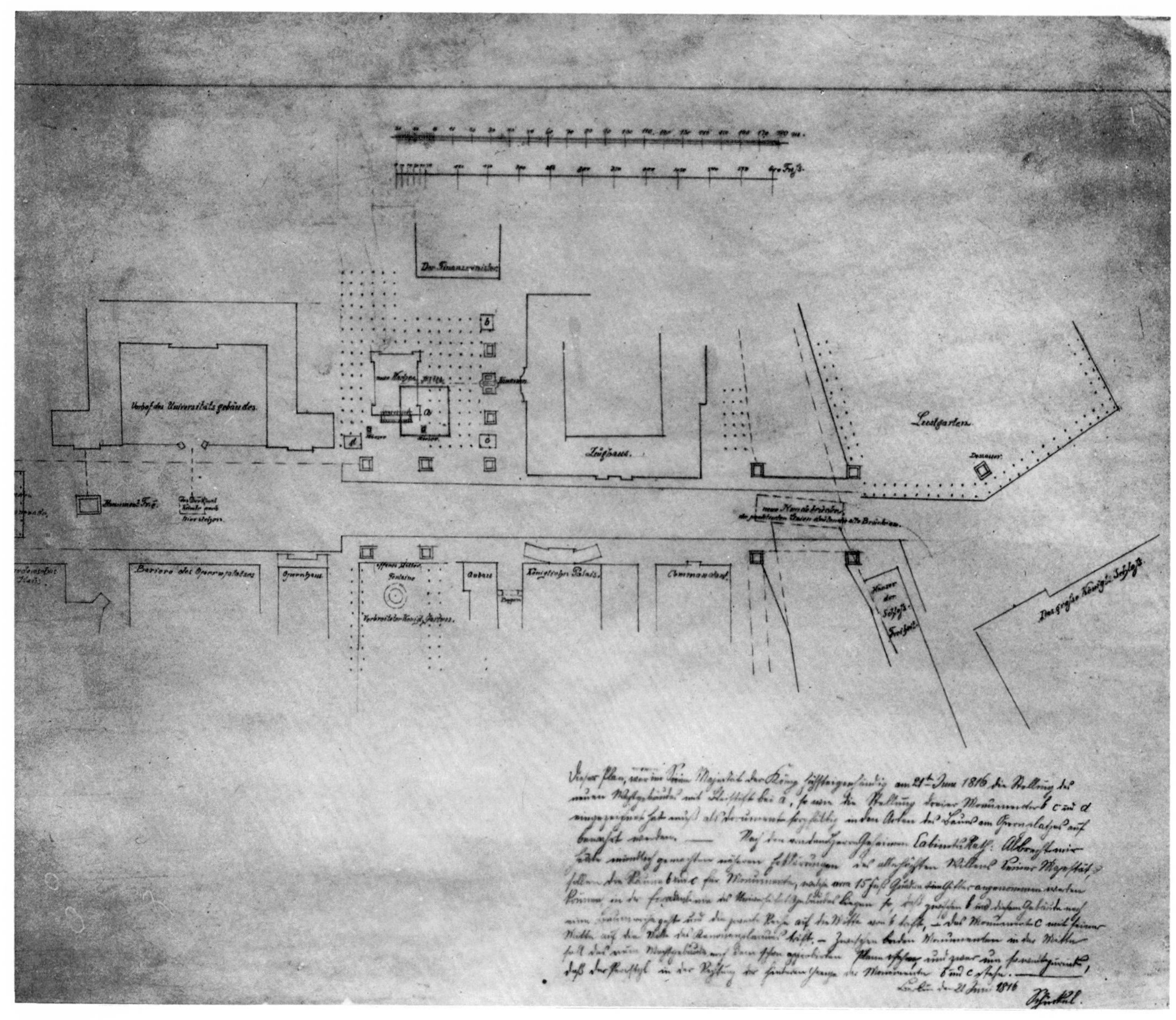

58. Neue Wache; second site plan, June 1816.

more area and additional improvements. The guardhouse is placed closer to the avenue (the overlapping rectangle, added in pencil, represents the position favored by the king), and the boundaries of its rectangular form are keyed to the pattern of surrounding structures. The southern edge is aligned with the rear facade of the university wing; its eastern flank is aligned with the west wall of the finance ministry. Moreover, the east-west center line of the guardhouse corresponds to the center of the side entrance of the Zeughaus. This manner of relating rectangular blocks within a grid pattern may have been in the academic tradition of Durand, but it was not Schinkel's sole consideration in siting the new building. The guardhouse is intentionally placed over the bed of the old canal, which was to be covered by a continuous subterranean vault. By means of inward slanting roofs and an interior drainage system, rainwater and sewage would be efficiently removed.[12] The building is also provided with an open interior court so that the activities of the military would be directed inward, leaving exterior spaces free for public use. East of the guardhouse, a large area of the chestnut grove, the Kastanienwäldchen, remains undisturbed, with a border of three freestanding statues and a group of cannons to separate it from a broad walkway along the flank of the Zeughaus. This public area is meant for pedestrian promenades, the trees providing welcome shade and the statuary relating its civic character to complementary groups along the avenue. Indeed, a distinguishing feature of the plan is Schinkel's masterful utilization of freestanding sculpture to define spaces, accentuate vistas, and organize a large urban segment into an environmental unit by the most economical means.

On his plan, the small squares indicating pedestals for statues mark important junctures and tie together the existing structures and Schinkel's suggested additions. A row of three monuments along the northern edge of the avenue continues at right angles the line which marks the boundary of the Kastanienwäldchen and also forms a transition between the university and the Zeughaus. Two of these simultaneously act as outposts for the guardhouse, through the intermediary of two mounted guns (*Mörser*), and as pendants to corresponding pedestals on the opposite side of the street. A circular fountain is proposed for the royal garden, to face the guardhouse on axis and complete this group—a small vignette within the larger scheme. The pattern of four related monuments here is repeated at the corners of a new bridge over the Kupfergraben, which would straighten and enlarge the extension of the Unter den Linden onto the island. The natural eastern termination of this expanded environment would be the existing statue of Leopold von Anhalt-Dessau by Schadow, which stood amidst the poplar trees planted in the Lustgarten by David

Gilly and faced the garden facade of Schlüter's Schloss. The suggested termination to the west would also be a single important figure, that of Friedrich II, shown in the center of the avenue opposite the west wing of the university (or, alternately, in line with the center of the court). Though this position is approximately the same as that proposed by Langhans for the competition of 1797, its promise would only be fulfilled some fifty years later when the equestrian statue of Friedrich by Christian Rauch was erected there.

Unfortunately, parts of Schinkel's comprehensive scheme would have infringed on the private property of the king. He had only recently had his private garden enclosed by a solid wall and neither the suggestion to replace it with an open metal fence (*offenes Gitter*) nor the proposal to substitute a fountain for the unsightly, polluted moat met with the monarch's approval. Despite the fact that Friedrich Wilhelm III had said as early as 1801 that he intended someday "to have the entire area rehabilitated," it is clear that the king had lost this foresight and initiative before his own architect presented him with a logical and beneficial overall plan. Friedrich Wilhelm's corrections of the plan and Schinkel's marginal note of disappointment unsuccessfully concluded the first environmental scheme for central Berlin.[13] The king's revisions were in keeping with his favorite dictum: "Je schlichter und einfacher desto besser." The simpler, the better, meant in this case that Schinkel's scheme to visually organize the area and relate the Unter den Linden to the island and the Schloss would have to be abandoned. The monarch was interested only in having the royal guardhouse positioned in such a way that he could easily observe his soldiers. He ordered the building to be placed even closer to the street, in the position marked *a* on the plan, and reduced Schinkel's extensive program of sculptural accents to three, marked *b, c, d,* within the immediate vicinity of the guardhouse. Construction of a new bridge across the Kupfergraben had to wait until 1819 (see Figure 20; the sculptural decoration of this bridge was not realized until after Schinkel's death). Needless to say, any changes in this waterway or embellishment of its banks for pedestrian promenades was also rejected by the king.[14] Such farsighted planning and unsolicited suggestions were not considered within a civil servant's domain.

Schinkel's final plan of the site of the Neue Wache (Figure 59) shows the building in the position desired by the king, surrounded on three sides by neat rows of trees. The guardhouse, the portico of the Opernhaus, and the curving ramp at the entrance to the Königliche Palais are all shown in outline, in contrast to the shaded forms of other buildings, as if to indicate a special relationship among them. A recent photograph (Figure

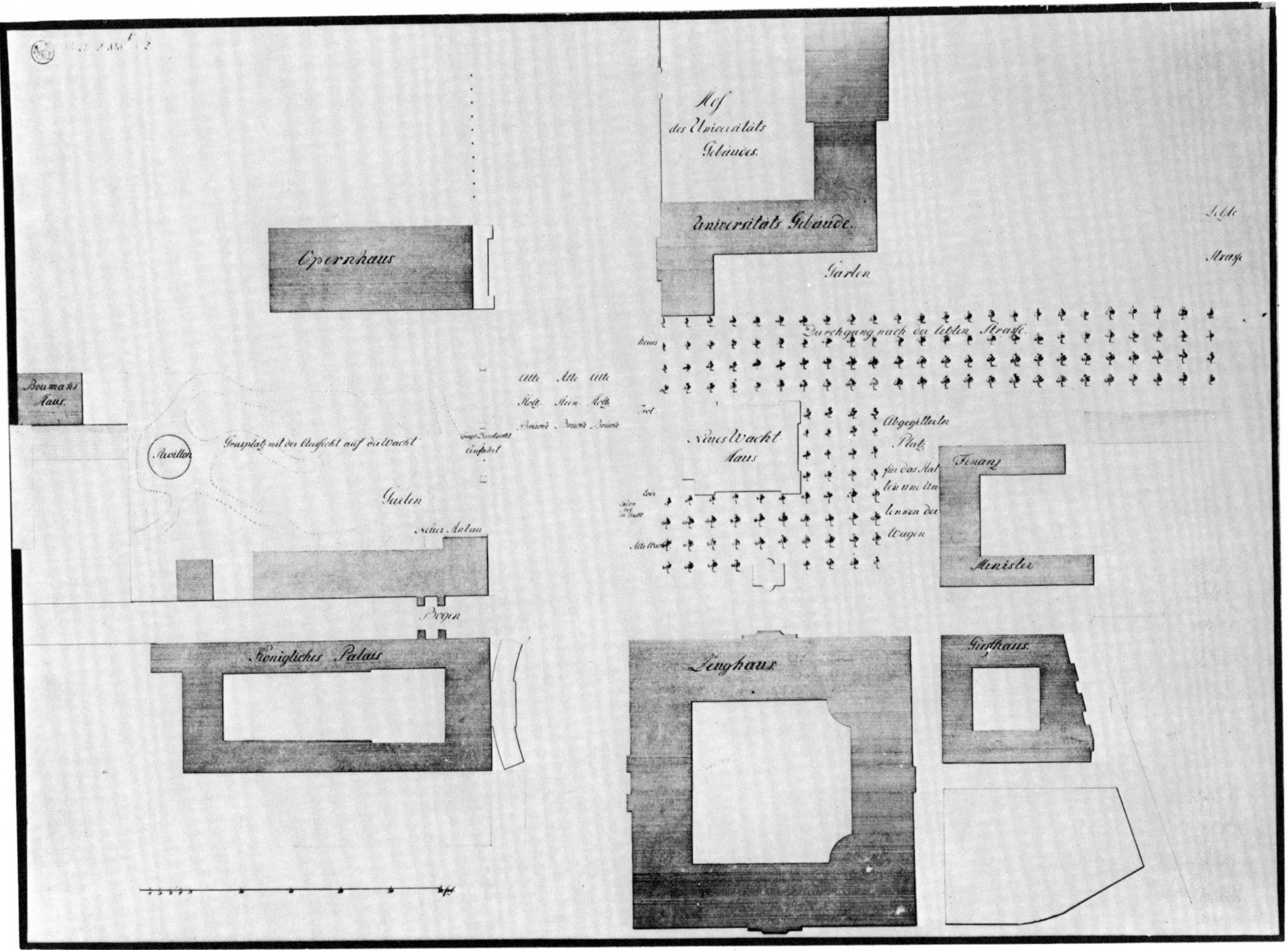

59. Neue Wache; final site plan, autumn 1816.

60. Neue Wache; view from site of the Königliche Palais.

60) shows the view the king had of the guardhouse and its shallow forecourt from his city residence across the street. While the bulk of the building is hidden by foliage, the frontal portico and corner towers framing it stand out like a stage backdrop for the enactment of the military ritual of the changing of the guard. The view from the Neue Wache entrance to the Opernhaus (Figure 61) reflects Schinkel's awareness of the stylistic characteristics of the surrounding buildings and his attempt to harmonize his own forms without becoming imitative.

61. Neue Wache; view through portico onto the Opernhaus.

In addition to the conscious correlation of the guardhouse to existing buildings, Schinkel again tried to enhance the open spaces of the area. In this last scheme he proposed new landscaping for the royal garden, including a circular pavilion at its southern edge. The curving paths and irregular planted areas were perhaps meant to remind the king of his favorite retreat, the Pfaueninsel, which was then being transformed by Lenné in the style of English landscaping.[15] For the city garden, the purpose is explicit. The area is designated "Grasplatz mit der Aussicht auf die Wacht" (green with view of the guardhouse), and the entrance to it is marked "Grosse Durchsicht" (major vista). For Schinkel, a proper view of his building was as important as the structure itself and, to the end, he insisted upon a setting which would accommodate this perspective.

Like the others, this arrangement was not completely accepted. Besides the guardhouse itself, only the widened avenue directly in front of it and the elimination of the old bridge at this point were realized.[16] More and more, it seemed, the Neue Wache was destined to become an isolated monument, serving its specific function but restrained from acting as a unifying force in the larger environment. While Schinkel was prevented from realizing the total scope of his envisioned changes, he nevertheless continued to view his new building as part of a larger scene. With the perception and skill of a panorama painter and perhaps also with the consciousness of the framed view of a stage designer, he drew a perspective of the Unter den Linden from the Zeughaus to the Brandenburger Tor (Figure 62). The portico of the Neue Wache is barely visible behind the monumental silhouette of the Zeughaus, but it appears to be properly balanced in height and visual emphasis in relation to its neighboring

62. Perspective drawing of Unter den Linden from the east, 22 July 1817.

structures. The main point here is not to show the Neue Wache as a single, serene, and isolated monument. Instead, Schinkel tried to test its visual and formal effect in the context of a larger and more important environment—that is, the total vista of a newly opened street, a continuum of space rather than parcels of plazas joined by bridges and interrupted by a canal. Despite restrictions and alterations, the result is more than a single, whimsical visual link between a royal residence and the guardhouse across the street. For Schinkel, the environment spans as far as the eye can see, and it embraces a colorful landscape of many buildings and spaces. In 1822 Heinrich Heine wrote of this very scene: "Truly, I do not know of a more impressive view than the one that unfolds when one stands near the Hundebrücke looking towards the Linden. On the right-hand side, the high and imposing Zeughaus, the new Wachtgebäude, the Universität and the Akademie. On the left, the Königliche Palais, the Opernhaus, the Bibliothek, etc. At this site, one magnificent building is followed by another of equal splendor."[17]

To fully appreciate the setting of the Neue Wache as an operative part of a living city, one would have to visualize it as did the people of nineteenth-century Berlin. Fortunately, an illuminating record exists in the giant canvas by Franz Krüger entitled *Parade Berlin*, painted in 1837 (Figure 63).[18] The royal regiments fill the avenue and extend as far as the eye can see; the citizenry crowd the plazas and sidewalks and hang from windows and rooftops. At the far left, the king, mounted on a white horse, awaits the approaching cavalry. All of the surrounding civic buildings lend the weight of their monumental facades to the display of autocratic power. In the clean air each detail stands crisply outlined and the clear sunshine reflects from bright walls and polished helmets. Compared to its condition half a century earlier (see Figure 53), the Unter den Linden had finally achieved a physical framework worthy of Prussia's *via triumphalis*.

Schinkel's Neue Wache takes its place among the older imposing structures, and Krüger even includes a portrait of its distinguished architect amidst the spectators standing near it.[19] Its portico is flanked by Christian Rauch's statues of Scharnhorst and Bülow, erected in 1822; opposite stands the figure of Blücher, completed four years later. All were important Prussian military leaders during the Napoleonic wars. These three figures on their high pedestals were the only ones retained from Schinkel's much more extensive sculptural program. And yet, the very nobility of the guardhouse and its commanding presence in the heart of Berlin made his first major building a splendid and lasting success. In 1842, soon after Schinkel's death, Franz Kugler paid tribute to his creative genius in this summation of the Neue Wache: "The totality of this build-

63. Franz Krüger. *Parade Berlin,* 1837.

ing combines earnestness, solidity and strength with an expression of magnificence which is appropriate to the two basic criteria by which it had been created: its representational purpose as the principal guardhouse of a royal residence and its integration into a splendid environment."[20]

The Transformation of Central Berlin

Schinkel's concern with totalities and his effort to coordinate comprehensive environments had been essential to his work and philosophy since his training under Gilly and Gentz. He had also learned to appreciate that his position as a state architect would rarely permit him to execute his projects according to his own intentions. Again and again he had to surrender to the bureaucratic conditions under which he worked, and the king for whom he planned was hesitant and unimaginative. Prussia under Friedrich Wilhelm III was not Bavaria under Ludwig I. Yet, ironically, in Prussia the architect had ideas which the king restrained; in

Bavaria the king had imagination which the architect, Leo von Klenze, lacked. Schinkel's peculiar position and the strict supervision which he endured must be kept in mind in order to appreciate his ultimate achievement. The design of the Neue Wache demonstrated not only his ability in terms of architectural design and his concern for the environment, but also his adaptability in acquiescing, albeit grudgingly, to the limitations of an uninspired monarch. Rarely, if ever, has so superior an architect been forced to practice the art of compromise more often than Schinkel. Nor, since Sir Christopher Wren, has there been one more determined to succeed. Unlike the so-called "visionary architects," including dreamers like Boullée and Lequeu or a score of others who sought grandeur and unreasonableness and were classified by Emil Kaufmann as masters in the Age of Reason, Schinkel deserves the title of Architect. He built buildings with reason and restraint. He made every effort to overcome difficulties in order to effect as comprehensive a solution as possible. And, even more important, he expressed confidence in his own ability and a sense of commitment to his professional obligations. It was his firm belief that an architect should be "one who endeavors to ennoble all human conditions." It follows that a person who confesses such a philosophy would inevitably seek every opportunity to reach beyond the prescribed limits of his duties as a state architect and civil servant. It not only meant that he would interpret every commission in the broadest possible sense, as exemplified in the plans for the Neue Wache, but he would also think in terms of large-scale and long-range planning proposals which would ultimately improve the total environment of central Berlin.

One of the most resolute statements in support of this attitude is Schinkel's rarely discussed *Bebauungsplan* (master plan) of Berlin which he composed during the later planning stages of the guardhouse and presented to the king in March 1817 (Figure 64).[21] It covers an area of about two square kilometers of the center of the city and should be analyzed in accord with Schinkel's own definition of purpose. In a letter to Christian Rauch he stated that he attempted "through this plan, to eliminate an intolerable hodgepodge of organization and a jumble of specific ordinances affecting the forms of the city."[22] In other words, he approached the king, who only six months earlier had ruined his plans for the environmental design of the Neue Wache, with a comprehensive study for the architectural replanning of the entire core of the capital. Schinkel may have had good reason to doubt that anything would come of his idealistic proposals. Indeed, he wrote in the preceding sentence: "But only God knows what the decision may be." No record indicates that he ever received an official response from the king.

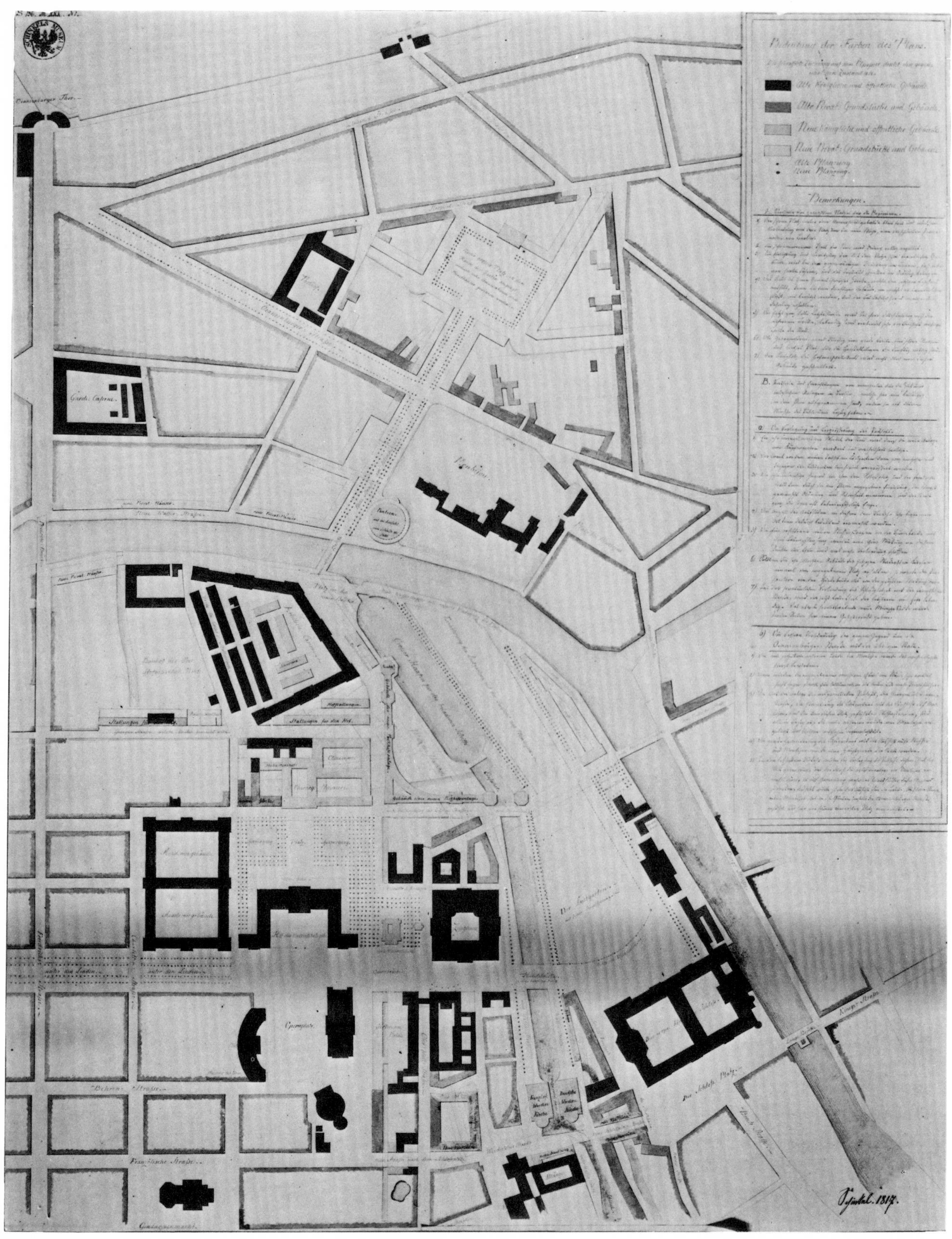

64. Master plan for the redevelopment of central Berlin, 1817.

Despite the neglect of this plan at the time of its conception, it is certainly of great significance. First, it summarizes Schinkel's planning ideas at the beginning of his career as a practicing state architect. Second, it is an important index to and source of many of his subsequent planning solutions.

The 1817 plan is the first master plan of central Berlin executed by an architect. Although numerous surveys existed, among them the comprehensive map by J. C. Selter of 1804 (see detail, Figure 13), no one had ever gone beyond topographical or picturesque recordings.[23] Schinkel's plan is not a document of history, but a statement of intent. Except for royal property, public buildings, and some major waterways and streets, he begins anew. He seems to show no respect for the crooked streets in Friedrich-Werder, the random pattern of commercial buildings at the northern end of the island, and the ever-present and disrupting moats. He proposes a complete transformation of the central area and the destruction of obstacles "no longer bearable."

According to his marginal notes, he focused first on an area already familiar to the king and himself. He called for the grouping of several hospital installations into a single unit north of the university, reinforcing his architectural proposals with arguments for economy. He also pointed out that the efficiency resulting from this coordination of medical facilities would enable him to utilize the remaining area for parks and promenades.[24] The military barracks behind the hospital would remain untouched. Toward the east, however, he proposed a totally new shipping and storage center: a harbor basin, bridges, cranes, and a continuous L-shaped complex of customs warehouses. This arrangement would not only eliminate the unsightly warehouses in Friedrich-Werder, further south, but would also permit the razing of Nering's crescent-shaped Orangerie which had been used as an annex of the Packhof on the island since around 1750. Finally, the proposal to build a new and enlarged storage area along the lower Kupfergraben would enable him to close the Pomeranzengraben which cut the island in two. With the coordination of hospitals, commercial buildings, and shipping facilities thus conveniently arranged, Schinkel could concentrate on the embellishment of the island.

He called once more for a new and wider bridge from the Unter den Linden to Schlüter's Schloss. Looking toward the south, two impressive churches were to flank the canal, replacing the old Packhof. All newly regulated embankments were to be planted with avenues of trees. Public promenades along the river had already existed in Friedrich Wilhelm's Lustgarten in 1648 (see Figure 2), and the similar treatment of riverbanks in Florence and Paris had elicited Schinkel's admiration.[25] For the rest of the area north of the palace, Schinkel simply suggested the removal of Gilly's ailing poplar trees and the termination of the planted section toward the south by a curving screen of *Bildsäulen* or freestanding sculpture. This emphasis on openness toward the north was intended to amplify the vista onto a new circular structure called the *Panteon* in the gardens of Schloss Monbijou.[26] A direct and unobstructed visual link was to be created across the northern half of the Spree island from the traditional royal apartments above Portal V in the old Schloss toward a focal point of symbolic significance some six hundred meters distant.[27]

Despite the fact that a somewhat superficial criticism has been leveled against Schinkel's monument,[28] its function as an element of environmental control reached far beyond a simple statement of visual accent and focus. Indeed, the presence of the Panteon signaled the incorporation of the Spandauer Vorstadt into the environment of modern Berlin. Reaching deep into the undeveloped urban fabric of this section, Schinkel proposed a series of interconnecting avenues and a spacious city square. The generous size of this plaza would have permitted private gardens in the center, similar to English examples. Along its borders he intended the construction of private residences. With its dominant axial exit toward the southwest and numerous secondary entries along its sides, this square seems almost to be a bourgeois version of the Place Stanislaus in Nancy. In Berlin, however, such a city square could have become a prototype for future residential planning and would perhaps have prevented Hegemann's despair over the city's notorious tenements, the *Mietskasernen*, erected at a later time.[29]

The innovations of Schinkel's plan of 1817 reveal his imagination and farsightedness and also the breadth of the changes which this young architect was willing to attempt. He proposed the systematic consolidation of areas of public service, and of commerce and residential units. Moreover, he projected extensive new areas of parks and promenades. He would have closed inefficient canals, improved facilities for river traffic, and provided open spaces in the very heart of the capital. Never before had anyone proposed such generous expanses and public uses for the northern half of the island. Never again would Berlin enjoy a more promising plan for the utilization of its river. Despite the extent of local control and urban improvement outlined and regardless of the number of individual items proposed, Schinkel's plan might have emerged as merely a statement of fragmentized units were it not for one additional major idea. This idea does not pertain to planning concepts which aim primarily at the creation of new vistas or the preservation of old historical monuments. Rather, it focuses on the essence of large-scale urban design. It demands the combination of improvement within individual environmental units with effective solutions for the transformation of the total urban scene. This combination in Schinkel's plan is the least obvious, yet most important, aspect and the foundation for its success. He attempted to achieve it in a number of simple ways: by broadening streets and building bridges, by razing slums and opening modern thoroughfares.

The interconnection of individual parts of the city, neglected for years, would be the essence of his plan. Near the Panteon he proposed a new bridge across the Spree, linking his new avenue into the Spandauer Vorstadt with the vital commercial center of the Packhof. Along the southern edge of this L-shaped complex, the Letzte Strasse (Dorotheenstrasse) would be transformed into a spacious thoroughfare and, continued across the Kupfergraben via a new iron bridge, it would "play a vital rôle, very effectively connecting important parts of the city," as Schinkel noted in the margin of the plan. A further extension of this street would cut across the island and continue over the Spree into historical Berlin to the east. He also realized the need for another traffic artery further to the south which could connect the western and eastern parts of the capital. For the first time an architect proposed joining Friedrichstadt with Friedrich-Werder, the island of historical Cölln and the old quarters of Berlin, east of the Spree. The broad Französische Strasse, bordering the Gendarmenmarkt at the north, was to break through barriers of moats and jumbled groups of buildings to Gentz's Münze at the Werdersche-Markt, continue through the mills of Friedrich-Werder and into the Schloss-Platz, south of Schlüter's palace. The Lange Brücke across the Spree would then lead this transverse axis to the distant St. Georgenthor (or Königsthor), the eastern entry to Berlin. On this route, Schinkel planned a pair of twin churches (one for the French, the other for the German congregations of the parish of Friedrich-Werder) over the narrowed Kupfergraben; he also hoped to reduce the uncontrolled sprawl of vendors' shacks by providing a series of modern commercial structures near the Werdersche-Markt.

Thus, by this master plan Schinkel attempted an organic coordination of several sections of the central city into a unified and harmonious environment for commercial and civic life. His daring proposals to transform the nucleus of the capital were the first to allow for the vital relationship between the river, the island, the palace and the Unter den Linden. Yet, the scope and vision of Schinkel's grand design was not appreciated by the king and, for the moment, nothing came of the plan of 1817.

Although the state's lack of funds and the hesitant attitude of his royal patron would continue to restrict Schinkel's promising potential as a city planner, several of his subsequent projects for Berlin reveal that his quest for the improvement of the city's environment had become an inseparable part of his philosophy as an architect. Apart from projects such as the Museum, where his plans embraced the entire area of the Lustgarten, there are a number of less conspicuous examples which indicate that he was willing to accept any challenge to bring unity to the sites for which he built. Among them, perhaps the most sophisticated, yet the least obvious, is his Schauspielhaus (1818–1821) at the Gendarmenmarkt.[30]

Schinkel received the commission for its design unexpectedly. His building was to replace the Nationaltheater, which had been gutted by fire in July 1817. Designed by Carl Gotthard Langhans, one of Berlin's first neo-Classicists, the older theater had been built as recently as 1800–1802. In contrast to Langhans' more famous Brandenburger Tor, the Nationaltheater was not a distinguished work. Its long, nondescript facade framed one side of the Gendarmenmarkt and featured a loosely attached portico at its center. The rectangular block was covered by the swelling curvature of an enormous *Bohlendach,* which quickly earned it the sobriquet "coffin lid" among the critical public of Berlin. A drawing of the building survives, presumably executed by the young Schinkel as early as 1800 (Figure 65).[31] Compared to Friedrich Gilly's competition entry for the same project (see Figure 71), Langhans' contribution appears even more pedestrian.

65. Nationaltheater by Carl G. Langhans, 1800–1802.

66. Schauspielhaus; view from the northeast, 1821.

Although this uninspired structure was gutted, the program for the new theater required the utilization of the still-existing foundations and the badly damaged sections of the lower walls. In addition, royal requests stated that the new building had to provide spaces for additional functions. Besides the theater proper, there was to be a large concert hall, a royal reception lounge, rehearsal rooms, offices, and areas for the construction and storage of stage scenery. In order to meet these demands and to avoid additional interference "von Seiten Allerhöchsten Ortes" (meaning the king), Schinkel resorted to a modern professional device. He requested a written guarantee that he, the architect, would be exclusively responsible for all decisions.[32]

The resultant design of the new Schauspielhaus became Schinkel's first international success (Figure 66). The elevated central portion of the building contained the major elements of stage, orchestra, and auditorium, while the symmetrically placed lateral wings housed the concert hall and rehearsal sections. Because of this complex program and the specific requirements and restrictions imposed upon the architect, the space given to the theater proper was reduced to about one-third of the total area.

Seen within its urban setting, the Schauspielhaus formed the central feature at the west side of the city plaza (Figure 67). It was flanked to the north and south by two almost identical churches of an earlier period. The Französische Kirche (1701–1705) at the north was designed by Louis Cayart for the Huguenot community in Berlin.[33] Its southern counterpart, the Deutsche Dom or Neue Kirche (1701–1708), was the work of Giovanni Simonetti, an Italian-trained mason and stucateur, who executed this structure after plans by Martin Grünberg. Only toward the end of the century, after 1781, did both churches receive their characteristic tall drums and domes, modeled after designs by Karl Philipp Gontard, a captain and architect in Friedrich II's army of military men and civil servants. Nicolai contends that Gontard, the teacher of Heinrich Gentz and an acquaintance of the famous Carlo Bibiena, had to draw the plans for these dominant cupolas "following the king's own idea."[34] In the context of our discussion of Schinkel's design for the Schauspielhaus, the presence of these tall centralized structures on either side played an important role. They challenged Schinkel in the overall composition of his new design. Somehow a correlation had to be achieved between the old and the new. Despite the fact that he insisted that the form of the theater should express its purpose—the exterior conforming to the interior tripartite division of functions—he also had to find some means of relating it to its neighboring structures.

A view across the plaza onto the Französische Kirche (Figures 68, 69; photos taken before and after World War II) reveals some basic principles of design by which Schinkel succeeded in complementing the existing architectural framework of this important city square. Most obviously, the new building was similar to its neighbors in its essentially classical appearance. Freestanding pedimented porticos, symmetrical balance of masses, and an emphasis on center and axis are basic in each design. Nevertheless, Schinkel's inventive transformation of Grecian and Renaissance inspirations resulted in a new civic structure that was clearly distinguishable from the Franco-Italianate character of the two existing religious buildings.

He claimed that he sought inspiration from Greece: "In general, concerning the style of the architecture in which I created the building, I tried to emulate Greek forms and methods of construction insofar as this is possible in such a complex work."[35] Even in specific reference to the characteristic treatment of the walls, an exquisitely proportioned grid of

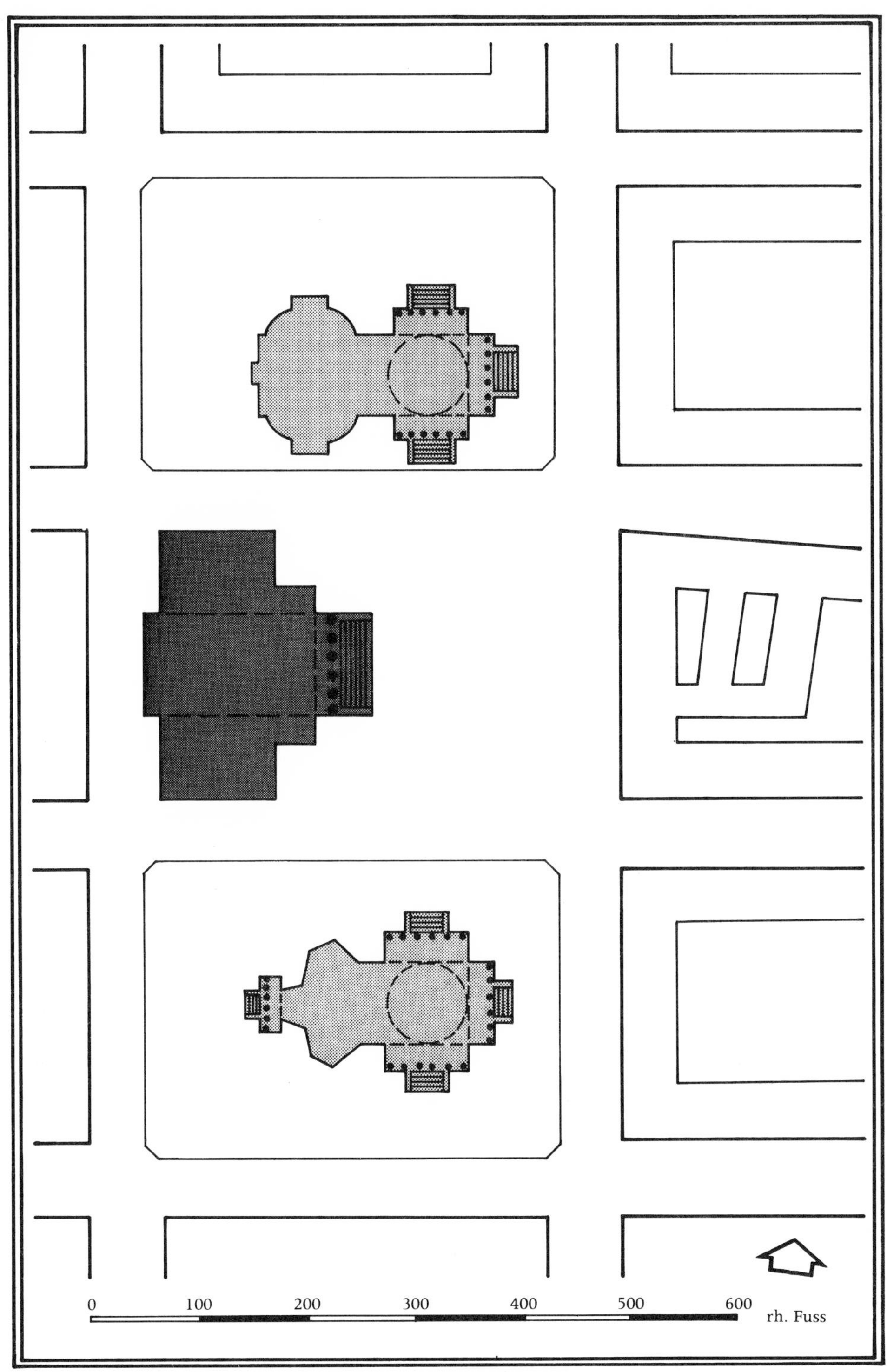

67. Site plan of the Gendarmenmarkt.

68. Gendarmenmarkt with Französischer Kirche and Schauspielhaus, prior to World War II.

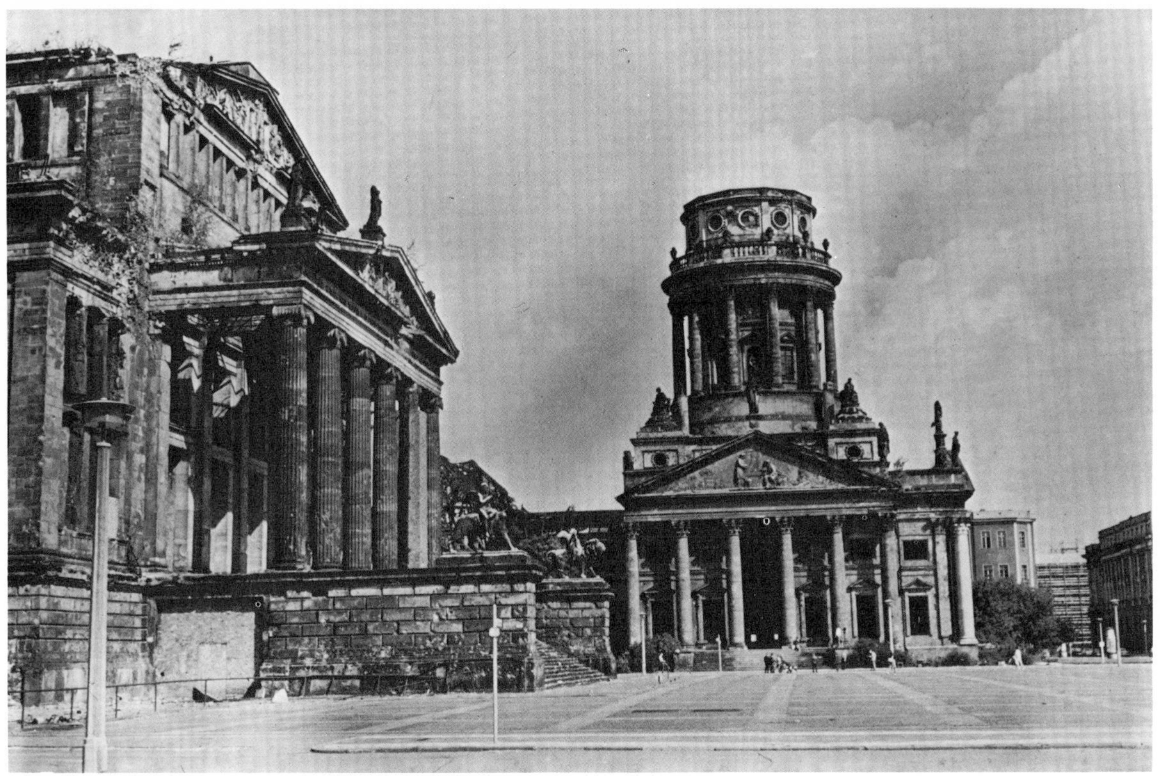

69. Gendarmenmarkt (now Platz der Akademie).

alternating pilaster-piers and window openings (see Figure 66), he cited a Grecian model.[36] At the same time, he pointed out that this treatment admitted a maximum of natural light. However, the sources of his inspiration are not so simple. In reference to the wall treatment, one could argue that the Roman works of Michelangelo were an equally important influence. The structural and decorative patterns of verticals and horizontals of the palace facade at the Capitoline Hill had been carefully drawn by Schinkel (see Figure 44). He had used the same system for the great basilica in his conceptual design, *Dom auf einer Anhöhe* (see Figure 45). At the Schauspielhaus in Berlin, it really mattered little whether he thought of the Michelangelesque pilaster-piers or the Palladian portico as being Greek in inspiration. In the end, he would transform these Classical elements into a style distinctly his own, as well as into components relating to and complementing the forms of existing structures.

Aware of the fact that the theater would have to dominate the plaza, Schinkel chose a pyramidal composition for the main facade, with the triangular pediment of the portico repeated above the clerestory, where it is crowned by a sculptural group at the apex. The richness of this composition and the breadth of the facade helped to balance the vertical emphasis of the domed churches flanking the square. The dominance of the theater was also effected by raising it on a podium, which Schinkel was able to justify on strictly practical and economic grounds, but which certainly served a visual function as well. This platform was extended into the plaza to form the spur walls of a grand staircase leading up to the main portico. The purpose of the portico also went beyond the mere embellishment of the theater's entrance. In echoing the porticos of the churches it effectively drew together three sides of the large plaza into a harmonious formal unity.

While the frame of the square itself was coordinated by these formal means, Schinkel was also aware of the more subtle relationships existing between the churches and other parts of his theater. A distinctive feature of the flanking buildings is the use of porticos on three sides below a centralized dome (see Figures 67, 68, 69). Approaching the square along one of the connecting streets—coming south from the Unter den Linden, for example—one would immediately be aware of the multiple porticos leading one's eye around the projecting mass of the church into the square and onto the raised portico of the Schauspielhaus. The sculptured pediments of the churches are not only repeated—twice—on the main facade of the theater, but they also appear on the lateral wings. Economic and spatial restrictions prevented Schinkel from using freestanding porticos on these lateral facades, but he did employ a subtle means of identifying their elevations with those bordering the square. A view of the south facade of the Schauspielhaus (Figure 70) reveals the heavy ashlar base below and an elegant pediment with sculptured accents above. Between, the main elevation is framed by the strong pilaster-piers of the typical "Schinkel corner" and consists of a complex rhythm of vertical supports and window openings. Four unbroken verticals extend below the sill line and rise above to the level of the building's continuous entablature. Thus, the composition is a very subtle reminder of the porticos which characterize the other facades and dominate the Gendarmenmarkt.

The view shown here also indicates that Schinkel had gone beyond the consideration of a site as a mere stage set for human activities. He realized that a building can be seen and experienced from angles other than the most obvious or most conventional. It is interesting that he includes in this view not only a corner of the important Neue Kirche, but also the less significant buildings which surround the plaza and face onto the Charlottenstrasse in order to place the Schauspielhaus into its real urban setting. In this respect, his attitude is markedly different from that of his master, Friedrich Gilly, who had designed a theater for the same site only twenty years earlier.

70. Schauspielhaus; view from the southwest.

In the competition for the original theater, Gilly had proposed a structure inspired by the geometric abstractions of recent projects by Boullée and Ledoux (Figure 71).[37] One is struck by the boldness of its major components: a massive cube in the center, flanked by two half-cylinders, and an entrance marked by a portico. The exterior composition is unified by means of a rusticated ashlar base and two horizontal bands, one continuing the top level of the lateral arcades, the other, converted into a frieze of low-relief sculpture, encircling the cube and the half-cylinders at their cornice level. In keeping with the tradition of French, so-called "revolutionary" Classicism, he emphasized the structure's severe geometric forms, plain surfaces, and concise contours. Unlike the French and especially Boullée, however, he avoided an axial front view and dramatized the visual appearance of his building by the use of his characteristic oblique perspective. The architecutral object thus emerges as a statement of form in space. But this space also, like the building, is essentially abstract. The real environment is not considered. Indeed, in this drawing Gilly did not hesitate to literally erase the cupola of the Neue Kirche, roughly sketched at the left. In so doing, he created a misleading image of the setting, while the building remains highly individualistic and strikingly effective as an isolated monument.

By contrast, Schinkel, the Romanticist of the younger generation,

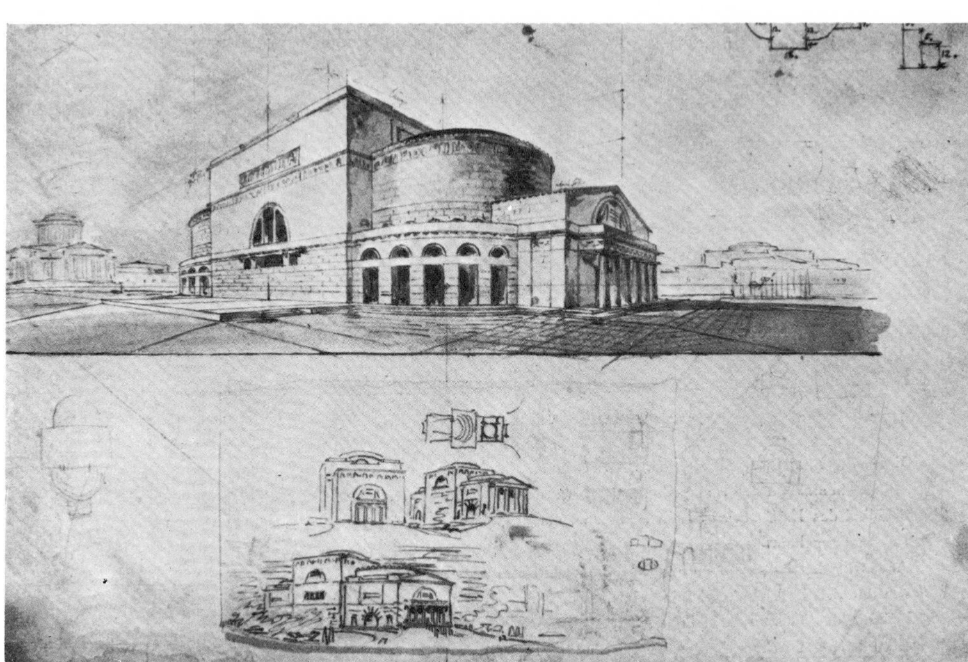

71. Friedrich Gilly. Project for the Nationaltheater, ca. 1798–1800.

72. Stage backdrop for the opening of the Schauspielhaus, 26 May 1821.

underscored his conscious endeavor to think in terms of totality by providing an especially enlightening document of his intentions. For the opening of the new theater in 1821, he designed a panoramic backdrop depicting the new architectural setting of the entire Gendarmenmarkt (Figure 72).[38] The audience, arriving for the opening-night performance of Goethe's *Iphigenie auf Tauris*, was confronted with a visual recording by Schinkel the painter of the results of urban planning by Schinkel the architect. They were made aware, in a most dramatic fashion, of the total urban setting of the theater in which they were seated—their vision expanded to include a distant horizon as well as the immediate spatial and formal relationships of the monuments framing the Gendarmenmarkt. Could they have left the theater and come out into the square untouched by what they had seen—what the architect had forced them to see? Just as Gilly's theater project may be looked upon as a testimony to the principles of the Age of Reason, Schinkel's vision of a comprehensive totality might be seen as an architectural tribute to the Age of Idealism, the age of Goethe.[39]

Schinkel's planning principles, which had found only limited application at the Neue Wache and somewhat greater relevance at the Gendarmenmarkt, were to be carried further in his next important commission: the total redevelopment of the Lustgarten area on the Spree island, north of the Schloss. Its principal component was to be a new public museum. This stately monument would be integrated into an urban environment consisting of new and old buildings and spaces. Ultimately, the program would also embrace the coordination of numerous streets and public spaces, the extensive replanning of canals and the improvement of river communication along the Spree. From the northern tip of the Spree island to the Werdersche-Markt at the south, there stretched a large area which would feel the impact of Schinkel's vision and skill as an architect and a planner (Figure 73).

This transformation of central Berlin occupied Schinkel throughout the decade of the 1820's. His new Museum was only completed in 1830. The construction of the new customs warehouses (Neue Packhof) was not finished until 1832, and the new building for the Bauakademie was to occupy him until 1836, five years before his death.

The Transformation of Central Berlin

An analysis of a planning project of this scope and consequence calls for an approach which permits emphasis on totality rather than on the investigation and description of individual parts. It is especially necessary to treat this project in its wider context since some of the most sensitive students and critics of Schinkel's work have failed to comprehend it as a composition of environmental totality.[40] Philip Johnson, for instance, has spoken eloquently of Schinkel's Museum alone, but, because of the radical changes which have occurred in the Lustgarten area since 1894, he was impressed only by its simple monumentality, subtle proportions, and the clarity and restraint of its details.[41] A younger generation of architects and planners, however, may profitably expand their view and benefit from a study of Schinkel's total program: the transformation of a major section of central Berlin, a project comparable in scope and consequence to many present-day efforts.

Consequently, the questions to be raised in our context do not pertain to individual buildings, specific details, or possible prototypes. It is of

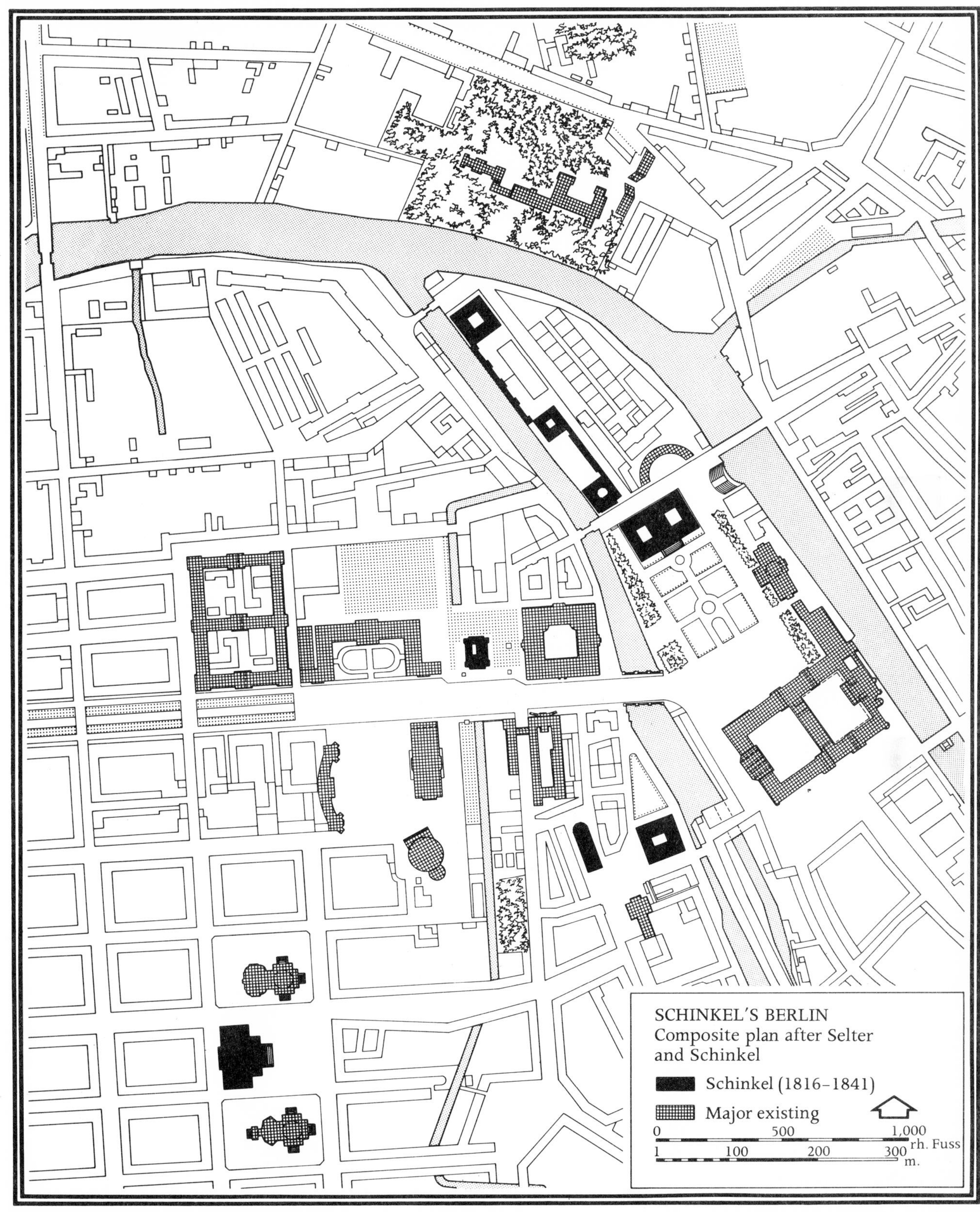

73. Schinkel's Berlin, 1816–1841.

greater importance to trace the ideas which gave impetus to this extensive architectural project and to reach an understanding of the principles and forces which led to Schinkel's solutions. Such an approach to his transformation of the greater Lustgarten area can provide an appreciation of the full impact of Schinkel's greatest triumph as an architect.

Some early attempts to improve the Lustgarten area have already been discussed. David Gilly had tried in 1798 to transform the unsightly parade ground of Friedrich Wilhelm I into a respectable civic plaza. His border lines of poplar trees were planted at the time when Schinkel was studying in his office (Figure 74). Soon afterward, Friedrich Gilly had proposed a modern bridge across the Kupfergraben (see Figure 19), which would have improved the connection between the Unter den Linden and the Schloss. Subsequently, it was Schinkel's third teacher, Heinrich Gentz, who restated in 1806 that a better link between the western sections of the city and the central island and palace was imperative for reasons of proper communication and the benefit of the visual appearance of the site.[42] Ten years later, Schinkel expanded his site plan of the Neue Wache into an environmental scheme, which proposed an uninterrupted connection between Knobelsdorff's Opernhaus in the west and Schlüter's Schloss on the island. Statues along either side of the avenue and atop the balustrades of a new bridge across the Kupfergraben were to effect visual unity and environmental comprehensiveness between hitherto isolated segments of Berlin's

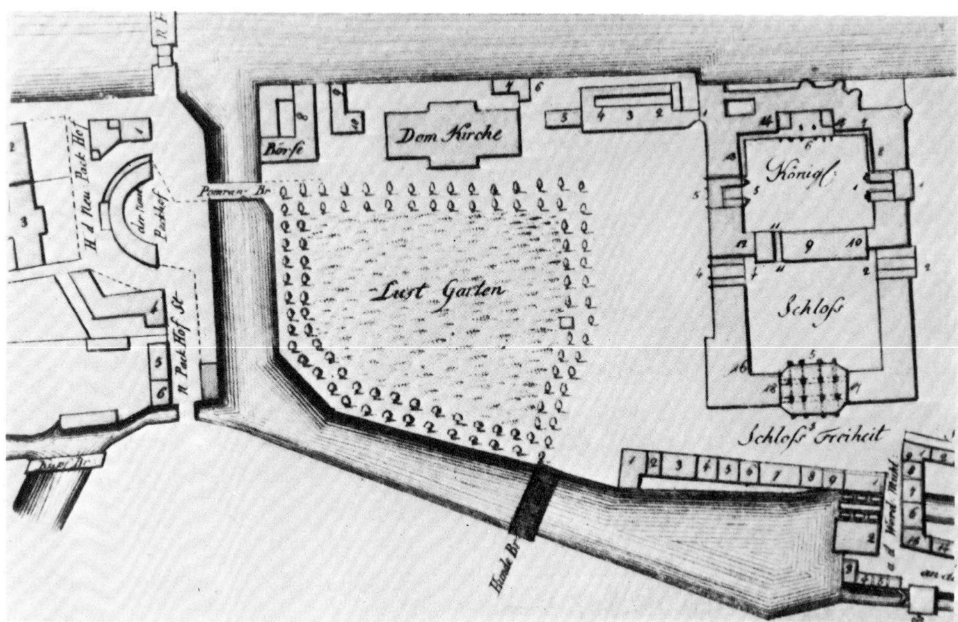

74. Map of Lustgarten area, 1812.

civic center (see Figure 58). After this project failed, he attempted once more in his city plan of 1817 to convince his hesitant royal patron that far-reaching steps would have to be taken to modernize central Berlin. Part of his scheme was a repeated plea for the improvement of the Lustgarten and the construction of a new bridge (see Figure 64). That same year he also recommended that the state should support the preservation of what he considered to be Andreas Schlüter's most outstanding works, the Schloss and the Zeughaus. Schinkel's interest in the area of the Lustgarten and its functional and aesthetic improvement gained renewed impetus in 1819 when he was finally commissioned to construct a bridge at the eastern terminus of the Unter den Linden (see Figures 18, 20). Gilly's and Gentz's proposals had thus been realized at last: the avenue and the island were finally effectively connected.

On 8 January 1823, Schinkel took another stand against the odds of repeated refusal and presented Friedrich Wilhelm III with a comprehensive master plan aimed at the improvement and transformation of a large area of central Berlin (Figure 75). He first had to convince the king to dismiss the costly plans for the installation of a public museum in the royal academy and stables. These two functions had been housed under the same roof in a building complex called by the irreverent Berliners "musis et mulis" (muses and mules), located on the Unter den Linden west of the university.[43] Schinkel proposed to divert these allocated funds from a remodeling job to the construction of a separate museum at the Lustgarten opposite the Schloss. He supported his request for this change with a series of drawings and a statement of purpose and intent. Most importantly, however, he supplied three additional documents of consequence: an explanation of the drawings, a summary of all advantages, and an account of the costs.[44] These writings have no equal in the entire Schinkel literature; they are masterpieces of rhetoric and forceful statements of persuasion.

Two basic characteristics are reflected in these written documents: first, the rationalism of an administrator; second, the creativeness of an artist and architect. Schinkel, the civil servant of the Prussian state, exposes his determination in the clipped rhetoric of his writing style, the compelling logic of his arguments, and the impressive listing of selected facts and figures. Rational persuasion is used to impress the ever-hesitant king. The first paragraph in his listing of advantages begins with a familiar Hanseatic merchants' phrase: "An Kosten werden gespart . . ." (As for expenses, we shall save . . .). The persuasion of statistics seems to dictate every line. Every positive fact and every calculation of savings stand out. He wrote that, instead of the unsatisfactory solution of incor-

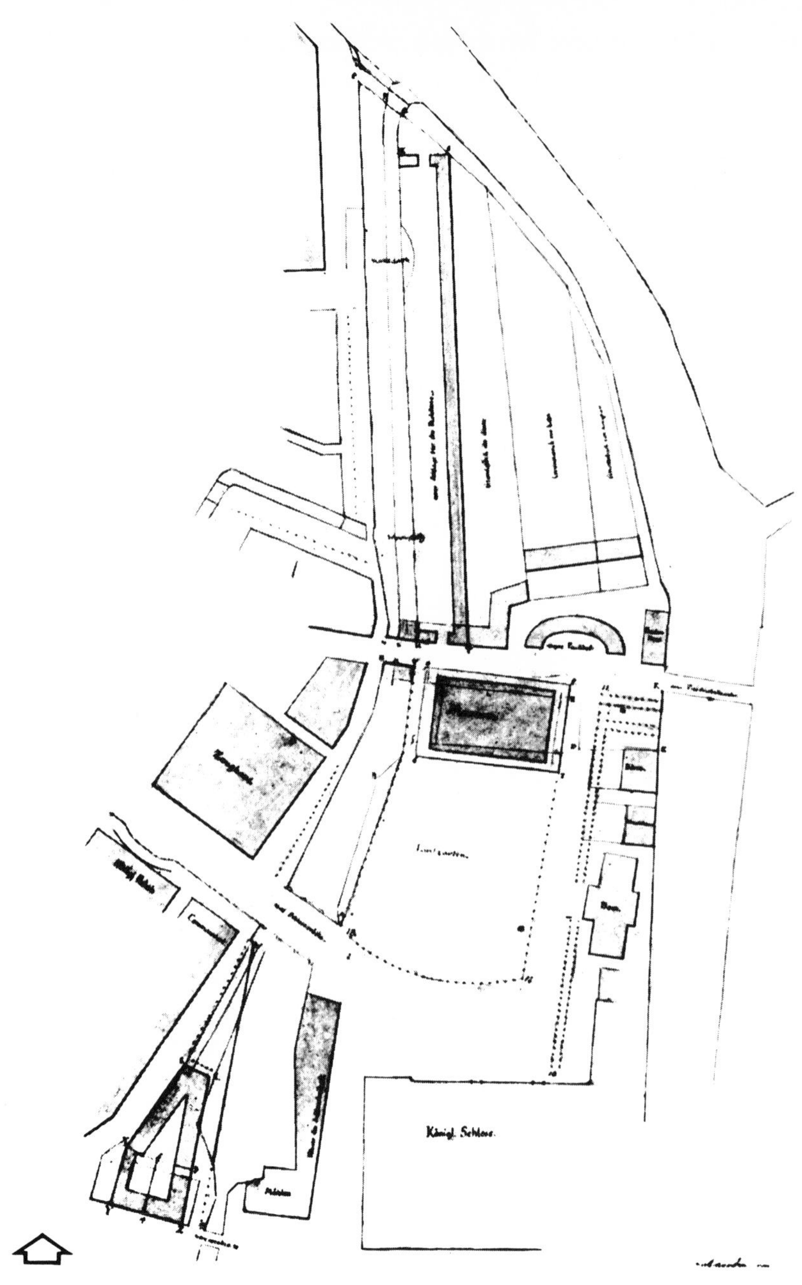

75. Master plan for the vicinity of the Lustgarten, 8 January 1823.

porating the museum into an existing building, he would not only produce a separate structure to serve this function, but that his building would bring eminence to its royal patron. It would be erected at the most prominent site in the capital, opposite the royal Schloss. Moreover, the allocated funds (700,000 *Thaler*) would suffice to cover all construction costs of the museum and, in addition, provide for urgently needed improvements in the facilities for river traffic along the Kupfergraben. Shipping, storage, and the transfer of goods, the taxes from which went to the royal treasury, would be facilitated by the erection of a new storage complex upstream. In turn, the site of the old customs warehouses at Friedrich-Werder could be sold or used to build a profitable apartment block. In addition, he noted cleverly, the site for the Neue Packhof at the northern end of the island appeared to be for sale. These favorable conditions, plus the fact that the allocated total sum would certainly cover this purchase as well, enhanced the program and encouraged immediate action. This summary intrigued the "thrifty king in frugal times." Indeed, it may have been a decisive key to Schinkel's final success. Despite the formality of calling an investigation committee (of which Schinkel was a key member) and the official registration of minor complaints, the king approved the project on 24 April 1823.[45] He expressed one basic concern: "In regard to the expenditures, I do hereby establish this irrevocable condition: the sum of 700,000 *Thaler*, which has been granted by me for the execution of the earlier project [that is, the remodeling of the Akademie building for the installation of the museum], must suffice for the execution of the current plan in its entirety, including the cost of the renovation of the Akademie. Under no circumstances can any kind of additional allocation be expected."[46]

Schinkel, the creative artist, manifested his talents and sensitivity not only in the drawings which accompanied his written proposals, but also in certain passages of his writings which were contained in letters to friends and in the official statements to the king. For instance, to Sulpiz Boisserée, whose collection of medieval paintings Schinkel had tried to secure for Berlin, he wrote enthusiastically in a letter dated 7 May 1823: "I should like to mention briefly that the construction of a large museum, based upon my design, has been approved. I hope to commence preliminary work soon and complete the entire structure in about five years. The preliminaries will effect important changes and improvements in the city and will ultimately provide the desired site for the museum, namely, the beautiful plaza at the Lustgarten, opposite the royal palace."[47]

But already in the initial correspondence with the monarch, it is easily discernable that Schinkel, the artist and architect, held sway over Schinkel, the administrator. He wrote that he wanted to erect a structure which would serve solely as a museum and whose character of unity would serve a single purpose. The site onto which it would be placed was by far more suitable than the originally designated location. He insisted that the beauty of the Lustgarten area would gain its completeness through the presence of this structure because the plaza would be closed at its fourth side. In addition, he intended that the extensive riverbanks of the Kupfergraben should henceforth be embellished with promenades, that the slums of Friedrich-Werder should be razed, and that the newly designated site of the customs warehouses should eliminate disturbing barges and commercial traffic south of the Schlossbrücke. Purpose and beauty, "Zweckmässigkeit und Schönheit," were the criteria by which Schinkel gauged his objectives.

Finally, he called for a correlation between diverse parts of the city and for overall unity. These were the key words expressed by Schinkel, the environmental planner. As before in his city plan of 1817, he demanded once again the elimination of the Pomeranzengraben, the seventeenth-century moat which divided the island in two. Its broad bed would provide ample space for the substructure and foundations of the Museum. Directly toward the north would be the modern and enlarged complex of the Packhof with easily accessible entry and exit for barges arriving from the Elbe and Havel rivers, the principal trade and communication routes, as he pointed out. These boats would be serviced in a broadened harbor basin, whose excess soil could fill parts of the closed canal and could also be utilized to raise the level of the Lustgarten. Also, the river communication from the south would be facilitated by the improvement of bridges and riverbanks from the locks in Friedrich-Werder to the Packhof basin in the north. Finally, Schinkel's master plan provided for a new bridge across the Kupfergraben south of the Neue Packhof leading to a broad street on the island behind the Museum. In combination with the Friedrichsbrücke across the Spree, he thus envisioned an uninterrupted east-west thoroughfare, which was to connect Dorotheenstadt in the west, the island in the center, and old Berlin in the east.

The Transformation of Central Berlin

Schinkel's master plan of 1823 and its carefully composed supporting statements thus combined the rationalism and the creativity of his complex personality. Addressing himself to the most urgent and timely architectural problems of central Berlin, he spoke persuasively in terms of practical data, such as savings and costs. As an artist and architect, however, he reiterated the lessons of his great teachers and added his own maxims of purpose and beauty. Finally, as a planner, he looked beyond a simple task, the construction of an impressive Museum, and called for the creation of a larger environment, of which this structure was to be an integral part.

With the king's acceptance of Schinkel's plan for the Museum building, he embarked upon the first phase of his long campaign to bring to fruition the numerous proposals contained in his master plan. The Museum (known as the Alte Museum since the erection of August Stüler's Neue Museum in 1841–1855) was constructed at the north side of the Lustgarten plaza, directly opposite Schlüter's Schloss. Designed as early as the end of 1822 and executed from 1824 to 1830, this building became one of Europe's first public museums.[48] It has been cited repeatedly as one of the most successful designs of its type, and critics commented favorably on its adaptable exhibition spaces as late as the mid-twentieth century.

In addition to the economy and practicality of its general layout, the plan and exterior composition of the Museum were conceived as basically complementary to the Schloss and also to the Zeughaus across the Kupfergraben toward the southwest (see Figure 73). The general formal definition of the Museum repeated the basic horizontal treatment of existing structures, their cornice levels all being of approximately the same height. The particular relationship of the Museum to its neighboring buildings was considered one of its most important attributes by Schinkel's biographer, Gustav Friedrich Waagen. In 1843 he wrote that Schinkel's outstanding qualities as a designer of individual buildings and his sensitivity to a "picturesque" overall composition had already been evidenced in his very choice of the building site. Waagen notes that Schinkel had kept in mind that his new monumental structure would rise within the vicinity of Berlin's finest buildings and that it could only enhance the overall effect of the heretofore undistinguished environment of the Lustgarten by acting as an important link in the context of the existing civic and royal structures of the area.[49] Schinkel himself, in recognizing the importance of the Zeughaus and Schloss and their particular formal qualities, had written that the Museum "had to be conceived as a noble form, not only for its own sake, but especially in response to its location at the most beautiful plaza of the capital, across from the royal palace and the Zeughaus."[50]

The one existing structure in the area which was different in character was the Domkirche (1747–1750) by Johann Boumann the Elder. Located at the eastern edge of the Lustgarten, the more compact, vertically emphasized religious structure acted as a foil for the lower, broader buildings surrounding it. When in 1819 Schinkel had been called upon to remodel the entrance facade of this church, he had employed one of his favorite architectural forms, an Ionic portico.[51] Characteristically, he

76. Perspective view of Museum am Lustgarten; first design, 8 January 1823.

then insisted on using this same Classical order in the colonnade of his adjacent Museum and included the portico of the Domkirche in his first perspective view of this new addition to the Lustgarten scene (Figure 76). Despite unfavorable criticism, he defended his choice of colossal Ionic columns as absolutely necessary for the creation of a sense of continuity between the portico of the church and the facade of his new building. In fact, he stated that he designed the columns of the Museum to be approximately the same height as those of the church entrance. Concluding his clearly stated argument for continuity in design, he rejected the criticism of the Museum colonnade with the comment that "the plaza on which the building is to stand, the most important public square in Berlin, demands something extraordinary. One must take care not to confuse the simple and monumental with the mediocre, which would degrade this major square instead of enhancing it."[52]

The Museum's impressive colonnade, with its spacious recess and richly decorated walls,[53] may have been closer in spirit to a Grecian stoa poikile than to the Palladian portico of the adjacent church. Yet, the subtle interrelationship of certain component parts in the design of these two buildings verifies one of his major principles: that architecture must be created in terms of coordination between units of a given site or area. Individuality of forms or even overall stylistic expressions should never be confused with the concept of monumental isolation as had been the case in the design of Gilly's theater some twenty years earlier.

And yet, Schinkel's Museum did differ from its neighboring buildings in one important respect. Like his Schauspielhaus at the Gendarmenmarkt, it was raised on a high substructure or podium. Jakob Hittorff considered this compositional element to be a conscious attempt on Schinkel's part to create a "theatrical effect."[54] Furthermore, during the evaluation of the project Alois Hirt criticized the podium as an extravagant visual feature which should be reduced to a maximum height of three feet above ground. In defending his design, Schinkel pointed out that the vaulted base would prevent condensation and dry rot and also act as a fireproof shell to house the heating equipment of the Museum. Its ample spaces would also provide profitable rental units.[55] Moreover, it is clear from a study of Schinkel's own perspective drawing of the Lustgarten from the west (Figure 77) that this high base also served a decidedly aesthetic function. He drew this view in 1823, prior to the construction of the Museum. He must have realized that only by elevating the colonnade well above ground level was it possible to view the frontal facade in its entirety from a distant observation point. At the same time, only a comprehensive view of the building, including the complete frame of the giant columned screen, could effect an impression of total formal unity—a concept foremost in the mind of a Classical architect.

This perspective view of the Lustgarten also demonstrates that Schinkel was conscious of the Museum in the context of the entire area and that his former activity as a panorama painter must have inspired him to present an architectural spectacle that went beyond the range of normal visual comprehension. Through the breadth of the view presented, one is made aware of the relationships between Museum, Domkirche, and Schloss and even the Zeughaus, a corner of which frames the composition at the left. Even the steeple of the old Berlin Marienkirche appears on the distant horizon, while the foreground plane is dominated by Schinkel's newly constructed Schlossbrücke. At the same time, he does not idealize the scene, but retains the nondescript multistory building at the right, which obscures the northwest corner of the palace and adds to the topo-

77. Perspective view of Lustgarten from the west, summer 1823.

graphical realism.[56] The Museum, then, while an outstanding work of architecture in itself, is also an integral part of a larger picture. Fritz Stahl cautioned against viewing it as a "monument," an isolated phenomenon. He insisted that "the outstanding achievement of the architect, of which the Museum is only a part, even if the most important part, is the Lustgarten. How many realize that this plaza as it is, or, rather, as it was before the new Domkirche was built, the pride of the city, admired by all foreign visitors and in its character the equal of any famous city square, is really the personal creation of Schinkel?!"[57]

The wide range of buildings and spaces which Schinkel encompassed in this view of the Lustgarten is comparable to his earlier rendering of the Unter den Linden (see Figure 62). In fact, the artist's vantage point in both cases is the same—one view looking west, the other exactly 180 degrees to the east. The two drawings, taken back to back, provide a comprehensive panorama of central Berlin. In the foreground and middleground of the later drawing, Schinkel portrayed a number of pedestrians, whose implied movement suggests that they could survey the spaces and forms of the Lustgarten scene in a continued sequential order. In the planning of the total environment it is apparent that the spatial relationship between the various structures, then, was as important as their formal balance.

In the presentation of his first master plan of 1823 (see Figure 75), Schinkel appears to have been fully aware of the fact that all of the monumental buildings at the plaza demanded a large open space—the Lustgarten itself, which would act as the unifying spatial element of the entire area. Since he wished his Museum to be a large dramatic addition to the site, it would have been impossible to squeeze it into any of the available spaces. However, by deciding to erect the Museum at the former site of the transverse canal, the appropriate physical distance from the long, impressive facade of the palace could be achieved. In addition, the new structure could act as a physical barrier, or *Riegel*, against the commercial Packhof and the east-west thoroughfare toward the north. In short, the Museum would serve both to close one side of the large plaza and also to separate public from commercial activity.

When the king authorized the construction of the Museum at the suggested site, Schinkel concentrated his planning efforts on the Lustgarten itself. His site plan of 1824 (Figure 78) is more precise in respect to

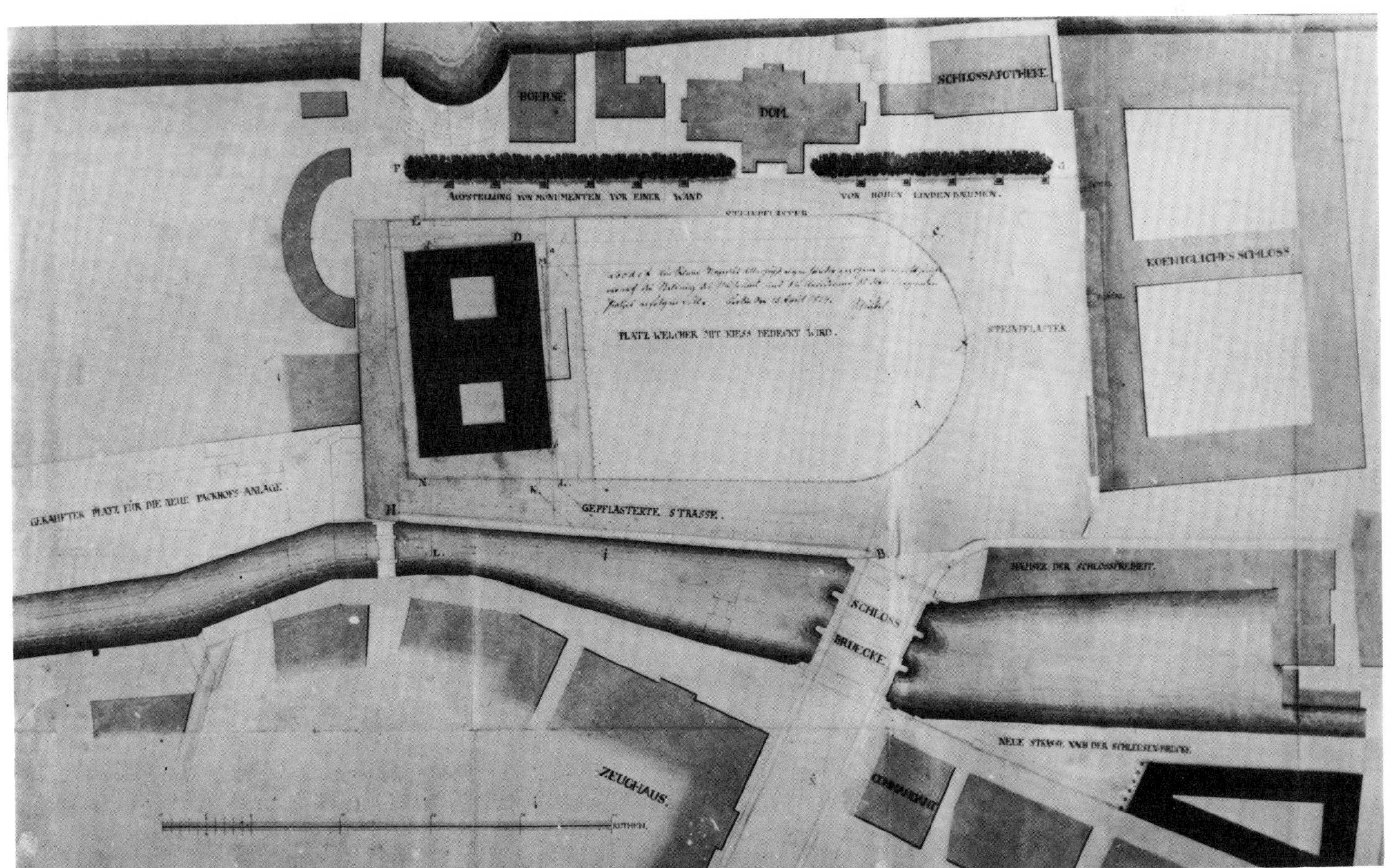

78. Revised site plan of the Museum, March and April 1824.

certain features of landscaping which were only vaguely suggested in the earlier master plan. One sees more clearly the important role of the portico of the Domkirche in the overall visual appearance of the plaza. In order to effectively relate the central section of the church to the other buildings, Schinkel intended to create a "third facade" along the eastern border of the square. This was necessitated by the fact that the buildings to the right and left of the Domkirche were neither properly arranged nor suitable in their architectural appearance to become part of the overall scheme. This third facade was to consist of a double row of trees, a *Baumwand*, which would effectively mask the awkward buildings and create a transition between the Schloss, the Domkirche, and the Museum. In front of this arborous facade were to be placed monuments on high pedestals, emphasizing its barrier-like character and relating this border with the statues of the Schlossbrücke, as seen from the ideal point of view (see Figure 77).

It is apparent from this plan that Schinkel's early scheme had not remained intact. In 1824 the discovery of faulty soil conditions at the western edge of the projected site of the Museum forced the architect to shift his building almost ten meters to the east.[58] In a brief statement to the king, he explained that the new location of the Museum would not affect the overall plan. "This distance," he wrote, "will have no effect whatsoever on the regularity of the planning scheme of the plaza, since perfect regularity is impossible due to the existing surroundings."[59] Although he had originally planned to place the Museum midway between the Kupfergraben and the row of linden trees, Schinkel now argued that, as long as the new building retained a parallel alignment with the palace, nothing would be lost in the overall spatial effect of the plaza. Furthermore, since "the Schloss, opposite the new structure, does not have a definite central element, which could perhaps also determine the center of the Museum," there was no need to be careful about relating any conspicuous features of the two facades. The new location would also present the opportunity to broaden the street along the Kupfergraben for better access to the Packhof. Although the king approved this new scheme, we learn from Schinkel's note written on the plan that he insisted the Museum be shifted slightly so that its main facade was no longer parallel to the palace, but its east side would be parallel to the adjacent row of trees. It was not a drastic change, but it loosened the formal composition somewhat. The spatial effect would now emphasize the open side of the plaza toward the Schlossbrücke in the west. At the same time, the central portico of the Domkirche would be accentuated even more as the centerpiece along the eastern border.

The final placement of the Museum can be seen on Schinkel's first plan

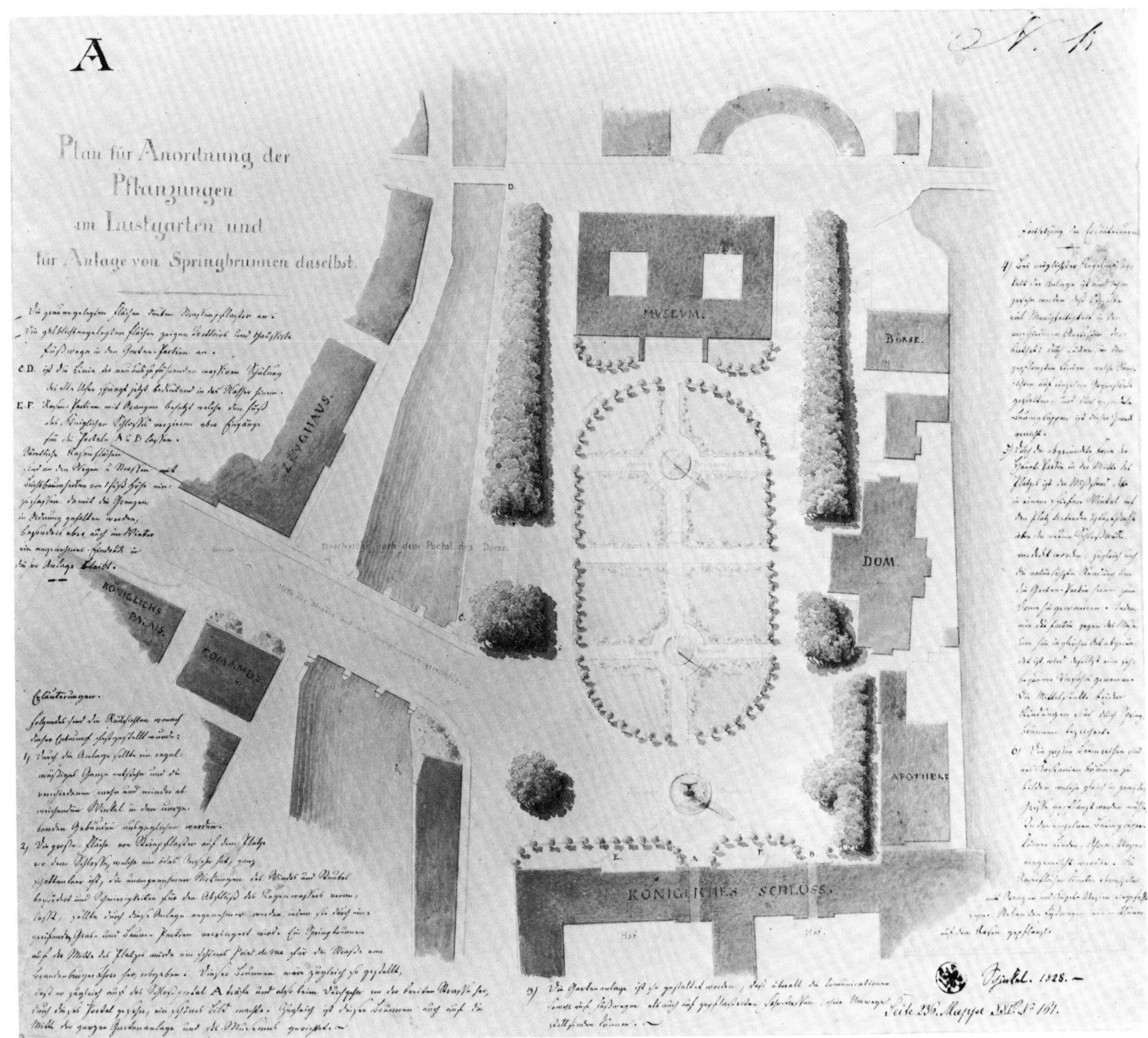

79. First landscaping proposal for the Lustgarten, 1828.

for the landscaping of the Lustgarten, which he presented in 1828 (Figure 79). Perhaps as a reaction to the shifting of his building, he now proposed to obscure oblique views of the Museum by adding a thick row of chestnut trees along the water's edge and by replacing the wall of linden trees at the east with denser chestnut trees as well. While a first glance at this landscaping project may suggest an overabundance of natural elements, these irregular forms of nature did assist him in the creation of a regimented and logical unity. In addition to the large masses of trees bordering the plaza, neat rows of deliberately spaced single trees outlined parterres in front of the museum and palace and the edge of an elongated oval in the center of the Lustgarten. Intersecting walkways crossed the central parterre and connected the major buildings and spaces. These patterns of promenades and planted areas within the Lustgarten transformed it into a "regulated whole" *(regelmässiges Ganzes)*, a key phrase in Schinkel's marginal notes. The manipulation of a pedestrian's visual comprehension of the plaza by means of the judicious placement of natural elements was obviously one of his major concerns. He noted that the landscaping scheme which he proposed "ought to achieve a regulated whole and balance the numerous awkward angles [inherent] in the disposition of the surrounding buildings."[60]

Thus, the former vastness of the square would now be replaced by a dense pattern of cross-axes, vistas, and accents. In reading Schinkel's enthusiastic description of the gardens of the Palais du Luxembourg, which he had visited in 1826, one is reminded of the colorful variety of shapes and elements which he may have tried to emulate in his spacious public gardens in the center of Berlin. "At the Palais Luxembourg we enjoyed the garden, a magnificent wide space, bordered by terraces and avenues of high trees and decorated with marble statues, grass, lilacs, roses, flowers of all kinds and pools." He concluded with a note specifically applicable to his scheme in Berlin: "From here there is a vista onto the Observatory in one direction, and, turning the other way, one has the most delightful view onto the Panthéon at the end of a high-vaulted avenue of trees."[61]

In Berlin, Schinkel was not able to build terraces nor to create visual axes which could unite his plaza with distant parts of the city. But outside views onto particular sections of his environmental scheme were certainly part of his conception. A break in the western screen of trees allowed a view onto the portico of the Domkirche and, in fact, emphasized the role of the high-domed church as the focal point of the vista from the Unter den Linden. An arrow on the plan and the inscription "Durchsicht nach dem Portal des Doms" indicate Schinkel's intention that the transverse axis of the plaza was not intended to be merely a self-contained planning element within the Lustgarten. Rather, it was to reach across the river and embrace the outer limits of the space. Finally, like the avenue which afforded the "most delightful view onto the Panthéon" in Paris, Schinkel underscored a vista from the Schloss to the distant Brandenburger Tor. A large fountain, on axis with the central promenade of his square, was placed in such a way that it would intersect a vista from the Unter den Linden in the west. "A fountain in the center of the plaza could become a beautiful *point de vue* when seen along the street from the Brandenburger

Tor. At the same time, this fountain would be placed in alignment with portal 'A' of the palace . . . Moreover, the fountain would be directed toward the center of the entire garden area and the Museum."[62]

I believe that Schinkel's intentions have been grossly misjudged by Rave and Ott. He was not, as both imply, only interested in creating a pretty bourgeois setting.[63] Once we are willing to penetrate the complexities of the project, the irregularities of the site, and his serious attempts to overcome them, we must acknowledge that the planning of the Museum and its environment resulted in at least two successes. First, a new public space had been envisioned in addition to an architectural masterwork. Seen in its own right, the whole Lustgarten area was to become a controlled visual experience, with nature playing a decisive role in relating both the masses of solid structures to one another and the open and confined spaces to the whole. Second, seen in the greater context of total environmental design, Schinkel sought to interrelate the plaza with major planning elements of the city. In connecting the Lustgarten with the Schlossbrücke and the Unter den Linden to the west and in proposing to accent their visual and spatial continuity with a fountain in front of the Schloss, he proved to be the first architect of Berlin whose principal aim was the correlation of the city's four major planning components: the river, the island, the building and the street.

It is all the more regrettable, therefore, that Schinkel's plans were altered once more by the king's pen. Clearly visible on Schinkel's plan *A* are marks which cross out much of the planting near the Schloss and two fountains—one at the critical *point de vue* toward the Brandenburger Tor. In October 1828 Schinkel submitted a revised and simplified landscaping scheme (Figure 80). Only one fountain is retained, at the main crossing of the promenades within a reduced planted area. Absent is the visual link between the Schloss and the Unter den Linden. Rejecting Schinkel's attempt at environmental planning, at overall formal and spatial integration, the king demanded an open plaza immediately north of the palace. Schinkel had to comply and, as a result, the scheme fell short of the impressive unity which its designer had originally intended. Despite these imposed revisions of his landscaping scheme and despite budget cuts limiting the embellishment of the Museum and the Schlossbrücke, his major structure for the Lustgarten can still be appreciated for its merits both as an isolated architectural landmark and as a unit within a larger, more comprehensive scheme of environmental planning.

While Schinkel's plans and his early perspective view of the Lustgarten have taught us to look at his building from a distance and see it within a larger context, a final drawing by the architect shows us the opposite point of view: the surrounding environment from within the Museum

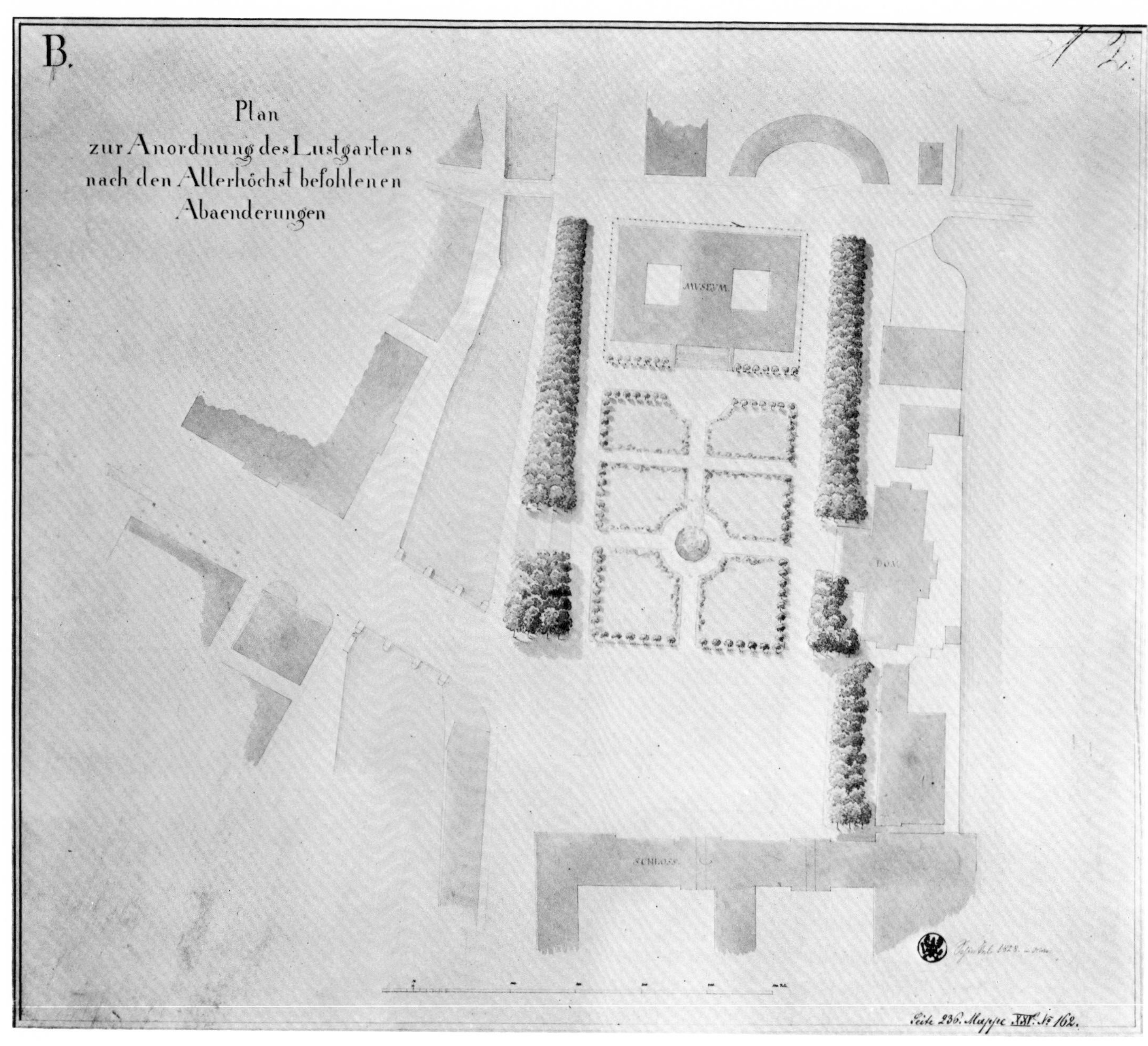

80. Second landscaping proposal for the Lustgarten, October 1828.

81. View from the upper vestibule of the Museum, 1829.

itself (Figure 81). From the semienclosed vestibule at the upper landing of the great staircase, one looks through the columned screen onto the plaza and the city beyond. It is as if Peruzzi's illusionistic wall painting at the Villa Farnesina in sixteenth-century Rome were brought to life and translated into real three-dimensional form in nineteenth-century Berlin.[64] From this upper platform, which Schinkel called a "resting place, which is like an *Altan*," one sees, carefully delineated, a panoramic view of the newly landscaped Lustgarten, a section of the Schloss and the distant towers of his own Werdersche Kirche. At the far right, between the last two columns, Schinkel even included a narrow segment of the Zeughaus. The choice of this vista seems intentional—not an axial view to the palace across the square, but an oblique angle showing the larger city environment, of which the new Museum is only one part.

Thus, although Schinkel used some traditional methods in composing his spaces, his vision was not solely dependent upon conventional relationships. Right angles and axial alignments were simply means of organizing what might otherwise become disparate elements haphazardly grouped together. Yet he realized that relationships existed among these elements which were independent of the imposed rational order. These were the visual relationships which the architect had to consider when placing his new building on the site. These were the relationships which the painter of panoramas and architectural landscapes and the designer of stage sets could envisage and control.

Upon its completion in 1830, the Lustgarten became an organized civic space, taking its place in the long history of city plaza development beginning in sixteenth-century Italy. Indeed, it was one of the last great urban plazas and one of the most significant examples executed in Germany in the nineteenth century. In comparison to Leo von Klenze's contemporary work in Munich or Friedrich Weinbrenner's plans for Karlsruhe, Schinkel's planning of the Lustgarten appears less static and monumental, his composition more picturesque or *malerisch*, to use his own term. His ability to coordinate the various elements, both old and new, into a single unity of formal, spatial, and visual relationships was undoubtedly due to his observations of such sites as the Campidoglio in Rome and his experiences as a painter of panoramas. His own rendering of the Lustgarten from the west (see Figure 77) indicates how sensitive he was to the panoramic effect of the total site, while his drawing of the upper vestibule is reminiscent of many of his sketches of sites in Italy, the view of Rome (see Figure 37), for example, where he could look out from a high point.

The Transformation of Central Berlin

The condition of Schinkel's Museum today can hardly suggest its previous role as an integral part of the Lustgarten and its foremost position within the greater environment of central Berlin. Though the building itself has been painstakingly restored, its original surroundings have been obliterated by thoughtless change and the destruction of war. A recent photograph (Figure 82) of the same view which Schinkel drew for his *Sammlung* in 1829 shows some trees of the present Lustgarten in the foreground and the vast empty space of the adjoining Marx-Engels-Platz, where the Schloss once stood. Recently constructed buildings for the Staatsrat and the foreign ministry of the DDR are seen in the distance.[65] Similarly, looking onto the Museum from the south (Figure 83), one has no idea of its original role in shaping the city's environment. Instead of a structure which once formed part of a scenic urban space, one beholds now the magnificent facade of a totally isolated work of architecture. Today, Schinkel's Museum is a monument in the true sense of the word.

82. View from the upper vestibule of the Museum.

83. Museum am Lustgarten; view from the former site of the Königliche Schloss.

A similar fate has befallen another portion of Schinkel's comprehensive plan of 1823. The site for which he proposed a new and modern complex for the city's customs warehouses at the northern end of the island is now occupied by two additional museums of world renown: the Pergamon-Museum, 1906–1930 (incomplete), by Alfred Messel and Ludwig Hoffmann; and the former Kaiser-Friedrich-Museum (now Bode-Museum), 1897–1903, by Ernst Eberhard von Ihne.[66]

As Schinkel's master plan and his original perspective drawing of the Museum indicate (see Figures 75, 76), his foremost concern for the utilization of the area north of the Lustgarten had focused on practical matters. He proposed to combine the commercial, storage, and shipping centers of Friedrich-Werder in the south and the additional Packhof facilities, located in Nering's Pomeranzenhaus (Orangerie) near the Lustgarten, into a single coherent unit. In his initial statement of 8 January 1823, he drew attention to the fact that, since most cargo vessels reach Berlin via the Elbe and Havel rivers, their efficient handling as well as commercial exchange would be better served at the northen end of the island, thereby avoiding the congested narrower canals and the necessity to pass the Schlossbrücke.[67] By combining this argument with his desire to salvage the site of the transverse canal for his projected Museum, Schinkel hoped to obtain royal approval of his plan. Improvements in matters of efficiency and advantages relating to commerce and income for the crown had always been favorite criteria in the decision making of the otherwise hesitant king. Schinkel's plans for relocating of the royal customs warehouses were thus approved, but realization of the new Packhof complex, unlike the Museum, took a considerable length of time. Construction of buildings according to final designs did not commence until 1830, and the project was not completed until 1832. Repeated alterations in general layout and in the design of individual units had prolonged their planning over several years.[68] However, the final form of the buildings and the successful coordination of the Packhof with the Lustgarten in the south resulted in "a totality of distinctly picturesque composition," to quote Kugler's succinct description.[69]

The original planning concept of the warehouse complex of 1823, which Schinkel published in his *Sammlung* two years later (compare Figures 75 and 84), seems to have been a simplified version of the extensive Packhof section which he first proposed in his city plan of 1817 (see Figure 64). The large L-shaped warehouse units of the earlier scheme, which he projected at the western bank of the Kupfergraben, were now reduced in size and transferred to the right bank. Although the impressive harbor basin of his 1817 plan was abandoned, he did propose to broaden

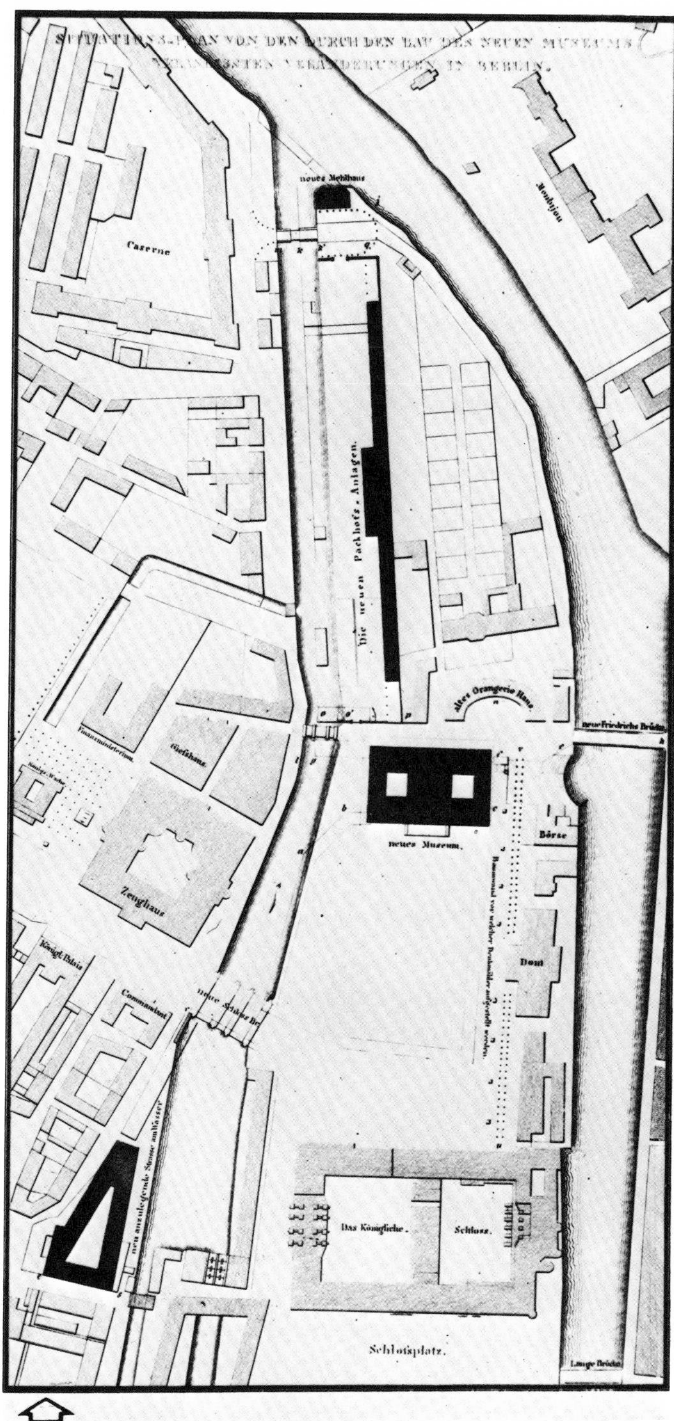

84. Master plan for the vicinity of the Lustgarten, 1825.

the Kupfergraben by nearly twice its original width in order to accommodate the new docking and loading facilities. The excess soil would be used to fill parts of the Pomeranzengraben at either side of the Museum. Finally, the appearance of Schinkel's Packhof project of 1823 can be judged from his early perspective drawing of the Museum (see Figure 76). According to this preliminary scheme, the warehouses were to be simple one-story structures consisting of a colonnaded storage gallery between projecting pavilions at either end. In contrast to the impressive and detailed rendering of the Museum, the commercial buildings were only vaguely suggested. They were hidden behind the Museum as unobtrusive appendages to the important Lustgarten redevelopment scheme.

Although several preliminary studies gradually improved the design, it was not until 1829 that Schinkel and his staff arrived at a solution which appeared to satisfy a complex range of specific functional demands. Instead of a single continuous row of buildings, the final plan consisted of a sequence of connected blocks (Figure 85). Closest to the northern end of the island, at the entrance to the harbor, was a five-story warehouse, the Magazin. Seen in plan, this structure resembles a miniature version of the Zeughaus at the other end of the canal—perfectly square with an open central court. Corresponding with the simple geometry of its outline is the grid pattern of its interior piers, whose module determines the placement of stairs and partitions. A low, narrow element along the quay connects this simple block with another square building toward the south. Unlike the warehouse, however, this structure is recessed from the waterfront; it is also smaller in size and more complex in plan. It contained the offices of the Hauptsteueramt, or main customs agency for foreign exchanges. Another low wing, containing apartments and separated from the water by a deep, open court, connected this building to the third cubic structure at the south. This was the main administration building, the Hauptstempelmagazin, and, although it is the same size and height as the office building, there is a curious angular adjustment of its south facade.

Why would Schinkel be inclined to distort his strictly rectilinear planning pattern and disturb his design with an apparent irregularity? In his own brief commentary which accompanied the plans, elevations, and perspectives of the Packhof in the twenty-first installment of his *Sammlung* in 1834, he simply stated: "The building closest to the Museum has been provided with a pediment, decorated with sculpture which symbolizes the function of the entire complex."[70] If the purpose of this pedimental sculpture was stated, the reason for the angular orientation of the building's gabled end was not—unless we recognize Schinkel's conscious attempt to correlate the Packhof with buildings and spaces

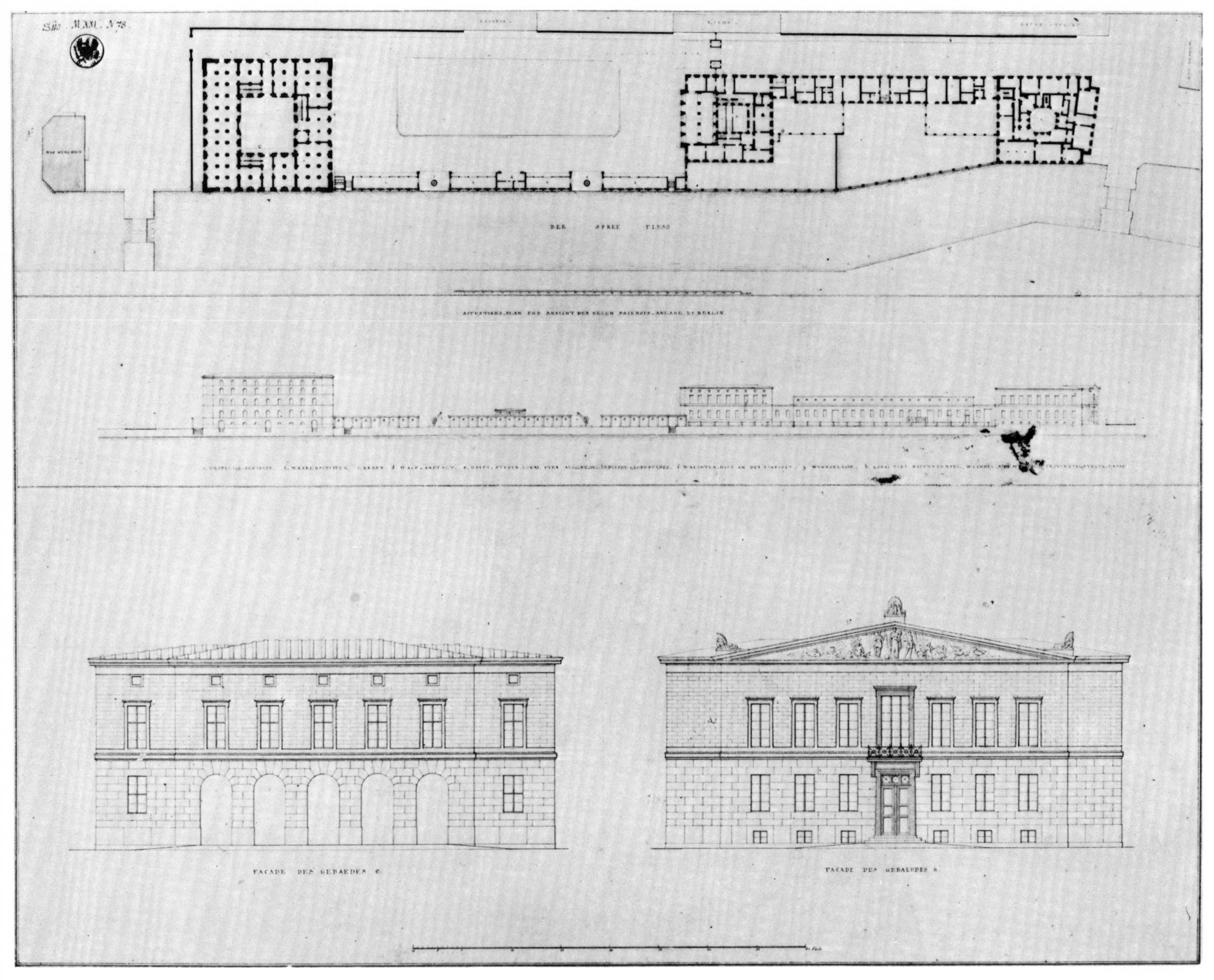

85. The Neue Packhof; final scheme, 1829.

toward the south. As a matter of fact, his site plan reveals clearly that the pedimented facade of the administration building runs parallel to the north facade of the Museum. Consequently, when seen from the Lustgarten approach in the south, the Museum and the principal building of the Packhof complex would stand in harmonious relationship to one another. Moreover, as the only decorated facade within the entire commercial complex, this south elevation would be in keeping with the more formal character of the Lustgarten environment (Figure 86). During the final phases of the design of the Packhof in 1829, Schinkel wrote that under no circumstances could he permit the facade of the major building to be exposed unless decorations were applied which would conform to the character of the Lustgarten and the entire environment. If no funds could be allocated for this purpose, it would be necessary to reduce building costs in general in order to effect this important measure.[71]

86. Trowitzoch. View of the Neue Packhof from the south, ca. 1835.

87. Perspective view of the Neue Packhof and Museum from the Schlossbrücke, 1834.

The full implication of Schinkel's mastery in integrating the new Packhof complex with the environment of the Lustgarten area is vividly demonstrated in his perspective view from the Schlossbrücke (Figure 87). Buildings as diverse as an armory, a museum, office blocks, and a warehouse are drawn into a harmonious architectural landscape without apparent conflict or friction between their respective functions or styles. It seems as if Schinkel, with what Ettlinger calls his "exacting sense of organic unity,"[72] succeeded in balancing masses and spaces into a loosely knit harmony. Waagen could speak of Schinkel's newly completed sequence of structures along the Kupfergraben as the finest vista in Berlin. He wrote enthusiastically about the *Spreelandschaft*, that new river landscape along the Spree: "The effect of these buildings is especially beautiful in a view from the Schlossbrücke, where, in combination with the Museum, they are seen in a harmonious relationship, one projecting from behind the other."[73]

It would be premature and uncritical to conclude Schinkel's planning efforts at the Packhof and Lustgarten with Waagen's favorable comment and the architect's own impressive view. This statement of planning and assimilation is too complex to be evaluated by visual and formal criteria alone, and an uncritical acceptance of this solution neglects certain features of its evolution. Waagen's praise and Schinkel's "classic" view could easily contribute to a typically modern failing: that architecture is considered good if praised by an "expert" and if drawn to its best advantage by the architect himself.

It is necessary to probe the validity of Schinkel's achievement beyond its success as a pictorial statement of abstract forms and the picturesqueness of its total visual appearance. This inquiry appears particularly important since the final masterful statement of environmental assimilation has little or nothing in common with the superficial early Packhof scheme. Even a cursory glance at Schinkel's first site plan of January 1823, and its published version of 1825 (see Figures 75, 84), reveals nothing of the scope and environmental implications that can be deduced from his final planning scheme. The two early versions consist of single building tracts strung along the entire length of a narrow riverfront property. Hidden behind the Museum and obscured from a distant view, they seem like appendages to the Lustgarten project—additions needed to secure approval for the Museum's construction. Neither of them indicates the importance and priority which Schinkel had assigned to his earliest warehouse and harbor complex in the city plan of 1817. Moreover, their architectural treatment seems second-rate and strictly utilitarian. If one compares the simple, gabled pavilion in Schinkel's first perspective of 1823 with the sequence of impressive three- and five-story cubes which appear in the final design of 1829, one may rightfully wonder at the cause of this dramatic change which occurred within the span of six intervening years.[74] How did Schinkel arrive at his distinctly modern planning pattern and its successful integration into that masterfully organized architectural landscape which he delineated from the Schlossbrücke in 1829? Somehow, it is not convincing that a greater attention to the diversified requirements for the Packhof assembly during these years of alteration and refinement could produce such drastic changes in planning concepts and architectural treatment. The abstract pattern and picturesque grouping of his final site plan and his demand for architectural sculpture cannot be explained by functional requirements and efficiency alone. Nor can the form of the individual Packhof units be explained solely by Schinkel's awareness of similar geometric shapes at the Zeughaus, Museum, and Schloss. These aspects may have played a certain role, but the basic concept of Schinkel's final scheme might well have been derived from sources outside the local sphere.

Where, in the 1820's, could an architect of western Europe have been inspired by the presence of efficient and aesthetically pleasing complexes of commercial buildings? Neither the riverfronts of the Arno and Tiber, nor the quays along the Seine could have offered Schinkel a model for his imposing project in Berlin. He had revisited Italy in 1824 and had admired Paris during another visit there in 1826. Yet, neither the recent transformation of the Piazza del Popolo in Rome nor the academic pursuits of contemporary architects in Paris offered a planning solution which projected commercial structures, such as warehouses, into the forefront of dignified urban scenes. Even England, Scotland, and Wales, which were Schinkel's next study grounds, could not furnish an example of environmental design where this problem had been successfully resolved.[75]

Britain, a traditional source of inspiration for Prussian architects such as Knobelsdorff, Erdmannsdorff, Langhans, Gilly and Gentz, would emerge as a challenge to Schinkel. Unlike his predecessors and teachers, who had been attracted by its Palladian elegance, the stately works of Robert Adam and William Chambers, and the charming gardens of William Kent, he found little inspiration in traditional concepts and standards. As an architect, he was apparently only impressed by the works of Inigo Jones. Waagen notes that Schinkel "referred with warm admiration to the beauty of proportions and decisiveness of character in the articulation of his buildings."[76] Robert Adam, on the other hand, was approached critically. Schinkel objected to his eclectic tendencies and commented on his lack of sensitivity for proportions in the design of the library in Edinburgh (1789). The Bank of England (1788–1832) by Sir John Soane did not impress him either. He considered the courtyards pleasing, but noted that many unnecessary elements had been included. Similarly, he seemed disenchanted with the prevailing disorder in Soane's own house. He expressed admiration for the residence of the Lord Mayor of London, the Mansion House (1739–1753), executed after designs by George Dance. On the other hand, the remodeling of Buckingham Palace received the epithet "ordinary," even though Schinkel met its designer, John Nash, while in London. Like the Anglophile Hermann Fürst von Pückler-Muskau, he found little positive to say of the architectural treatment of the concurrent structures around the impressive Regent's Park. He commented that they were pulled together in palace fashion, being nothing but private dwellings three to four windows wide and joined by a common architecture.[77]

These observations and opinions, however, represent only one facet of the professional nature of this neo-Classical architect. Schinkel had been sent to France and England by the king specifically to investigate the interior arrangements of recently established museums—to gather ideas for the new Museum in Berlin. Judging by the content of his diaries, however, a much more important part of his time and interest focused on aspects of industrial design and new mechanical methods of manufacturing, as well as the techniques used in the construction of English factory buildings. Although he was hardly as enthusiastic about the promise of Europe's industrial giant as his inquisitive traveling companion, Peter Christian Beuth, the founder and director of Prussia's Gewerbeinstitut, there is no question of his genuine admiration for the engineers and inventors of a modern, progressive age.[78]

Schinkel was interested in examples of environmental control, especially if they could be useful models for his own work in Berlin. Traditional centers of eighteenth-century town planning, such as the remarkable efforts of the Woods and Palmer in venerable Bath, impressed him unfavorably. He perceptively analyzed, criticized, and sketched the fashionable resort. He noted in his diary on 28 July 1826 that, although the architecture of Bath was highly praised in England, he considered it monotonous and totally immersed in English triviality. He did find the orientation of this city on hilltops and in valleys pleasant, but he felt that there was a shortage of lakes, that a natural skyline of definite character was lacking, and that certain branches of the city sprawled haphazardly into the surrounding valleys and hills. These parts were connected physically, but there was no master plan for the entire city. In some respects, the less publicized planning schemes, such as the recent expansion of Edinburgh by Gillespie Graham, appealed to Schinkel more than the famous sites. He enthusiastically described and sketched Graham's utilization of a broad slope by creating a series of terraces.

Neither Bath nor Edinburgh could have influenced Schinkel's project in Berlin since the functional requirements of the Packhof and the Prussian topography were completely alien to these impressive schemes. His remarks merely exemplify his perceptive awareness of aspects of environmental design in a foreign land. On the other hand, it may have been the total absence of any planning consideration in the case of another English example which challenged Schinkel's ability as an environmental planner of commercial buildings along the Kupfergraben: his expression of disgust upon seeing the industrial buildings in Manchester, recorded on 16 July 1826. This page from his diary (Figure 88) contains the well-known drawing of a series of factories and mills along a canal in the heart of this "progressive" industrial town. These factories, noted Schinkel in a line frequently quoted, are nothing but "monstrous masses of red brick, built by a mere foreman, without any trace of architecture and for the sole purpose of crude necessity, making a most frightening impression."[79] His sketch of this desolate assembly of strictly utilitarian buildings is further supplemented by a brief note which mentions that some of these buildings are seven to eight stories high, that they are fireproof, and that their length and depth corresponds to the size of the royal Schloss in Berlin.

One can assume from this last reference that, while in Britain, Schinkel was preoccupied with his own concurrent project for Berlin. He probably noticed the obvious similarity between the Manchester mills and his own Packhof buildings. In both cases, the problem had been to find a solution

88. Page from Schinkel's diary of 16–18 July 1826.
Factories and mills at Manchester, England.

for the design of efficient commercial structures along a waterfront. In Manchester, this problem was solved by strictly utilitarian means: the adoption of a simple structural grid; the use of segmental brick vaults, cast-iron columns and girders; and, finally, a curtain wall of brick.[80] This kind of builder's functionalism has been praised by Giedion as one of the pioneering statements in the history of modern building. In the 1820's, Schinkel recognized the potential of English factory construction. The plan and structure of the warehouses at the Packhof, and later of the Bauakademie, attest to his respect for progressive building methods and the utilization of modern materials. He was the first architect in Prussia to import British construction materials, such as Portland cement, in order to improve the local building technology.

Schinkel never subscribed to the use of modern methods or materials as an end in itself, only as a means of attaining good architecture. And since, in his philosophy, architecture was placed in the service of human needs and treated as an instrument for the improvement of man-made environments, the appearance of the Manchester buildings could have only evoked his utmost contempt. These structures had, he felt, been erected solely for utility and profit. "How depressing is the sight of such an English industrial town! We did not come across anything which could have delighted the eye," was his reaction to a similar situation at Birmingham. For once, Schinkel, the architect and humanist, could not share the enthusiasm of his friend and traveling companion Beuth, the reform-minded promotor of industry, who acclaimed English factories as "the wonders of a new age."[81]

In Schinkel's view, the inventiveness and progressive techniques of English building construction could be adopted, but the inhuman aspects of its appearance demanded drastic transformation. This was the greatest challenge which confronted him in Britain. He reacted by designing a complex of commercial structures along the Kupfergraben which satisfied the need for efficient, economical construction, but which rejected the grim utilitarianism of the factories along the shipping canal in Manchester. His careful siting of a series of simple cubes along the waterfront and his conscious endeavor to elevate these functional blocks to the level of dignified architecture make the Packhof project unique in the area of commercial construction in the early nineteenth century (Figure 89). The transformation of the northern half of the island constitutes a masterwork of urban planning and represents Schinkel in his maturity as a designer of specialized environments.

This assessment of Schinkel's ability may seem even more justifiable after examining the last section of central Berlin which he transformed

89. View of Packhof buildings along the Kupfergraben from the northwest, 1834.

and considering his repeated proposals for the improvement of Friedrich-Werder, one of the oldest quarters of the city. Located between medieval Cölln on the island and the newer Friedrichstadt toward the west, Friedrich-Werder had been one of the three semi-independent ducal communities surrounded by Friedrich Wilhelm's seventeenth-century fortifications. It had traditionally served as a center for shipping, storage, and commerce (Figure 90). Its nucleus was the old Packhof site, south of the Hundebrücke, and the Werdersche-Markt, west of the locks and mills along the Kupfergraben. In keeping with its early founding, Friedrich-Werder reflected a semimedieval character in its buildings and street patterns as late as the nineteenth century. A detail of the J. F. Schneider plan of 1802 (Figure 91) clearly reveals the abrupt change from the neat grid system of modern Friedrichstadt to the jumbled composition of Friedrich-Werder toward the east. The most obvious problem, a legacy from earlier times, was the absence of a connecting thoroughfare between the older and newer sections of the capital. To correct this situation and improve a number of additional aspects, Schinkel focused his attention on this area as early as 1817, and he worked there as late as 1835.

Unlike the Lustgarten environment, which had challenged him with its vastness of open spaces and the commanding presence of historic buildings, Friedrich-Werder demanded the skillful and cautious hand of a

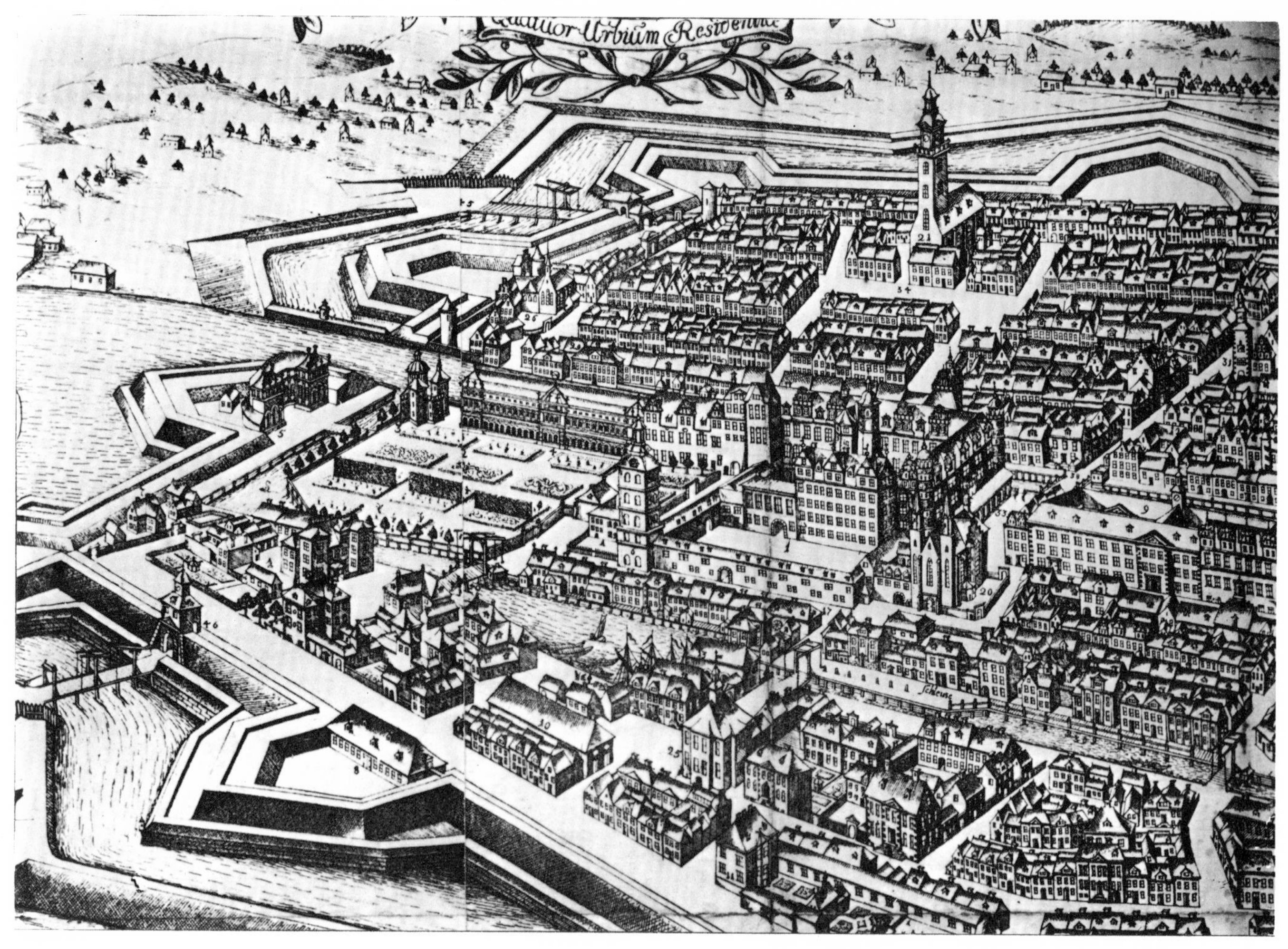

90. Johann Bernhard Schultz. Detail from aerial view of Berlin, Cölln, and Friedrich-Werder, 1688.

surgeon who could cut through densely crowded urban tissue and remove the cancers of commercial blight. In the final analysis, it was here that Schinkel's mastery of environmental planning would be tested. Friedrich-Werder had to be improved and reassimilated. It would become a case study of urban renewal, rather than a site of public display. It was at Friedrich-Werder that Schinkel would ultimately erect his favorite building, the Bauakademie. Although it was not begun until 1832, some of the preparatory steps leading to the reorganization of Friedrich-Werder can certainly be traced back as far as 1817. In his master plan for Berlin of that year (see Figure 64), Schinkel attempted for the first time to initiate vital changes in Friedrich-Werder. He indicated that the Französische Strasse should break through from Friedrichstadt to the island, providing an uninterrupted connection between the western and eastern sections of

91. J. F. Schneider. Detail from map of Berlin and environs, 1802.

the city. At the same time, he proposed to relocate the old Packhof as well as the unsightly mills and locks between the Werdersche-Markt and the Schloss-Platz. Two churches for the French and German congregations of the community were to take their place along the river. Schinkel's idealism seemed to have no bounds; he even proposed a modern market building along his new street to replace the temporary shacks of vendors. As mentioned before, his efforts were not appreciated and no changes were made.

Perhaps, as a consequence, his plan of 1823 (see Figure 75) is much more abbreviated and realistic. He repeated his request to relocate the customs warehouses, although the development of their original site, which was a parcel of royal property, is less ambitious than his proposal of 1817. The published version of his new scheme (see Figure 84) shows only a large triangular apartment block and a new street along the Kupfergraben. Conspicuously absent are details and, above all, proposals for further development of the surrounding environment. Aiming primarily at the realization of the Museum and the transformation of the northern half of the island, Schinkel may have purposely avoided an ambitious project for the area of Friedrich-Werder in order to assure his limited, yet important, goal. As an experienced Prussian civil servant, he knew that the construction of the Museum and of a modern Packhof could not permit excessive additional expenditures for improvements in the south. He may also have reasoned that the original site of the Packhof could not be utilized for new construction until its units were moved into new quarters. Both considerations proved to be correct. The Museum required all of the allocated sum of 700,000 *Thaler*, and the new Packhof was not finished until as late as 1832.

Since the erection of the apartment block was delayed, the area of the Werdersche-Markt would probably not have been substantially changed until some later date had Schinkel not been ordered to prepare designs for the rebuilding of the Friedrich-Werdersche Kirche.[82] The result of his painstaking efforts and frustrating attempts to satisfy the taste of the king and the crown prince is the simple, neo-Gothic church which he designed in 1824 (Figure 92). Friedrich Adler, among the last of Schinkel's students, cited the Friedrich-Werdersche Kirche in 1869 as a design in which Schinkel demonstrated that he would fulfill a royal order in regard to the choice of style, but he would not fall victim to the outright copying of historic examples in Prussia or elsewhere.[83] Perhaps it was a later pastor of the church, Johannes Krätschell, whose simple but perceptive statement reflected Schinkel's personal sentiments. He called this neomedieval building "Schinkel's Gothic *Schmerzenskind*."[84]

The architect's personal preference would have been a building in the

92. Friedrich-Werdersche Kirche; final design; view from southeast, 1828.

classical style. Among the numerous schemes which he prepared for the Werdersche Kirche, his favorite design was a simple structure with some early Christian overtones, including a freestanding campanile (Figure 93). In both site plan and perspective view this tower can be seen to play a pivotal role in the organization of the square. A vertical accent, reminiscent of the campanile at San Lorenzo which Schinkel sketched in Italy (see Figure 39), the tower called attention to the public plaza and gave a definition to this old quarter of Berlin which it had not previously possessed. Being completely detached from the church—joined to it only by means of a high wall—it could be seen as a separate and distinct form, relating as much to the civic character of the public square as to the religious function of the church.

93. Classical design for Friedrich-Werdersche Kirche, ca. 1824.

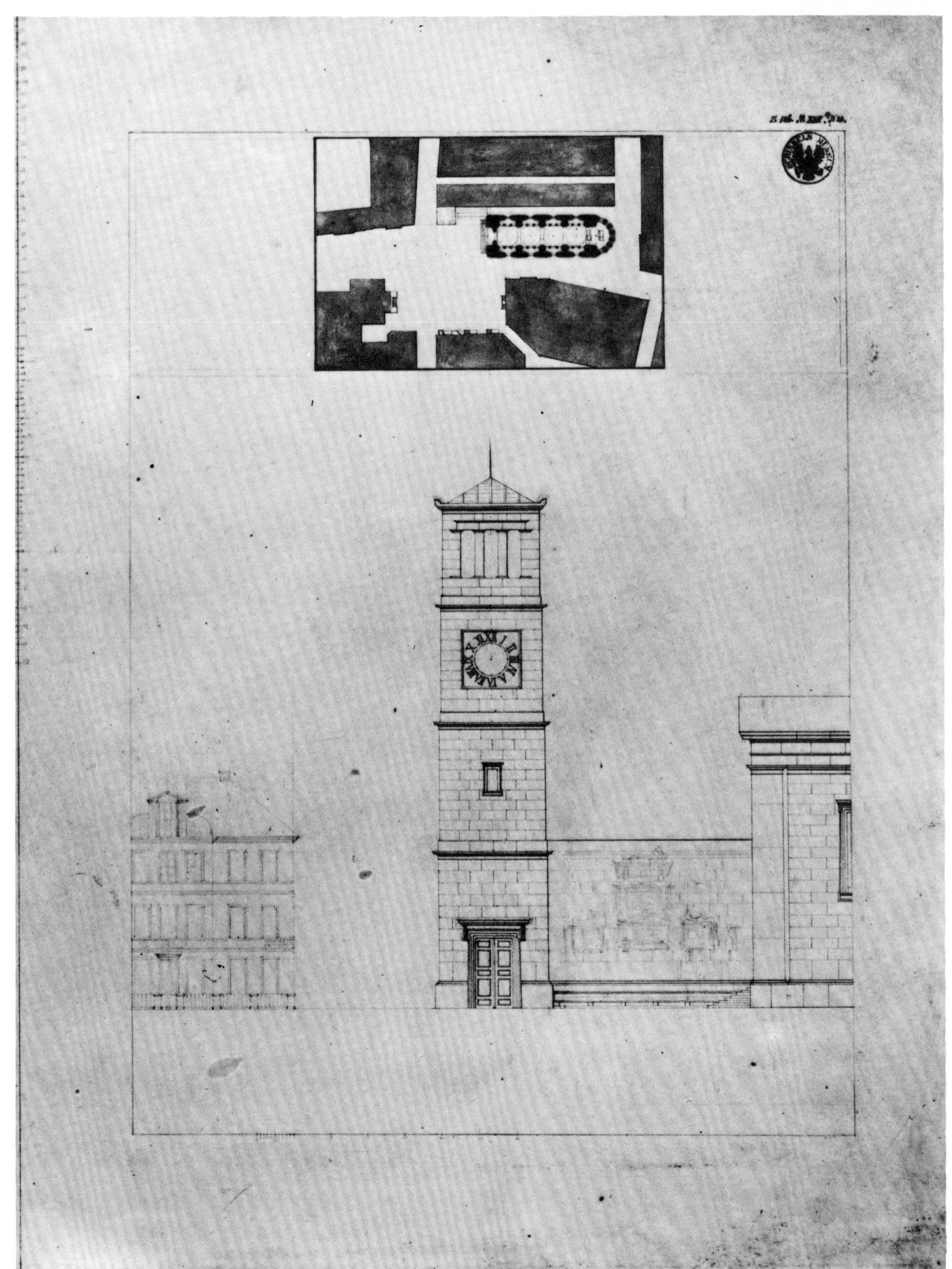

The church itself is severely simple in basic form. Schinkel stated in his explanations of the design that the location of the building would "make a rich architecture unpalatable," and demanded instead "an extremely plain exterior." Considering that a more obvious choice would have been a conventional projecting portico to emphasize the main facade, it is interesting to see that Schinkel turned instead to the unprecedented use of a large niche under a round arch surmounted by a simple pediment.[85] Since he stated that "the nature of the site . . . was a principal determinant in the proposed organization of the building," we must look to the existing structures surrounding the square for a key to his conscious austerity of design. One particular building whose style and formal presence must certainly have aroused Schinkel's attention and response was the Neue Münzgebäude by Heinrich Gentz (Figure 94). The sculptured frieze above its rusticated ground floor was executed by Gottfried Schadow after designs by Friedrich Gilly. It was built between 1798 and 1800 and, among other functions, it served as the first home of Berlin's Bauakademie. It was in this building that Schinkel attended classes conducted by Gilly, Langhans, and Gentz. Thus, some twenty-five years after his initiation to architecture, this commission forced him to cope with a building which had once personified the ideals of a modern style. Although the mint building by Gentz is rarely listed among outstanding examples of the revolutionary age, its uncompromising block-like form, its plain surfaces, and its crisp lines relate closely to better-known designs by Friedrich Gilly.

It is not surprising that Schinkel's design for the projected Werdersche Kirche was a simple frame with pediment, arch, and frontal stairs, facing onto the same city square which had formerly been dominated by his master's monument alone. This classical version would have resulted in a complementary, rather than rudely abrupt, stylistic and formal relationship between the two buildings. The harmony which he tried to effect is underscored by the site plan, which shows Gentz's block at the lower left and Schinkel's classical church diagonally across the city square (see Figure 93).

Further proof of Schinkel's concern for the classical spirit of Gilly and Gentz within the environment of the Werdersche-Markt is a tentative design for the royal stables, which he projected for the site of the old Packhof in 1827 (Figure 95). For this desirable piece of royal property, the crown prince had already sketched an extravagant neomedieval *Burgenschloss*, complete with curving walls, turrets, and crennelations, as a private residence for his brother, Prince Wilhelm.[86] Schinkel may have tried to forestall the possible realization of a second neomedieval structure

94. Heinrich Gentz. Münzgebäude, 1798–1800; view from northwest.

95. View of projected royal stables at the site of the old Packhof, 1827.

in the heart of Friedrich-Werder by proposing a stately classical monument for the stabling of the royal horses, a project which would have been a compliment to Schlüter, Gilly, and Gentz. The high pavilions at either end resemble the elevation of Schlüter's palace across the river; the magnificent portals with coffered barrel vaults on axis are literal quotations from Gilly's triumphal arch; the creative assimilation of forms responds to Gentz's Münze at the Werdersche-Markt. But neither the crown prince's dream castle nor Schinkel's stables would be erected at this site. Instead, the triangular plot along the west bank of the Kupfergraben would be utilized for the Bauakademie, a cornerstone in the urban structure of modern Berlin.

Early in 1832 Schinkel presented a final plan for the rehabilitation of the area of the Werdersche-Markt (Figure 96). With the Packhof moved to its recently completed quarters and construction of a new Bauakademie already approved, Schinkel hoped to effect a combination of building and planning measures which would have greatly benefited both the services and the appearance of a crucial area of the city. Much of Friedrich-Werder would be transformed into a community of highest architectural standards. Once more he urged the extension of the Französische Strasse in order to create a major east-west artery between Friedrichstadt and the island. Detailed proposals for the utilization of property north and south of the street were precisely outlined as part of the plan.[87] At the new corner created by the intersection of the Französische Strasse and the Oberwallstrasse he proposed the erection of a storage building for the scenery and decorations of the nearby Schauspielhaus. On the opposite side of the

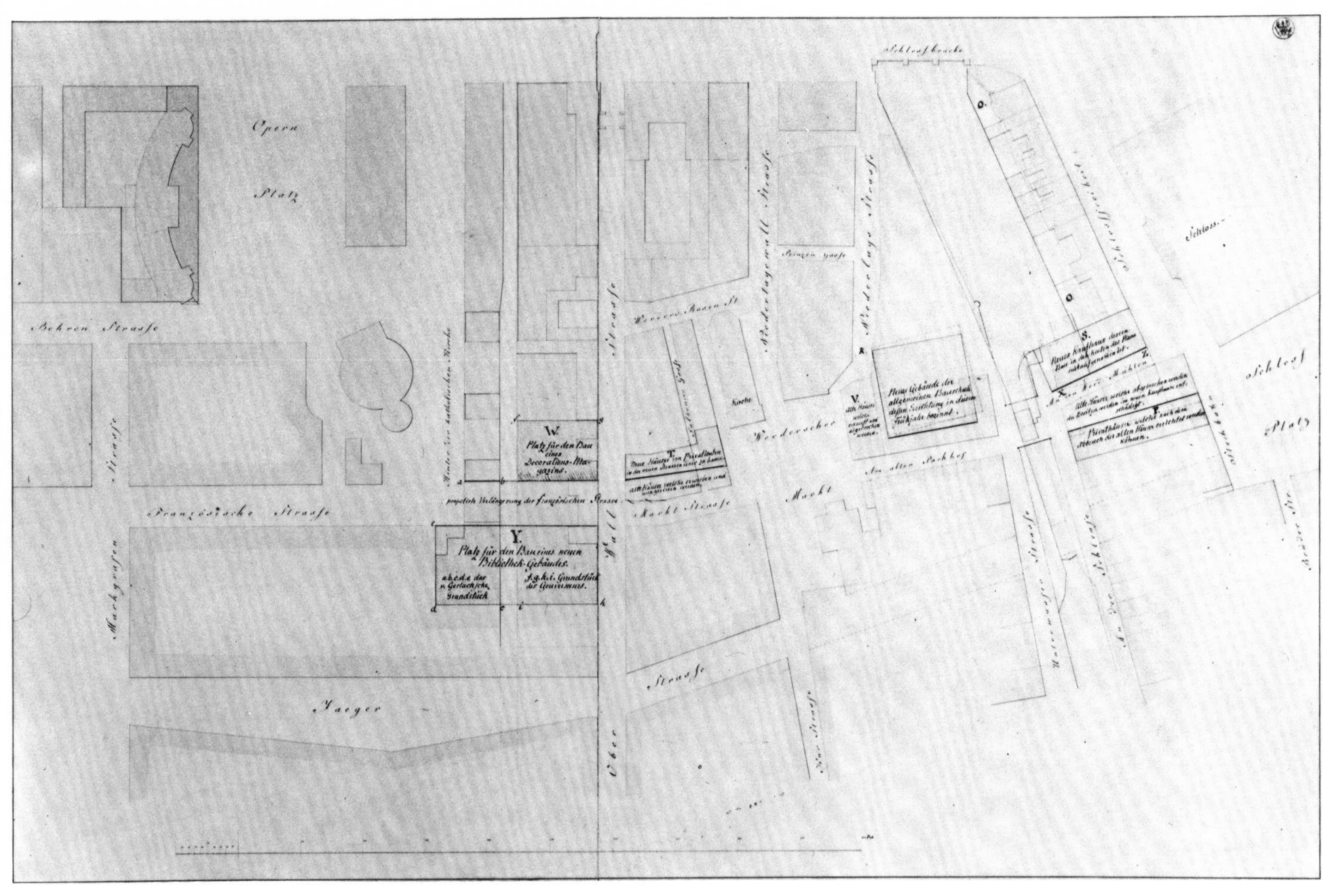

96. Master plan for Friedrich-Werder, winter 1831/32.

street would rise a new library, which was needed for two reasons: Crown Prince Friedrich Wilhelm wished to expand the old royal Bibliothek at the Opernplatz and use it as his private palace, and the original library needed enlargement, improvement, and modernization. Continuing toward the east, Schinkel advocated the elimination of several existing houses to increase the width of the former Markt Strasse, which led directly into the Werdersche-Markt. These buildings were to be replaced by private residences whose facades would conform to the border line of the new street, which is marked on the plan by a heavier line. A group of town houses at the east edge of the market square, next to the Bauakademie, would likewise be eliminated. This would enlarge the plaza and clear it of any obstructions between the church and the projected school of architecture. At the same time, the street called *Am alten Packhof* would be broadened to provide sufficient space for the continuation of the main thoroughfare toward the east. Gentz's Münze would remain untouched. Finally, the narrow passage across the Kupfergraben was to be opened into the Schloss-Platz and enhanced by a new Kaufhaus at the north and modern residences at the south of the broadened thoroughfare.

In short, Schinkel advocated the combining of the construction of the Bauakademie with a major renovation of Friedrich-Werder. The east-west artery here would correspond to the thoroughfare across the island in the north, which had been created as part of his extensive Lustgarten-Packhof scheme. In this way the Unter den Linden could be reserved as a permanent public avenue free of commercial traffic and use, its representational and formal character preserved. Schinkel concluded his specifications for this plan by pointing out that the combined advantages could be achieved at a lower cost per year than the average amount which had been allocated by the crown for embellishments of the city over the previous fourteen years. Once more the results were disappointing. The king approved nothing but the construction of the Bauakademie.[88] Waagen lamented justifiably over the rejection of Schinkel's outstanding plan: "It is an irony of fate that in Berlin, where most streets are wider than necessary, one of generous width is missing precisely at the very place where a proper thoroughfare is urgently needed, namely, at the locks, the junction between the old and new city. In order to overcome this ever apparent problem, Schinkel had proposed a plan to raze the townhouse of the Gouverneur and to use its site for the extension of a projected street, which was to terminate at the Schlossplatz. Unfortunately, this idea . . . was not realized."[89]

The rejection of Schinkel's proposals as outlined in the plan of 1832 did not deter him from restating several of the major planning objectives for the improvement of Friedrich-Werder, and the opportunity to do this came during the course of the following year, when he prepared drawings of the Bauakademie (called Allgemeine Bauschule until 1848) for publication. One of the sheets he drew to illustrate this building in his *Sammlung* is composed of a section, floor plans, and a site plan (Figure 97).[90] In the accompanying text he began his explanation of the project in a typical manner by listing first the advantages to the city, which he considered to be a natural extension of the building itself. He suggested that the increased width of the street south of the Bauakademie should be extended to the Markt Strasse at the western entry to the square. Ultimately, this street "could be continued in the same width at the opposite side of the market square and serve as a direct connecting link with the Französische Strasse." As before, he proposed that the houses bordering this street on the north be set back and that those facing onto the square adjacent to the church be remodeled in order to conform to the formal character of their

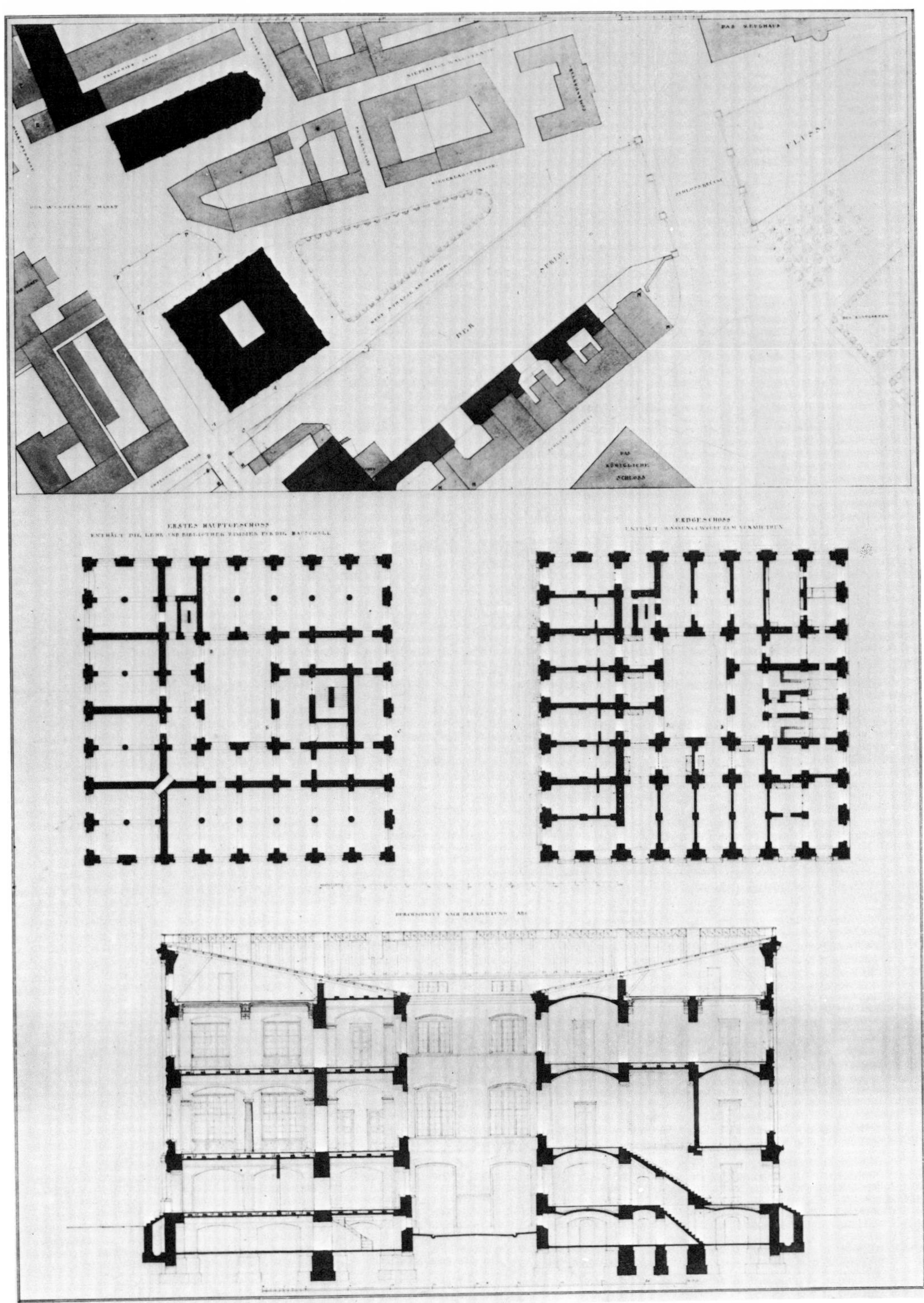

97. Bauakademie; site plan, floor plans, section, 1831.

important location.[91] The houses next to the Bauakademie (marked *F* on the plan) were to be razed in order to assure that the Werdersche-Markt would thus "attain its final completion." By this he implied that he considered the Bauakademie to be an integral part of the formal composition of the market square. In the opposite direction, east of the new building, he indicated again an enlarged bridge and restated his suggestions to replace the mills with a Kaufhaus and to improve the private property along the eastern bank of the Kupfergraben with "decent facades." Unlike Friedrich Gilly, who had once considered replacing the buildings in this area with others of his own design (see Figure 19), Schinkel suggested that the owners of these houses should be reimbursed for their efforts by the provision of some free land along the bank of the narrowed canal. Although he supplied no specific designs, he contended that the view from the Schlossbrücke onto this section of the island bordering the royal palace should be considerably improved. The result of the complete neglect of his advice is vividly documented in a watercolor by F. W. Klose, done after 1853, of the environment east of the new Bauakademie, whose southeast corner appears at the left (Figure 98).[92]

98. F. W. Klose. View of the palace cupola from the Bauakademie, ca. 1853.

At the Werdersche-Markt itself, Schinkel seems to have been more successful. His site plan gives some indication of his determined efforts to achieve that "final completion" of which he had written. It is hard to find a sympathetic line about the neo-Gothic church in his extensive writings, but he nonetheless consciously sought some harmony of spirit between it and the newer Bauakademie. He underscored the formal relationship of the two buildings by defining their areas in solid black and by emphasizing the exterior piers which characterized their perimeters. In another way, he harmonized their exteriors by constructing both of brick, "devoid of paint or plaster." This kind of relationship between structure and material assured a sense of unity between two major buildings of the city square, which was evident in the past and has remained so until recently. Eduard Gaertner's painting of 1868 (Figure 99) and a photograph taken prior to the destruction of the damaged Bauakademie in 1961 (Figure 100) reveal that Schinkel attempted to create a strong

99. Eduard Gaertner. *Bauakademie,* 1868.

100. Bauakademie and Friedrich-Werdersche Kirche; view from the southeast.

relationship between the favorite building of his career, the Bauakademie, and his Gothic "Schmerzenskind," as Krätschell had called the church.

There remains an obvious question: by what means, if any, did Schinkel try to correlate his most recent addition to the Werdersche-Markt with the Münzgebäude by Gentz? The answer, I believe, does not necessarily lie in their mutual block-like appearance, nor in the use of a balustrade around the roof. A closer link could possibly exist in their mutual acceptance of plain surfaces, the extensive area of window openings, and the carefully balanced amount of architectural decoration. Rave's eloquent essay on its ornamental system and two photographs of details of its south facade (Figures 101, 102) show clearly to what extent Schinkel understood that architecture can never rely solely on "structural honesty" and a relentless order of repetitive modules.[93]

Like Gilly and Gentz before him, or Louis Sullivan later in the century, Schinkel demanded that art and architecture be closely bound in order to form an inspiring and organic unity.[94] Once more it was Waagen who sensed this quality first and summarized the character of the Bauakademie in this penetrating paragraph: "To be sure, the building as a whole, based on a square format, does create an impressive and noble effect as a massive structure with a carefully articulated crowning. However, only if seen from nearby is it possible to become aware of its foremost appeal: the exquisite finesse of its articulation and ornamentation. The method of dividing the facades into floor levels and window bays—the latter being of unusual width—is here as novel as it is purposeful. Doors and windows have been accentuated by the use of architectural relief sculpture, whose depicted subject matter relates directly to the function of the building."[95] The Bauakademie's terra-cotta spandrels and the frieze around the Münzgebäude are therefore important manifestations of a similarity of attitude, principle, and style between two masters who complemented the environment of a city square with outstanding examples of their respective careers.

In the final analysis of Schinkel's Bauakademie as a statement of environmental design, it is necessary to realize that this building was not solely oriented toward the Werdersche-Markt in the west. As a matter of fact, the site plan and his written explanations indicate that he attempted to create a link with the Schlossbrücke and the Lustgarten area toward the north. A simple triangular plaza (later known as the Schinkel-Platz) extended from the main facade of the Bauakademie along the newly created Neue Strasse am Wasser and connected his modern building with the Baroque Zeughaus. The communication between these two buildings and indeed with the distant Packhof structures at the northern end of the

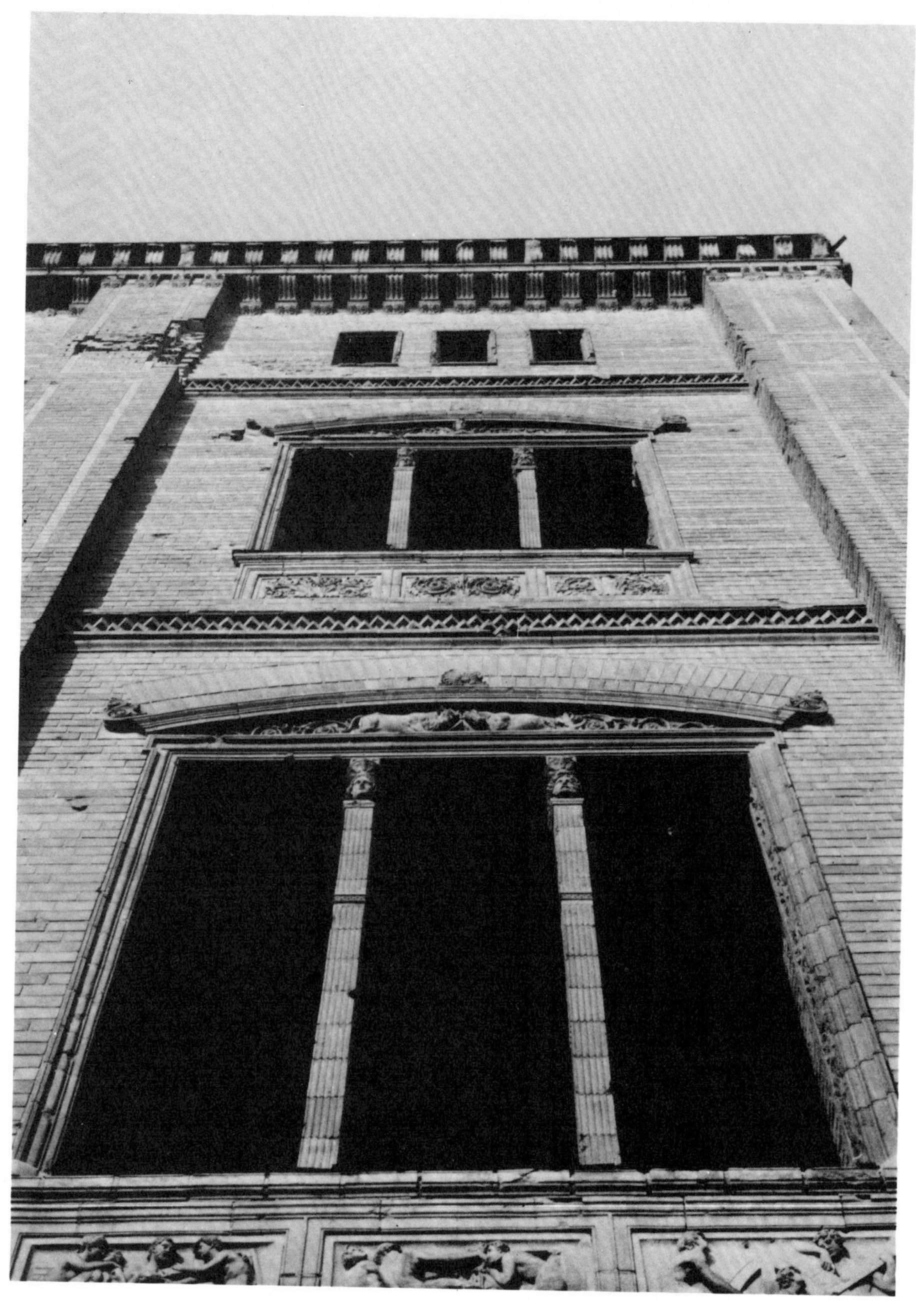

101. Bauakademie; detail of south facade.

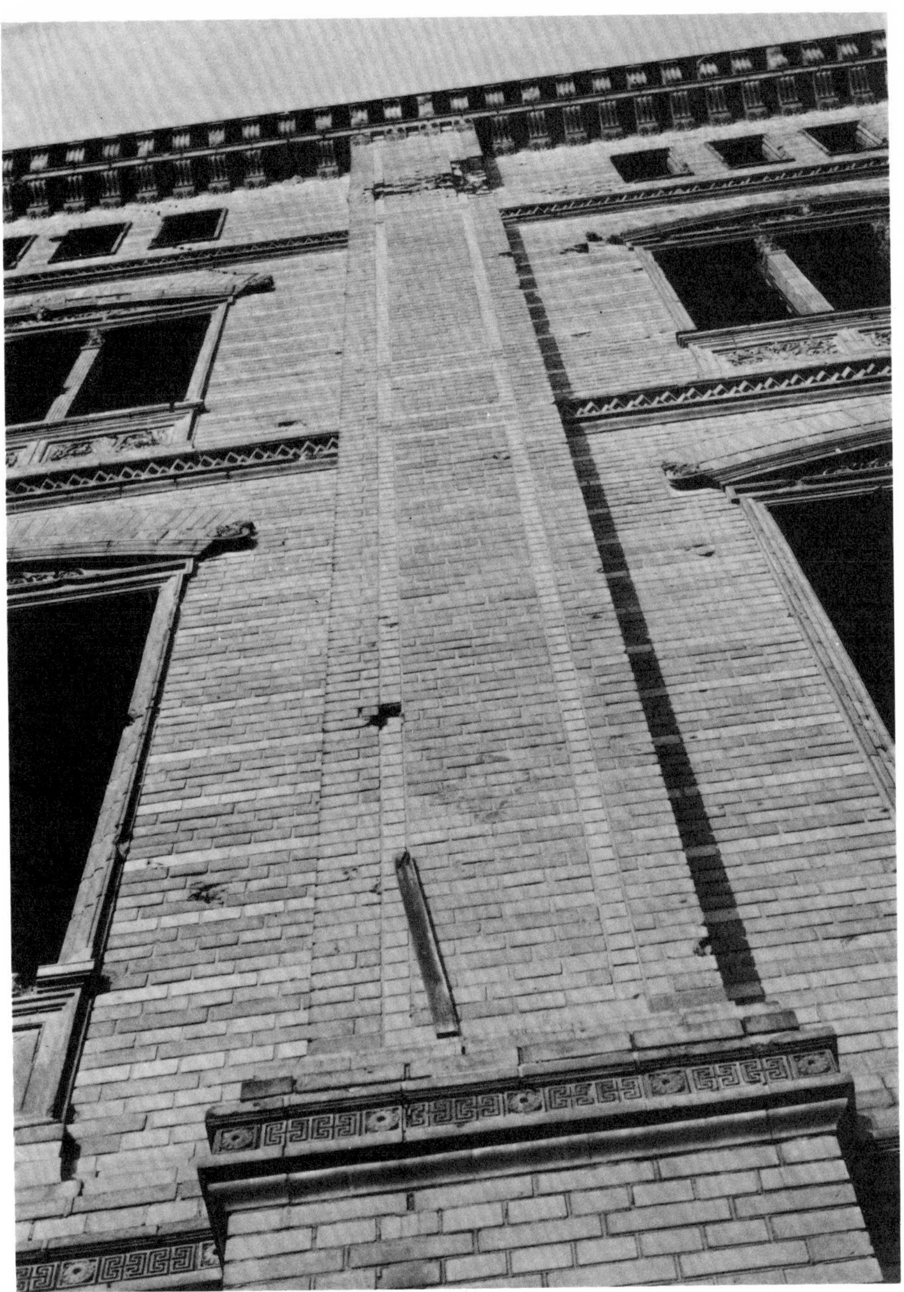

102. Bauakademie; detail of south facade.

PERSPECTIVISCHE ANSICHT DES GEBÄUDES DER ALLGEMEINEN BAUSCHULE IN BERLIN.

103. View of the Bauakademie and its environment from the northeast, 1831.

island was enhanced by the use of a square plan, a central court, and the characteristically cubic outline of his building's mass.

The character of the environment into which it was placed is seen in his general view of the Bauakademie, which he drew as early as 1831, five years before its completion (Figure 103). Against the backdrop of Friedrich-Werder, a formerly neglected area of commercial blight, rises the four-squared mass of his modern building, transforming the entire scene. In the foreground extends the newly reshaped embankments of the Kupfergraben and in the background rise the towers of his church. Unlike J.-N.-L. Durand, who illustrated this building only in plan and elevation in the 1833 edition of his famous *Recueil et parallèle* . . .,[96] Schinkel portrayed it both as a three-dimensional form and as part of a total urban scene. Just as he had drawn the Paris theater some twenty-five years before, he now presented the Bauakademie as part of an environmental context, going far beyond the building's own physical limits. Indeed, seen in this context of formal and spatial interrelationships with its neighboring buildings, both near and far, one can readily agree with Friedrich Adler's perceptive observation that the Bauakademie constituted a cornerstone in the environmental planning of modern central Berlin.

Upon its completion early in 1836, twenty years had passed since Schinkel had begun the second and major phase of his career as an architect and planner. These years had witnessed the realization of his masterworks: the Neue Wache, the Schauspielhaus, the Museum, and the Bauakademie. In addition, one could list numerous projects which he envisioned for the Prussian capital. Among them were a modern Kaufhaus on the Unter den Linden (1827), a city palace for Prince Wilhelm at the Opernplatz (1829), and several projects for a new Bibliothek behind the university (1835–1839). Constantly struggling against the realities of financial restrictions and repeated curtailments by a vacillating and reluctant monarch, he nevertheless succeeded in unifying the core of Prussia's capital city into a comprehensive organism of buildings, spaces, streets, and waterways. His intelligence and his tenacity were not only persistent characteristics of his will to succeed, but they also guided him in the timing of his proposals, the diplomatic argument of their advantages, and the utilization of every promising circumstance. From the time of his unrealized project for the Dom als Denkmal für den Freiheitskrieg in 1814 to his repeated demands for the improvement of Friedrich-Werder in the 1830's, Schinkel's qualities as a flexible and rational civil servant seem to have been as important as the creative imagination which finally gave substance to his principles and ideals.

These principles and ideals focused on an architecture of totality, that is, the utilization of architecture to create unified urban environments. This meant that Schinkel was not a planner in the traditional sense. Unlike Leo von Klenze in Munich or Friedrich Weinbrenner in Karlsruhe, Schinkel transformed areas within the established urban fabric, rather than adding new sections of a comprehensive design. Not a single commission given to him in Berlin or elsewhere called for the execution of an entire quarter or even a large-scale urban unit. Had it not been for his own initiative, constant urging and repeated requests for the expansion of royal commissions, the center of Berlin would have remained an agglomeration of isolated and fragmented parts. Unlike Ludwig I of Bavaria, Friedrich Wilhelm III never ordered his architect to design a monumental civic plaza or to unify parts of his capital by means of impressive avenues.[97] Consequently, Berlin does not possess the equivalent of the Königsplatz in Munich or the rue de Rivoli in Paris. It remains Schinkel's legacy that he was able to sustain creative imagination against the odds of bureaucracy and transform parts of the old fabric of central Berlin into a new and organic totality. His own subtle sense of beauty enabled his buildings to blend into the total landscape of the city's most representative section. This legacy did not remain unnoticed. Theodor Fontane, the poet of the

Mark Brandenburg and one of the most perceptive admirers of Schinkel, concluded a summary of his work in Berlin with a simple but penetrating comparison. Sir Christopher Wren, he observed, superimposed his famous buildings upon London and thus succeeded in changing the outward physiognomy of his city. Schinkel's works, however, transformed the essential character of Prussia's capital, or, as Fontane put it, Berlin "reflects Schinkel's stamp on its innermost structure."[98]

The same intuitive feeling for organic integration and continuum, instead of abrupt change and stark individualism, is also characteristic of Schinkel as an architect of individual buildings. He did not subscribe to the excessive grandeur and monumental fantasies which had guided the vision of many a man who preceded him. Robert Adam, for instance, did not appeal to him, as he might have to Friedrich Gilly, though Schinkel did appreciate the clarity of his details and the precision of his proportions. The same is true for his attitude toward other masters of the eighteenth century. Soufflot's church in Paris seemed too monumental; Soane's early work in London, too pretentious. But he nonetheless learned from them. Though he never referred to Piranesi or the Bibienas, these artists, too, provided a firm cultural and artistic background from which he drew inspiration. In short, Schinkel did not restrict the range of his vocabulary of form, expression, and style to the lessons he received from the Gillys and Gentz. He traveled extensively and absorbed an unlimited number of impressions. He found delight and inspiration in the simplicity of an Italian farmyard, the majesty of Michelangelo's Campidoglio, and the logic of an English factory. Finally, Schinkel was equally absorbed in reading and theoretical studies. His incomplete teaching manual on architecture reveals that the lessons of Winckelmann, Fichte, Goethe, and Durand had been firmly understood and then reinterpreted in his own creative way.[99] As a result, he would emerge as an inventive assimilator, rather than a highly individualistic genius or a dogmatic academician. His buildings are never "pure" in style. Unlike Weinbrenner, whose designs were primarily based on French neo-Classical models and thus very "clumsy" or "*ungeschickt*" according to Schinkel, he himself manipulated forms and spaces according to practical need, symbolic association, and his own uncommon sense of beauty. His Neue Wache is neither Greek nor Roman and his Schauspielhaus synthesizes Grecian, Palladian, and modern elements. His Bauakademie, far from being merely a statement of rationalist simplicity, is the rich and complex work of a mature architect.

This same characteristic of inventive assimilation marks Schinkel's planning philosophy. Since he was essentially an architect and landscape painter, rather than a speculative builder and planner like John Nash,

Schinkel aimed first at the perfection of the individual unit and, secondly, at its integration into an overall urban environment. This tendency, which was already evident in his early sketches of Italy, would become a standard quality of his planning statements in Berlin. Whether we think of his master plan of 1817, or smaller projects such as the Neue Wache, existing buildings and spaces would always constitute the basis of the environment which he organized for his new structures. Again and again he gave evidence of his cognizance of and respect for the existing architectural framework. Be it the cornice line of the Zeughaus or the porticos of the churches at the Gendarmenmarkt, he used existing components as guidelines for his own creations. Superficial connections such as free-standing, decorative colonnades were as alien to his spirit as the "sham facades" which he criticized in Bath and at Regent's Park in London. Instead, he turned to nature and recommended that trees and promenades should serve as unifying elements. Sculpture and fountains could be added to underscore visual and spatial organization among loosely linked building groups.

It is perhaps in this particular area that we find at once the greatest promise and the ultimate weakness of his planning schemes. Schinkel's employment of natural elements to enhance, unify, and relate parts of an urban environment is a lesson which could well be applied to the persistent problems of our own planning situations. Yet, the use of landscaping and sculpture in a modern city is even more vulnerable to the deterioration of time and the vagaries of man's taste than standards of style and scale in the design of architectural monuments. In specific reference to Schinkel's projects in central Berlin, the loss of a sequence of trees and the neglect to install his specified sculptures were already recognized by Waagen as detrimental to the completeness of the Neue Wache. Likewise, a single stroke of the king's pen through the outlines of a proposed fountain at the Lustgarten immediately destroyed a significant environmental concept. Although a substantial bridge was built to connect the Unter den Linden with the island, a single fountain could subtly have unified the river, the island, the building, and the street.

The Transformation of Central Berlin

It is not surprising, therefore, that future generations could swiftly change or destroy the character of Schinkel's urban environments. Disrespect, "progress," and a lack of sensitivity had reduced central Berlin to a state of spatial and formal compartmentalization by the time a generation of modern architects and critics began to look at his work during the first half of our century. An aerial view of central Berlin in 1936 (Figure 104) shows a pattern of starkly isolated blocks separated by "efficient" traffic arteries. The personal triumph of Schinkel's career, the

104. Aerial view of central Berlin about 1936.

Lustgarten and its environment, had been effectively destroyed. His sensitivity for continuity of scale had been disrupted as early as 1894. In that year, Julius Raschdorff replaced the old church, and his new Domkirche, a neo-Baroque giant, outraged in height and fancy all subtlety of scale and simplicity of form that had once united the total architectural scene. Subsequently, during the Nazi regime, the Lustgarten itself was reduced to a grid of stone pavement for political rallies and parades.[100]

The Transformation of Central Berlin

Today, twenty-five years after the holocaust of 1945, Schinkel's recently restored Museum is the lonely survivor of a once-splendid urban area. Gone are the Packhof buildings, the Königliche Schloss and the Bauakademie.[101] The Museum has irrevocably lost its communication with the spatial and physical context which originally formed a comprehensive, organized, urban environment. As a result, Schinkel's major achievement as an environmental planner has been effectively destroyed, while his imaginative ideas and solutions live on in his drawings and writings.

Similarly, individual projects and total complexes of Schinkel's career outside the physical framework of central Berlin have suffered under the impact of war and neglect.

In Berlin itself, at the Pariser Platz, his city palace for Graf Redern (1830) was razed in 1906 to make room for the fashionable Hotel Adlon (in turn largely destroyed by 1945). Nearby, his extension of the Wilhelmstrasse (1820) north of the Unter den Linden, originally designed as a complete environmental unit of shops and residences, was gradually destroyed beginning in 1867. One should add that his compromise project for the Potsdamer Tor at the Leipziger Platz remained largely intact until most recent times, though Alfred Messel's Wertheim department store (1897–1904) changed the character of the old residential square somewhat. The two Grecian gatehouses, though badly damaged, survived the war; one was razed in 1945, the other as late as 1961. In addition, it must be noted that Schinkel proposed a number of planning schemes for outlying areas from the Tiergarten to the Köpenicker Vorstadt; they were rarely carried beyond initial planning stages.

Outside Berlin, in Prussia's provinces as well as in numerous German states and foreign countries, Schinkel's works have met a similar fate. Many of his buildings were destroyed during World War II, some have been altered beyond recognition, and others had to remain projects on paper (see Appendix). In the final assessment of Schinkel's importance, the student of his life and work must always return to central Berlin. No matter how charming a single country seat, how forthright an isolated lighthouse, or how resolute a distant restoration project may appear, it is Schinkel's comprehensive approach to an urban problem which marks his ultimate success. The transformation of central Berlin, therefore, should be recognized as the major legacy of his unique and fruitful career as one of Europe's greatest architects of the nineteenth century.

In the context of this study, one final question should be raised. How, if at all, could Schinkel's work as an architect and environmental planner of nineteenth-century Berlin emerge as a meaningful inspiration today? More specifically, which principles might apply in the restless drive to improve, rehabilitate, and save our cities?

I believe that the most valuable lesson to be drawn from Schinkel's achievement focuses on his outstanding ability to assimilate his own new additions into the urban fabric of existing buildings and spaces. In contrast to many present-day seekers of fame, he valued the total context more than praise of an isolated monument. In his writings he spoke repeatedly of advantages which would arise from the organization of a plaza or the improvement of waterways, bridges, and streets, and his own work confirmed this goal. Despite his constant concern for professional excellence and an uncompromising discipline in the design and execution of the total fabric of his own buildings, Schinkel always looked beyond the narrow limits of a floor plan or the outlines of a single facade. With the skill of a panorama painter and the imagination of a stage designer, he readily embraced the rhythm of scale and proportion relating to the total scene rather than to the visual accent of a specific angle.[102] Time and again, his projects in Berlin and elsewhere proved his mastery in coordinating nature and architecture and his concern for the completion of totalities, rather than a preoccupation with isolated, self-contained entities and details. The concept of environmental totality in Schinkel's sense was not, however, restricted to visual, formal, and spatial aspects alone. Nor was his theory of function and purpose bound to efficiency and rationalism alone. Architecture had to perform a role which reached far beyond these narrow boundaries. A building had to manifest the spirit of a monument, and the architect himself had to be qualified to facilitate and to enhance every aspect of human need and aspiration. His credo of an architect's responsibility toward his profession and society rings with the fervent idealism of the age of Goethe and Byron. It also bears a touch of umblemished innocence which characterizes a bygone era of creative individualism and hope. Although taste, commitments, and standards seem quickly to vanish in our age of mass destruction and urban renewal, it becomes increasingly apparent that the principle of excellence could eventually restore a truly humane purpose to architecture and art.[103]

In the final analysis, a modern student of Schinkel's architecture should be conscious of the total context of his achievement. He should realize the conditions of his time, the prevailing sentiments of his era. He should be aware of the realistic restrictions under which he worked and should try to assess his solutions in the light of specific local and cultural limitations. By all means he should avoid the oversimplification of strict categorization and resist the temptation to place this man into a general national or international current of Romantic-Classicism. Rather, as is true of any real artist, Schinkel should be seen as a creative assimilator whose vision and critical observation were proof that eternal principles could be reinterpreted in the everchanging rhythm of human life and needs. Seen in this context, specific stylistic solutions or aesthetic formulations for individual buildings appear largely irrelevant as indications of his legacy for today. It is inconsequential whether he used the Doric or Ionic order, modern or protofunctionalist schemes. It is important that he emulated principles rather than imitated forms. Even more significant is his sense of responsibility toward man, his concern for the improvement of man's environment rather than for material gain and exhibitionism. Finally, modern students could draw from a study of Schinkel's life and work an understanding of the fact that great architects of all times have possessed a will to learn all the lessons that life and art could teach, and that each one's final achievement emerges as the only valid test of their successful application. Seen in this light, Schinkel's transformation of the urban environment of central Berlin is his legacy to our modern age and a testimony to the ideals which he expressed so well:

> As in any branch of art, life has to be visible in architecture. One has to recognize the process by which the idea is formulated, and the way in which the entire imagery of nature is ready and eager to satisfy this idea. A work of architecture must not stand as a finished and self-sufficient object. True and pure imagination, having once entered the stream of the idea that it expresses, has to expand forever beyond this work, and it must venture out, leading ultimately to the infinite. It must be regarded as the point where one can make an orderly entry into the unbreakable chain of the universe. Striving, budding, crystallizing, unfolding, driving, a splitting, fitting, drifting, floating, pulling, pressing, bending, bearing, placing, vibrating, connecting, holding, a lying and resting—where the latter, which contrasts with the kinetic properties, must be an intentional and obvious repose, and therefore also a living action—these are the ways in which architecture must manifest life.[104]

Schinkel's Motto

Unser Geist ist nicht frei, wenn er nicht Herr seiner Vorstellungen ist; dagegen erscheint die Freiheit des Geistes bei jeder Selbstüberwindung, bei jedem Widerstande gegen äussere Lockung, bei jeder Pflichterfüllung, bei jedem Streben nach dem Besseren und bei jeder Wegräumung eines Hindernisses zu diesem Zweck. Jeder freie Moment ist ein seliger.

Appendix

Karl Friedrich Schinkel, 1781–1841
Biographical Notes and Chronological Survey of Buildings and Projects

In the following summary of events important in Schinkel's life, the listing of his executed works and unrealized projects is as comprehensive as possible. In his later years, especially in his position as director of Prussia's Oberbaudeputation, Schinkel supervised innumerable building projects throughout the kingdom and depended upon the support of a large staff of assistants. For those important works which bear his own stamp, the essential data of design, construction, and subsequent history are given. Where applicable, the location of extant buildings is cited with the designations Berlin/West or DDR (Deutsche Demokratische Republik) referring to present political boundaries.

1781 *13 March*
Schinkel is born at Neuruppin/Mark Brandenburg, the second of five children of Johann Cuno Christoph Schinkel (1736–1787) and Dorothea Schinkel, née Rose (1749–1800). His father is superintendent of churches and schools (*Archidiakomus*) at Neuruppin. His mother's family is noted for its professional members (teachers, scientists, etc.).

Publication of *Die Räuber*, the first play of Friedrich Schiller (1759–1805).

Publication of *Kritik der reinen Vernunft* by Immanuel Kant (1724–1804), dedicated to Karl von Zedlitz, Prussia's minister of education and ecclesiastical affairs under Friedrich II.

1786 *17 April*
Death of Friedrich II at Sanssouci; he is succeeded by Friedrich Wilhelm II, son of Prince August Wilhelm.

September
Departure of Johann Wolfgang von Goethe (1749–1832) on a journey to Italy and Sicily (until April 1788).

1787 *25 October*
Death of Schinkel's father as a result of injuries received during rescue efforts in a fire which gutted major parts of Neuruppin. The family moves into the Prediger-Witwenhaus, a home for ministers' widows. The young Schinkel witnesses the rebuilding of Neuruppin in an austere neo-Classical style under the auspices of Friedrich Wilhelm II.

1788 Construction (until 1791) of the new Brandenburger Tor at the Quarrée (later Pariser Platz) after designs by Carl Gotthard Langhans (1732–1808). Badly damaged during World War II; restored by 1958.

1789 *14 July*
Storming of the Bastille in Paris.

1792 Schinkel attends (until 1794) the Gymnasium at Neuruppin in a new neo-Classical building.

1793 *21 January*
Louis XVI, King of France, guillotined in Paris.

16 October
Marie Antoinette, Queen of France, guillotined in Paris.

Founding of the Bauschule, predecessor of the Bauakademie, in Berlin by Oberbaudirektor David Gilly (1748–1808).

1794 Schinkel's mother moves the family from Neuruppin to a home for ministers' widows in Berlin at Papenstrasse 10. He attends (until 1798) the Gymnasium zum Grauen Kloster, Berlin's oldest high school.

Erection of the Quadriga, designed by Gottfried Schadow (1764–1850), atop the Brandenburger Tor. It was removed by Napoleon in 1807, returned to Berlin in 1814, reinstalled with modifications by Schinkel, reconstructed after World War II according to the original design and re-erected in 1958.

Heinrich Gentz (1766–1811) returns to Berlin after extensive travels to Rome, Sicily, Paris and London.

1796 Ludwig van Beethoven (1770–1827) visits Berlin and performs at the royal court and at the Singakademie.

1797 Death of Schinkel's only brother, Friedrich Wilhelm August, at the age of fifteen.

David Gilly designs Schloss Paretz, near Potsdam, for Friedrich Wilhelm III and Queen Luise of Prussia.

June
Exhibition of competition entries for a memorial monument to Friedrich II at the Akademie der Künste in Berlin. Schinkel sees Friedrich Gilly's

entry and decides to become an architect; he is discouraged by relatives who want him to prepare for a career as a merchant or brewer.

16 November
Death of Friedrich Wilhelm II; he is succeeded by his son, Friedrich Wilhelm III (the effective ruler since 1796).

1798 *March*
At Easter Schinkel leaves the Gymnasium against the advice of relatives in order "to devote himself to architecture." He joins the studio and household of David Gilly, learns the rudiments of drafting, and studies and copies drawings from the collection of Friedrich Gilly.

December
Friedrich Gilly returns to Berlin from a study tour (since May 1797) to Paris, London (?), and central Germany. He assumes the major role as Schinkel's teacher until his departure for Karlsbad in the summer of 1800.

Heinrich Gentz designs the new Münzgebäude (royal mint) for Berlin. Construction until 1800; demolished, 1886.

1799 Alexander von Humboldt (1769–1859), natural scientist and author of *Kosmos* (pub. 1845–1859), embarks on an expedition to the Spanish colonies of South America, visits Mexico and the United States prior to his return to Berlin in 1804. The results of this journey are published as a thirty-volume corpus entitled *Voyage aux régions équinoxiales du nouveau continent, fait en 1799–1804* (Paris, 1834).

1 October
Opening of the Bauakademie, officially known as Allgemeine Bau-Unterrichts-Anstalt für die gesamten Königlichen-Staaten. Schinkel joins the first class and also continues as an apprentice in the Gillys' studio. Among the principal professors and lecturers are:
David Gilly (1748–1808), Landhausbau and general construction, bridges, locks, canals (Wasserbau), and building economics;
Friedrich Gilly (1772–1800), design, optics (perspective), theaters;
Carl Gotthard Langhans (1732–1808), mathematics, design;
Heinrich Gentz (1766–1811), architectural practice, town planning;
Aloys Hirt (1759–1837), history, aesthetics, theory of art and architecture;
Friedrich Wilhelm Becherer (1747–1823), architectural design;
Johann Albert Eytelwein (1764–1848), mathematics, structure.

1800 *8 March*
Death of Schinkel's mother in Berlin.

April
Construction of Nationaltheater am Gendarmenmarkt, designed by Langhans, opening 1 Jan. 1802.

3 August
Death of Friedrich Gilly (born 16 Feb. 1772) in Karlsbad.

17 November
Schinkel is cited as the best of eighteen students recommended for awards at the Bauakademie.

Schinkel completes unfinished projects of Friedrich Gilly, possibly including a town house for the master carpenter Steinmeyer at Friedrichstrasse 103, Berlin. Constructed, 1800–1803; demolished 1892.

Schinkel designs the Tempel der Pomona, an Ionic garden pavilion, for Herrn von Oesfeld on the Pfingstberg near Potsdam. Executed, 1800–1801; survived World War II; presently in poor condition.

Schinkel designs a dairy building at Bärwinkel in conjunction with the estate of General von Prittwitz at Quilitz (later Neu-Hardenberg)/Mark Brandenburg. Executed, 1800–1801; later partially remodeled; damaged during World War II; restored. He also designs three service buildings for this estate. Executed, 1801–1803; restored after World War II (for further additions, see 1814 and 1820).

Schinkel designs the restoration of the manor house at Herzborn, near Wriezen. Executed, 1801; later altered; preserved.

Schinkel also lists in his "Selbstbiographie" (1825) intermittent activity as a furniture designer and decorator of porcelain for these years (until 1803).

1801 Schinkel probably continues his studies at the Bauakademie, now located in Heinrich Gentz's Münzgebäude am Friedrich-Werderschen Markt.

Through his acquaintance with the philosopher Karl W. F. Solger (1780–1819), Schinkel is introduced to the theoretical and philosophical writings of Friedrich W. J. von Schelling (1775–1854), especially his *System des Transzendentalen Idealismus* (pub. 1800).

Schinkel designs the remodeling of Schloss Buckow, near Lebus/Oder, for Herrn von Flemming. Executed, 1801–1803; badly damaged during World War II; ruins razed, 1947–1948.

1802 Schinkel designs Schloss Köstritz in Thuringia for Heinrich Graf von Reuss-Schleiz-Köstritz. Not executed (possibly a student project); several renderings of exterior and interior views are preserved in the Staatliche Museen zu Berlin, DDR.

Schinkel designs a service building for the manor at Behlendorf, near Lebus. Executed, 1802; later partially remodeled; minor damage during World War II; restored.

Schinkel designs a service building for the manor at Haselberg, near Wriezen. Executed, 1802; destroyed during World War II.

Schinkel becomes acquainted with the teachings and writings of the philosopher Johann Gottlieb Fichte (1762–1814), a lecturer in Berlin since 1799. He reads Fichte's works during his Italian travels, 1803–1804.

25 November
The anthropologist and philologist Wilhelm von Humboldt (1767–1835) arrives in Rome to assume his post as the Prussian diplomatic emissary to the Holy See (until 1808); from 1806 he is ambassador with ministerial rank.

1803 *1 May*
Schinkel leaves Berlin accompanied by J. G. Steinmeyer, the son of a client, for a two-year study tour of Saxony, Austria, Istria, Italy, Sicily, and France. In October he arrives in Rome and meets Wilhelm von Humboldt. He also becomes acquainted with the Austrian history painter, Joseph Anton Koch (1768–1839). Drawings, letters, and diaries relating to this trip are preserved in the Staatliche Museen zu Berlin, DDR.

1804 *May*
Schinkel leaves Rome and spends the summer traveling in Sicily.

May–June
Friedrich von Schiller visits Berlin and Potsdam; he contemplates changing his residence from Weimar to Berlin.

Madame de Staël (1766–1817), exiled by Napoleon in 1803, visits Berlin. She establishes contact with members of literary circles in the capital, especially Friedrich Karl von Savigny (1779–1861). Her work on Germany, *De l'Allemagne*, is published in 1810.

2 December
Coronation of Napoleon in Paris.

Schinkel is in Paris during the month of December.

Death of Immanuel Kant in Königsberg/East Prussia.

1805 *March*
Schinkel returns to Berlin from Paris via Strassburg, Frankfurt, and Weimar, but finds no employment as an architect since Prussia is threatened by war with Napoleon. His plans to publish a portfolio of drawings of medieval monuments in Italy cannot be realized because the publisher, Johann Friedrich Unger, dies.

Schinkel possibly renders assistance to David Gilly on a project for Schloss Owinsk/Warthe (now Poland).

Schinkel designs a country house for Herrn Tilebein near Stettin/Pomerania. Executed, 1805–1806; present condition unknown.

9 May
Death of Friedrich von Schiller at Weimar.

1806 *Spring*
Heinrich Gentz asks Schinkel for assistance in preparing the final presentation drawings for a memorial monument and park dedicated to Friedrich II near the Zeughaus, Berlin.

8 October
War begins; Napoleon advances through Thuringia and Saxony toward Prussia.

10 October
Battle near Saalfeld; death of Prince Louis Ferdinand of Prussia.

14 October
Napoleon defeats Prussian army near Auerstedt. The royal family leaves Berlin for Königsberg.

27 October
Napoleon enters Berlin, occupies the Königliche Schloss and declares the Continental Blockade.

1807 *14 June*
Battle of Friedland; remnants of the Prussian army are defeated by Napoleon and Prussia sues for peace. By the Treaty of Tilsit nearly half of its territories are lost to France.

July
Heinrich Baron vom und zum Stein (1757–1831) becomes Prussia's minister of foreign affairs and publishes (Oct.) the Reform Edict.

Johann Gottlieb Fichte delivers his celebrated patriotic lectures, *Reden an die Deutsche Nation*, in Berlin.

Schinkel executes numerous drawings, lithographs and paintings, including a series of "perspektivisch-optische Gemälde" of historical sites such as Jerusalem, Constantinople, Philae.

December
Christmas exhibition in Berlin sponsored by Wilhelm Ernst Gropius, an entrepeneur and manufacturer of theater masks. Schinkel exhibits a large painting of the Ponte Molle in Rome.

1808 *5 May*
Death of David Gilly in Berlin.

Schinkel establishes friendly association with the Gropius family. He joins their household at Breite Strasse 22 and continues his activities as a painter.

August–December
Schinkel designs and executes a large panorama of Palermo and vicinity. Permission from Friedrich Wilhelm III, residing in exile at Königsberg, to exhibit this work in the Königliche Schloss in Berlin is denied.

1 October
Death of Carl G. Langhans at Grüneiche, near Breslau.

December
Christmas exhibition in Berlin sponsored by Gropius. A special wooden shelter is built near the St. Hedwigs Kirche for the exhibition of Schinkel's *Panorama von Palermo*. Original lost; a small copy in the form of a copper engraving done by Schinkel in 1816 is the only record of this work; later copies, including one executed in St. Petersburg in 1844, also lost.

1809 *17 August*
Schinkel marries Susanne Berger (1782–1861). Their children are: Marie, born 1810; Susanne, 1811; Karl Raphael, 1813; Elisabeth, 1822 (marries Alfred Freiherr von Wolzogen, editor of *Aus Schinkel's Nachlass*).

Schinkel redesigns parts of the Königliche Palais (former Kronprinzen Palais) for Friedrich Wilhelm III, prior to the return of the royal family to Berlin. For further additions, see 1824.

Schinkel prepares designs for an addition to the Prinzessinnen Palais; two versions are preserved. The palace extension, known as the *Kopfbau*, is executed (1809–1811) according to the design of Heinrich Gentz; later altered; damaged during World War II; restored in 1960's. Location: Berlin/DDR, Unter den Linden, opposite Zeughaus.

With J. G. Steinmeyer, Schinkel prepares a public exhibition of a number of large-scale painted scenes with dramatic lighting effects and music, including *Markusplatz zu Venedig, Schweizerthal am Fusse des Mont Blanc* and three views of the *Dom von Mailand*. The royal family attends the presentation; Schinkel is introduced to Queen Luise.

Schinkel becomes acquainted with the members of a literary circle in Berlin known for its strong romantic sentiments. The group included Achim von Arnim (1781–1831), Bettina von Arnim (1785–1859), Friedrich Karl von Savigny and Clemens von Brentano (1778–1842).

1810 Founding of Friedrich Wilhelm-Universität (based upon a royal decree of 1807), located in the former Palace of Prince Heinrich on the Unter den Linden, Berlin. Wilhelm von Humboldt is in charge of its organization; Johann Gottlieb Fichte is appointed professor and rector (1810–1814). The university becomes a center for the cultivation of German patriotism despite the French occupation of the city.

15 May
Upon the recommendations of Wilhelm von Humboldt, director of the office *Kultus und öffentlichen Unterrichts* in the ministry of the interior, and Peter Christian Wilhelm Beuth (1781–1853), Friedrich Wilhelm III confirms Schinkel's appointment to Prussia's Oberbaudeputation (office for the financial regulation and supervision of state and royal building commissions, founded 1806) with the rank of Geheimer Oberbauassessor.

He is charged with the supervision of the design and "aesthetics" of civic, royal, and religious buildings in Prussia. In addition, he is responsible for the control of architectural preservation throughout the kingdom *(bauästhetische und denkmalspflegerische Kontrolle).*

19 July
Death of Queen Luise of Prussia (born 1776) at Hohenzieritz, near Neustrelitz/Mecklenburg.

Schinkel collaborates with Friedrich Wilhelm III and Heinrich Gentz in the design of a mausoleum for Queen Luise at Schlosspark Charlottenburg. Constructed, 1810–1811; limestone portico replaced by granite, 1828 (old portico re-erected as a memorial on the Pfaueninsel/Havel); additions, 1841 and 1889; interior sculptures by Christian Daniel Rauch (1777–1857); building restored after World War II, now open to the public. Location: Berlin/West, Schlosspark Charlottenburg.

Exhibition of paintings by Caspar David Friedrich (1774–1840) is held at the Akademie der Künste in Berlin. Friedrich Wilhelm III purchases two of the best paintings for his private collection. Schinkel's own work is obviously influenced after he sees this exhibition of Romantic landscapes.

December
Christmas exhibition in Berlin sponsored by Gropius; Schinkel exhibits a large painting of the *Markusplatz zu Venedig.*

1811 Schinkel's activities are largely dictated by his position in the Oberbaudeputation. Owing to the continued French occupation, however, there is little new construction.

13 March
Schinkel is appointed to the Königlich Preussische Akademie der Künste in Berlin.

July
Schinkel travels with his wife to Dresden, Prague, Salzburg, and Bad Gastein; in Bohemia he is accompanied by the poet Clemens von Brentano; he visits art galleries and continues his landscape painting.

Schinkel prepares and publishes designs for the reconstruction of Cölln's old Petrikirche (recently destroyed by fire). For additional efforts, see 1814.

Schinkel designs a cast-iron memorial monument to Queen Luise at Gransee/Mark Brandenburg and another memorial, the Luisenpforte, at the royal estate of Paretz, near Potsdam.

3 October
Death of Heinrich Gentz in Berlin.

1812 *June*
Napoleon invades Russia, captures Moscow (14 Sept.).

Schinkel prepares first design for the Singakademie in Berlin; not realized. For additional designs, see 1821.

Schinkel designs first scheme for the partial remodeling of the interior of the former palace of Prince Heinrich in Berlin (orig. 1748–1753 by Johann Boumann), which had housed the Friedrich Wilhelm-Universität since 1810. Second scheme of 1813 executed; building damaged during World War II; restored; now Humboldt-Universität. Location: Berlin/DDR, Bebelplatz, Unter den Linden.

Schinkel executes a large drawing of the west facade of the cathedral of Strassburg and another of the cathedral of Milan.

December
Christmas exhibition in Berlin sponsored by Gropius; Schinkel exhibits a panorama with moveable figures and special lighting effects entitled *Die Sieben Weltwunder.*

1813 *16 March*
Prussia joins Russia (Treaty of Kalisch) and declares the Freiheitskrieg (War of Liberation) against Napoleon. From Breslau Friedrich Wilhelm III issues the proclamation "An Mein Volk."

27 April
The French garrison leaves Berlin and the fortress of Spandau.

Schinkel trains for the Landsturm (national guard) with Achim von Arnim and Friedrich Karl von Savigny, but is never sent into combat.

Schinkel collaborates with Friedrich Wilhelm III in the design of the Iron Cross (Eiserne Kreuz), Prussia's famous military citation.

Schinkel proposes an extensive remodeling scheme for the interior of Langhans' Nationaltheater am Gendarmenmarkt, Berlin; not accepted.

Schinkel designs and executes (until 1814) a cycle of six oil paintings, *Die Tageszeiten,* for the Berlin town house of Jean Paul Humbert, a silk manufacturer. These paintings were exhibited in the Schinkel-Museum located in the former Kronprinzen Palais, 1931–1945; lost after World War II.

Schinkel executes the oil painting *Mittelalterliche Stadt am Wasser*; now at Neue Pinakothek, Munich; copy by August W. Ahlborn at Schloss Charlottenburg, Berlin/West.

23 August
Prussian forces defeat the French in the battle of Gross-Beeren, south of Berlin.

16–19 October
Völkerschlacht (Battle of Nations) near Leipzig; Napoleon is defeated.

December
Christmas exhibition in Berlin sponsored by Gropius; Schinkel exhibits

a large panorama, *Der Brand von Moskau*, animated by special lighting effects; it is a popular success.

31 December
Prussian expeditionary force, under the command of Field Marshall von Blücher (1742–1819), crosses the Rhine at Kaub.

1814 *27 January*
Death of Johann Gottlieb Fichte in Berlin.

31 March
Paris is captured; Austrian, Prussian, and Russian forces occupy the city.

11 April
Napoleon abdicates at Fontainebleau and is exiled to Elba; Bourbon dynasty restored in France.

Convening of the Congress of Vienna (until March 1815); Wilhelm von Humboldt is a leading Prussian delegate.

Schinkel submits designs for a national memorial church (Dom als Denkmal für den Freiheitskrieg) in Berlin with lengthy commentary and specifications. Project probably suggested by Friedrich Wilhelm III; later disregarded.

Schinkel proposes a large war memorial church outside Berlin; not realized. Project is later reduced in scope and built as the Kreuzberg monument at Tempelhof, south of the city; see 1818.

Schinkel prepares a second design for the reconstruction of the Petrikirche, Berlin-Cölln; not realized.

Schinkel designs the church at the village of Neu-Hardenberg. Executed, 1814–1817; additions, 1823; slightly damaged during World War II; restored. Location: Marxwalde, near Müncheberg, DDR.

December
Christmas exhibition in Berlin sponsored by Gropius; Schinkel exhibits a large panorama, *Schlacht von Leipzig*, a vivid pictorial commentary on the most dramatic event of the previous year.

1815 *12 March*
Schinkel is promoted to the rank of Geheimer Oberbaurath, in charge of the Berlin Bureau of the Prussian Oberbaudeputation.

20 March
Napoleon re-enters Paris.

18 June
Battle of Waterloo; Wellington and Blücher defeat Napoleon.

22 June
Napoleon abdicates; exiled to St. Helena.

6 July
The coalition troops re-enter Paris. Second peace treaty of Paris; Wilhelm von Humboldt is appointed Prussia's ambassador to France.

The most active period of Schinkel's career begins.

He prepares a study for the preservation of national historic monuments (Grundsätze zur Erhaltung alter Denkmäler und Altertümer unseres Landes) and thus lays the foundation for government protection of architectural monuments in Prussia.

Schinkel participates in a competition for a Walhalla in Bavaria. Accepted design by Leo von Klenze (1784–1864) executed, 1830–1842.

Schinkel begins designing stage settings for the Nationaltheater am Gendarmenmarkt in Berlin, now under the supervision of the Generalintendant der Schauspiele, Karl Graf von Brühl (1772–1837). He continues intermittently until 1832; some original sketches for stage scenery are preserved in the Staatliche Museen zu Berlin, DDR.

Schinkel designs twenty-six scenes for Mozart's opera *Die Zauberflöte* (opening in Berlin, 1 Jan. 1816).

Schinkel designs the remodeling of the interior of the city palace of Prince August, uncle of Friedrich Wilhelm III, on the Wilhelmstrasse in Berlin. Executed, 1815–1817; some work continued until 1834; used as Reichsjustizministerium during 1930's; destroyed during World War II.

Schinkel executes two companion oil paintings: one depicting man's classical heritage, *Griechische Landschaft mit Theater und Aufgang zur Akropolis* (lost since 1945); the other depicting Germany's medieval past, *Mittelalterliche Stadt an einem Fluss* (now in Schinkel-Pavillon, Schlosspark Charlottenburg, Berlin/West).

December
Christmas exhibition in Berlin sponsored by Gropius; Schinkel exhibits a panorama of *St. Helena*.

1816 *2 April*
Friedrich Wilhelm III commissions Schinkel to design the Neue Wache (new royal guardhouse) opposite his palace at the Platz am Zeughaus. Final design executed, 1817–1818; from 1918 to 1930 used for various purposes; remodeled by Heinrich Tessenow as Ehrenmal für die Gefallenen des Weltkrieges, 1930; known as Reichsehrenmal, 1933–1945; damaged and vandalized during World War II; partial collapse of portico, 1950; building restored, 1950–1960; rededicated as Mahnmal für die Opfer des Faschismus und Militarismus, 8 May 1960; since October 1969 also Grabmal des Unbekannten Soldaten und Unbekannten Widerstandkämpfers.

27 April
Dedication of a cast-iron memorial monument to the dead of the War of

Liberation, designed by Schinkel for Spandau. Preserved; now know as Schinkel-Denkmal, Heinrichsplatz, Berlin-Spandau.

Schinkel submits to the king several schemes for the renovation of the interior of the Dom am Lustgarten (orig. 1747–1750 by Johann Boumann); accepted design executed, 1816–1817.

Schinkel prepares a site plan for the Grosse Stern (traffic circle) in the Tiergarten, as part of a total replanning scheme for the Tiergarten area (begun 1814); project partially realized after his death.

June
Schinkel goes to Heidelberg at the request of Prussia's Chancellor, Prince Carl August von Hardenberg (1750–1822), to try to obtain for Berlin the Boisserée collection of about 250 early Netherlandish and German paintings. Negotiations fail; collection purchased by Bavaria in 1827; now at the Alte Pinakothek, Munich.

12 July
Schinkel visits Goethe at Weimar.

He continues to Cologne and inspects the cathedral for possible restoration and completion. He then visits Mainz, Trier, Maria Laach, towns in the Netherlands, and Xanten. Numerous sketches from this trip are preserved in the Staatliche Museen zu Berlin, DDR.

2 August
Premier performance in Berlin of E. T. A. Hoffmann's opera *Undine* with stage scenery designed by Schinkel.

1817 Schinkel visits Stettin and other towns in Pomerania on an official inspection trip.

Schinkel designs a Rathaus for Berlin; not realized.

Schinkel designs the Lehr-Eskadron-Kaserne und Militärstrafanstalt, Berlin, Lindenstrasse. Executed, 1817–1818; later changes; destroyed during World War II.

Schinkel designs the remodeling of the interior of the city palace of Prince Friedrich, nephew of Friedrich Wilhelm III, Berlin, Wilhelmstrasse. Executed, 1817ff.; main facade remodeled, 1852; used as the Reichsanstalt für Ernährung und Landwirtschaft in 1930's; interior gutted during World War II; ruins removed.

Schinkel executes the oil painting *Triumphbogen für den Grossen Kurfürsten und Friedrich den Grossen* (now in Schinkel-Pavillon, Schlosspark Charlottenburg, Berlin/West).

Schinkel presents recommendations for the preservation and restoration of the Cistercian monastery church of Chorin/Mark Brandenburg. Restoration and archaeological excavations continued as late as 1959. Location: Chorin, near Eberswalde/DDR.

Schinkel designs stage scenery for the opera *Alceste* by Christoph Willibald Gluck, performed at the Nationaltheater, Berlin.

27 July
The Nationaltheater am Gendarmenmarkt is destroyed by fire; numerous stage settings designed by Schinkel lost.

19 November
Friedrich Wilhelm III instructs Graf von Brühl, Generalintendant der Königlichen Schauspiele, to initiate preparations for the reconstruction of the building, henceforth referred to as the Schauspielhaus.

Winter
Schinkel prepares the Grosse Bebauungsplan (master plan) for central Berlin, incorporating new hospitals, warehouses, markets, streets and canals; not realized.

1818 *April*
Schinkel designs the new Schauspielhaus at the Gendarmenmarkt; executed, 1819–1821; opened, 26 May 1821; exterior refurbished, 1883–1884; drastic remodeling of interior, 1904–1905; original interior of Konzertsaal restored by 1935; interior gutted, exterior severely damaged during World War II; restoration in progress, entire interior to become one large concert hall. Location: Berlin/DDR, Platz der Akademie.

Summer
The sculptor Christian Daniel Rauch returns from Italy and establishes permanent residence in Berlin; frequent collaboration between Schinkel and Rauch in subsequent years.

18 August
The royal guard occupies its quarters in the Neue Wache.

Schinkel designs a war memorial for the Kreuzberg, south of Berlin, in commemoration of Prussia's participation in the War of Liberation (1813–1815). Executed in cast-iron, 1819–1820; dedicated, 1821; landscaping added later; high platform and stairs added (1878) by Heinrich Strack (1805–1880). Location: Berlin/West, Tempelhof near Zentralflughafen.

Schinkel designs a series of houses and shops for the extension of the Wilhelmstrasse, north of the Unter den Linden, including the Marschallbrücke across the Spree River. Partially executed, 1819–1822; individual units altered; demolished 1867; bridge replaced.

Schinkel designs new gatehouses for the Hallesche Tor at the Belle Alliance Platz (formerly Rondeel) and proposes the redevelopment of the area; not realized.

Schinkel proposes the renovation and remodeling of the interiors of the two churches at the Gendarmenmarkt, Berlin; not realized.

Schinkel designs the parish church of Gross-Beeren. Executed, 1818–1820; restored, 1930; damaged during World War II; restored. Location: Gross-Beeren, near Teltow/DDR.

Schinkel submits proposals for the reform of architectural education (Reform des staatlichen Architekturunterrichtes) at the Bauakademie, Berlin.

1819 Schinkel is appointed a member of Prussia's Technische Deputation im Ministerium für Handel, Gewerbe und Bauwesen, a state agency for the promotion of commerce, industry, and building construction, directed by Peter Christian Beuth.

9 September
Schinkel is made an honorary member of the Königlich Bayerische Polytechnische Verein, Munich.

Publication of the first portfolio of Schinkel's designs of projected and executed works, *Sammlung architektonischer Entwürfe* (28 portfolios issued intermittently until 1840).

Schinkel travels to East Prussia to inspect the Marienburg (1308–1457), formerly the principal seat of the Grand Masters of the Teutonic Order. He submits to the king recommendations and designs for the restoration of the great refectory (Remter) and its facade. Executed after 1845; reconstruction and conservation work continued throughout nineteenth and early twentieth centuries; parts destroyed during World War II; partially restored; now museum. Location: Malbork, Poland.

Schinkel designs a new bridge to replace the Hundebrücke over the Kupfergraben in Berlin. Executed, 1819–1823; known as the Schlossbrücke. Eight sculpture groups on pedestals installed, 1853–1857; removed and stored, 1943; not yet replaced. Bridge damaged during World War II; restored 1950ff.; now Marx-Engels-Brücke. Location: Berlin/DDR, connecting Unter den Linden and Marx-Engels-Platz.

Schinkel submits to the king a design for a new church at the Spittelmarkt, Berlin; not realized.

Schinkel designs the remodeling of the facade of the Dom am Lustgarten, Berlin. Executed, 1820–1822; building demolished, 1893. New Domkirche, 1894–1904, by Julius Raschdorff; badly damaged during World War II; partially restored.

The sculptor Friedrich Tieck (1776–1851), a lifelong friend of Schinkel now residing in Berlin, executes a marble portrait bust of Schinkel. Exhibited after his death in the peristyle of the Museum am Lustgarten; now in the National-Galerie, Berlin/DDR.

Gasparo Spontini (1774–1851), formerly a conductor in Paris, becomes Generalmusikdirektor of the royal opera in Berlin. Schinkel designs stage scenery for his opera *Olympia*.

30 December
Theodor Fontane, poet and author of *Wanderungen durch die Mark Brandenburg* (pub. 1862–1882), is born at Neuruppin (dies in Berlin, 1898).

1820 Schinkel designs a monument for the grave of General Gerhard Johann David von Scharnhorst (1755–1813). Erected at the Invaliden Friedhof, Berlin, 1824; sculpture of a reclining lion by Friedrich Tieck added by 1834; preserved. Location: Berlin/DDR, Scharnhorst Strasse near Walter Ulbricht Stadion.

6 April
Festival commemorating the tercentenary of the death of Raphael is held at the Akademie der Künste, Berlin; decorations designed by Schinkel.

Summer
Schinkel visits Goethe at Weimar in the company of Friedrich Tieck and Christian Rauch.

Schinkel designs the remodeling of Schloss Neu-Hardenberg (formerly Quilitz) for Prince Carl August von Hardenberg. Executed, 1820–1823; slightly damaged during World War II; restored and altered after 1952; now used as a school. Location: Marxwalde, near Müncheberg/DDR.

Schinkel designs government buildings in Aachen and a high school (Gymnasium) in Düsseldorf.

Schinkel designs an observatory and the Anatomie in Bonn; executed, 1820–1822. The Anatomie later became the Akademische Kunst-Museum; altered.

Schinkel designs the renovation and expansion of Schloss Tegel for Wilhelm von Humboldt. Executed, 1821–1824; celebration held upon its completion, 31 Oct. 1824; interior vandalized and library plundered during World War II; restored; privately owned; open to the public. Location: Berlin/West, Tegel.

Schinkel begins preparing drawings and text for the publication of an "Architektonisches Lehrbuch," intended to be a substantial work on architectural theory and practice. He works actively on it until about 1830, when other duties interrupt. It was never published, but the manuscript and numerous drawings are preserved in the Staatliche Museen zu Berlin, DDR.

20 December
Schinkel is appointed professor of architecture and a member of the senate of the Akademie der Künste, Berlin. The appointment is largely honorary; he does not lecture, but occasionally participates in juries and final examinations.

1821 *31 March*
Dedication of the Kreuzberg monument.

26 May
Opening of the Schauspielhaus. The overture to Gluck's opera *Iphigénie en Aulide* (1774) preceded a performance of Goethe's *Iphigenie auf Tauris* (1787). Goethe, unable to attend, sent a prologue. It was read as the dedication in front of the painted backdrop, which was designed by Schinkel and depicted the Gendarmenmarkt environment.

18 June
Premier performance of Karl Maria von Weber's opera *Der Freischütz* at the Schauspielhaus, with stage scenery designed by Schinkel.

August–September
Schinkel travels to Stettin, Pomerania, and the island of Rügen; numerous drawings from this trip survive, including the oil sketch *Stubbenkammer auf Rügen.*

Schinkel submits second design for the Singakademie, Berlin; not accepted. He subsequently assists his student, Carl Theodor Ottmer (1800–1843), in preparing the accepted design. Executed, 1824–1827; damaged during World War II; restored; now Maxim Gorki Theater. Location: Berlin/DDR, adjacent to Zeughaus.

Schinkel prepares first design for the Friedrich-Werdersche Kirche, Berlin. The king rejects the neo-Classical design and orders a new version in neo-Gothic style (see 1824).

Schinkel designs the St. Nicolai-Kirche in Magdeburg-Neustadt. Executed, 1821–1824; interior gutted during World War II; restored, 1947–1953. Location: Magdeburg-Neustadt/Saxony-Anhalt, DDR.

Schinkel and Beuth begin publication of *Vorbilder für Fabrikanten und Handwerker,* a series of pamphlets consisting of engraved plates and essays, issued intermittently until 1837 by the Technische Deputation für Gewerbe. They served as guides or models for the products of the newly developing light industries of ceramics and glassware, metalwork, textiles, and architectural ornament. This is an early, perhaps the first, instance of an architect furnishing the designs for a wide variety of objects in an attempt to raise the standards of quality of mass-produced articles (a century before the founding of the Bauhaus).

1822 Schinkel assists Hermann Fürst von Pückler-Muskau (1785–1871) in planning for the expansion of his estate near Bad Muskau/Niederlausitz. Designs for a country house and service buildings by Schinkel not realized. Lifelong friendship between the two men is sustained through mutual interest in antiquity, architecture, and nature. Parts of the renowned park at Muskau have been restored and are open to the public. Sections of the former estate east of the Neisse River are under Polish jurisdiction; condition unknown.

Schinkel assists the architect Johannes Peter Cremer in the design of a colonnaded hall surrounding a natural spring (Elisenbrunnen) at the spa of Aachen. Erected, 1824–1826; severely damaged during World War II; now restored.

Schinkel designs the Zivilkasino, Potsdam. Executed 1822–1824; severely damaged during World War II; ruins removed, 1946–1947.

Schinkel designs the hunting lodge, Château Antonin, at Ostrów, near Poznań (Poland), for Anton Heinrich Fürst von Radziwill (1775–1833), a noted composer and musician. Executed in wood, 1822–1824; preserved.

Schinkel designs a town house for the master mason, Adler, in Berlin, Neue Wilhelmstrasse. Executed, 1823; demolished, 1867.

Schinkel assists the architect Johannes Peter Cremer in the design of a Schauspielhaus Im Kapuzinergarten, Aachen. Executed, 1822–1825; altered, 1873–1874.

Schinkel designs the remodeling of an existing building to accommodate the Gewerbe-Institut, Berlin, Klosterstrasse. Destroyed during World War II.

Schinkel designs the Artillerie- und Ingenieur-Schule (later known as Kriegsakademie), Berlin, Unter den Linden. Executed, 1824–1825; destroyed during World War II; site cleared, 1949.

27 March
Friedrich Wilhelm III orders the remodeling of parts of the Akademie building on the Unter den Linden in Berlin for the installation of a public art museum. Schinkel begins work on this project.

November–December
Independently Schinkel prepares designs for a separate museum building at the Lustgarten (possibly suggested by Crown Prince Friedrich Wilhelm).

1823 *8 January*
Schinkel presents his design for the Museum am Lustgarten to the king as part of an environmental plan of central Berlin.

4 April
Friedrich Wilhelm III approves the Museum project. Chronology of the building:
Spring 1824, drainage of Pomeranzengraben, work on foundations and piles;
1824–1826, construction of exterior and peristyle;
1826–1827, work on interiors after Schinkel's return from studying museums in France and England;
1828, design of frescoes for peristyle;
1829, creation of a commission headed by Wilhelm von Humboldt to supervise installation of art works;
3 August 1830, royal opening of the Museum;
1 June 1831, public opening of the Museum;
1843, installation of bronze sculpture, *Amazonenkämpferin* by August

Kiss, flanking the frontal stairs; 1861, installation of bronze sculpture, *Löwenkämpfer* by Albert Wolff, opposite the Kiss group;
1841–1845, construction of Friedrich August Stüler's Neue Museum, resulting in alterations to north wing of Schinkel's building (now called the Alte Museum) to accommodate a connecting passageway. (The Neue Museum was damaged in World War II; reconstruction scheduled for 1971.)
1841–1847, Schinkel's peristyle frescoes partially executed under the supervision of Peter von Cornelius (1783–1867); remainder not completed until after 1864;
1876–1884, changes in the upper galleries;
1880, new roof constructed, courtyards enclosed;
1939–1945, building damaged during World War II;
8 May 1945, ammunition truck explodes near east facade, furniture stored in interior ignites, interior gutted, exterior shell rendered insecure; bronze gates at entrance stolen;
1951, first measures to secure existing shell;
1953, roof rebuilt;
1958–1966, restoration of interior and exterior; installation of new interior stairway; upper vestibule entrances closed; improvements in lighting; restored decorations of rotunda based on original designs; frescoes in peristyle lost, not restored;
October 1966, reopening of Museum.
Location: Berlin/DDR, Museumsinsel, Lustgarten.

Schinkel designs the remodeling of parts of the interior of Schloss Bellevue (1785–1786, by Philipp Michael Boumann), Berlin, Tiergarten, as a palace for Prince August, uncle of Friedrich Wilhelm III. Completed by 1824; damaged during World War II; exterior restored; no original interiors exist except a salon by C. G. Langhans. Since June 1959 it has served as the official residence of the president of the Federal Republic of Germany during state visits to West Berlin.

Schinkel designs a villa for the merchant Behrend in Berlin-Charlottenburg. Executed, 1823; demolished, 1905.

Schinkel prepares an environmental plan for the Leipziger Platz and Potsdamer Tor, Berlin. Gatehouses executed by 1824; landscaping after 1825 by Peter Joseph Lenné (1789–1866); gatehouses badly damaged during World War II; removed by 1961.

28 November
Dedication of the new Schlossbrücke; Schinkel designs festive decorations to adorn the bridge on the occasion of the arrival of Princess Elisabeth of Bavaria for her marriage to Crown Prince Friedrich Wilhelm of Prussia.

1824 *28 January*
Schinkel is appointed Associe Étranger de l'Académie Royale des Beaux-Arts de l'Institut de France.

19 April
Death of George Gordon, Lord Byron, at Missolonghi.

7 May
Premier performance of Beethoven's Ninth Symphony in Vienna; score dedicated to Friedrich Wilhelm III of Prussia.

8 May
The king accepts Schinkel's neo-Gothic design for the Friedrich-Werdersche Kirche in Berlin. Executed, 1825–1830; interior gutted and exterior damaged during World War II; restoration in progress since 1950. Location: Berlin/DDR, Werderscher-Markt.

Founding of the Architekten- und Ingenieur-Verein in Berlin with Schinkel's active support.

24 July
Schinkel is made an honorary member of the Royal Academy of the Fine Arts, Copenhagen.

Schinkel designs the remodeling of a suite, known as the Historischen Räume (Bibliothek, Sternensaal, Tee-Salon), in the Königliche Schloss for Crown Prince Friedrich Wilhelm and his wife, Princess Elisabeth of Bavaria. Executed, 1824–1827; remodeling caused the loss of some fine Rococo decoration designed by Knobelsdorff and executed by Johann August Nahl (1710–1785) for Friedrich II; later altered; suite gutted during World War II; ruins of the Schloss razed, 1950–1951.

Schinkel designs the remodeling and expansion of a country Schloss at Klein-Glienicke with gardens and park buildings for Prince Karl of Prussia, son of Friedrich Wilhelm III. Kasino (garden pavilion) executed, 1824; Schloss completed, 1826; Belvedere, called the "Grosse Neugierde" and modeled after the Choragic Monument of Lysikrates in Athens, added, 1835; complex damaged during World War II; Schloss restored by 1950 (now a convalescent home for athletes); Kasino and Belvedere restored after 1960. Location: Berlin/West, Klein-Glienicke, Potsdamer Chausee at the bridge to Potsdam.

Schinkel designs a guest house, known as the Kavalier- und Danziger-Haus, on the Pfaueninsel for Friedrich Wilhelm III, incorporating the facade of a Danzig patrician house. Executed, 1824–1825; restored after World War II; entire island is a public park. Location: Berlin/West, Pfaueninsel in Havel River, near Klein-Glienicke.

Schinkel designs a garden pavilion, known as the Sommerhaus or Neue Pavillon, in the park of Schloss Charlottenburg for Friedrich Wilhelm III, inspired by Villa Reale Chiatamone, a Neopolitan seaside villa which the king occupied during a visit to Italy in 1822. Executed, 1824–1825, including furnishings; interior gutted during World War II; restored, 1957–1970 (now known as Schinkel-Pavillon, a museum displaying the artistic heritage of Berlin in the first half of the nineteenth century). Location: Berlin/West, Schlosspark Charlottenburg.

June–November
Schinkel visits Italy for the second time accompanied by Dr. Gustav Friedrich Waagen (1794–1868), an art historian and first director of the Museum am Lustgarten; August Kerll (1782–1855), a government official in Berlin; and Henri-François Brandt (1789–1845), a medalist at the Berlin mint. Their itinerary includes Köln, Strassburg, Freiburg, Stuttgart, Basel, Lake Como, Milan, Genoa, Pisa, and Rome, where Schinkel cooperates with the Danish sculptor Bertel Thorvaldsen (1768–1844) in designing a funerary monument for Pope Pius VII (1800–1823). Further travel to Pompeii, Paestum, Naples, and return via Florence, Mantua, Munich, and Weimar, where Schinkel again visits Goethe.

Upon his return to Berlin, Schinkel designs the partial remodeling, including the chapel, of the Königliche Palais (former Kronprinzen Palais) for Friedrich Wilhelm III. Executed, 1825–1826; major revisions by Heinrich Strack, 1856–1857; used as modern art gallery and the Schinkel-Museum of the National-Galerie, 1931–1945; gutted during World War II; reconstructed according to Strack's design after 1966. Location: Berlin/DDR, Unter den Linden, opposite Zeughaus.

1825 *30 May*
Schinkel is made an honorary member of the Accademia di S. Luca, Rome.

Schinkel writes a brief "Selbstbiographie" for publication in *Brockhaus-Lexicon* (Leipzig, 1826).

Schinkel executes the oil painting *Blick in Griechenlands Blüte;* given by Friedrich Wilhelm III as a wedding present to his daughter, Princess Luise, upon her marriage to Prince Friedrich of the Netherlands.

Schinkel designs a public meeting hall, Volkssaal Am Sogenannten Klosterbergegarten, Magdeburg. Executed, 1825; damaged during World War II; restored.

Schinkel designs a Leuchtturm (lighthouse) at Arkona on the island of Rügen. Executed, 1825–1827; preserved.

Schinkel furnishes designs for a Stadttheater in Hamburg. Executed, 1825–1827; altered, 1873–1874; damaged during World War II; rebuilt and expanded by 1950. Location: Hamburg, Karl-Muck-Platz.

1826 *21 March*
Friedrich Wilhelm III authorizes a stipend for Schinkel to travel to France and England to study public museums and their interior arrangements.

April–August
Schinkel travels extensively through west German provinces, France, England, Scotland, and Wales, accompanied by Peter Christian Beuth. He meets leading architects in Paris and John Nash in London. He visits cultural and industrial centers and comments critically on architecture, society, industry, and town planning. Original diaries preserved in the Staatliche Museen zu Berlin, DDR.

Upon his return to Berlin, Schinkel plans in detail the interior arrangements of the Museum am Lustgarten. He incoporates features of modern English fireproof construction which he observed during his trip.

Schinkel urges the introduction of gas lighting for major streets in Berlin based upon his studies in Britain; installed by a London firm in 1827.

Schinkel refines plans for a new Packhof (royal customs warehouses) along the Kupfergraben north of the Museum. Initial project, 1817; changed, 1823; final design, 1829; executed, 1830–1832; partially demolished to make way for Kaiser Friedrich and Pergamon Museums; last Packhof building demolished, 1938.

Schinkel submits design for the town hall of Kolberg, Pomerania (now Kolobrzeg, Poland), incorporating original Gothic parts. Executed, 1827–1832, under the supervision of E. F. Zwirner (1802–1861); restored after World War II.

Schinkel designs Schloss Charlottenhof in the park of Schloss Sanssouci, Potsdam, for Crown Prince Friedrich Wilhelm. Executed, 1826–1827, by Ludwig Persius (1803–1845) under the supervision of the crown prince. Schinkel proposes a "Villa des Plinius" at Charlottenhof, 1833; not realized. For further additions, see 1833.

Schinkel designs the Infanterielehrschule, later known as the Unteroffizierschule (noncommissioned officers academy), in Potsdam. Executed, 1826–1828; later enlarged and remodeled; preserved.

Schinkel prepares first designs for the Nikolai-Kirche in Potsdam (similar to a church project by Friedrich Gilly of 1796; Gilly's drawing was copied by Schinkel in 1801). Revised scheme, 1829; executed, 1830–1837; cupola with iron supports added, 1843–1849, by Ludwig Persius and Friedrich August Stüler (1800–1865) following plans by Schinkel. Severely damaged during World War II; reconstruction of cupola, 1956–1958, after original structural drawings of 1848 from the Borsig ironworks; interior still under reconstruction. Location: Potsdam/DDR.

1827 *26 March*
Death of Ludwig van Beethoven in Vienna.

Schinkel continues work (begun in 1822) on various designs for a memorial monument to Friedrich II in central Berlin, possibly in collaboration with Crown Prince Friedrich Wilhelm (until 1830); not realized.

Schinkel prepares a design for the royal stables at the site of the old Packhof in Friedrich-Werder, Berlin; not realized.

Schinkel proposes a Kaufhaus on the Unter den Linden, adjacent to the university; not realized.

Schinkel designs Schloss Putbus on the island of Rügen for Wilhelm Malte Fürst von Putbus. Executed under the supervision of J. G. Steinmeyer, 1827–1832; destroyed by fire, 1865; rebuilt in altered form, 1867; vandalized during World War II; demolished, 1962.

Schinkel designs the remodeling of the city palace of Prince Karl of Prussia in Berlin, Wilhelm-Platz. Executed, 1827–1828; alterations of interior, 1883 and 1889; used as the Reichs-Propaganda-Ministerium in the 1930's; destroyed during World War II.

1828 *6 April*

Festival commemorating the tercentenary of the death of Albrecht Dürer is held at the Akademie der Künste, Berlin; Schinkel designs the decorations.

Schinkel designs a town house for Tobias Christoph Feilner, a manufacturer of stoves, bricks, and terra-cotta ornament, in Berlin, Hagenhegergasse (Feilnerstrasse after 1848). Executed, 1828–1829; destroyed during World War II; fragments of terra-cotta ornament preserved at the Märkische Museum, Berlin/DDR.

Schinkel designs a cycle of frescoes for the peristyle of the Museum am Lustgarten (until 1831); executed, 1841ff.

Schinkel prepares two designs for the landscaping of the Lustgarten. Plans altered by Friedrich Wilhelm III; executed, 1829–1830.

Schinkel designs Schloss Werder. Executed 1828; renovated and expanded, 1950–1951; now serves as a recreation home for teachers. Location: Werder, near Potsdam/DDR.

Schinkel designs the parish church at Straupitz. Executed, 1828–1832; damaged during World War II; restored, roof and windows replaced. Location: Straupitz, near Lübben/Niederlausitz, DDR.

Schinkel designs the renovation of the exterior of the monastery church (orig. fourteenth century) at Dobbertin. Executed under the supervision of Demmler; preserved. Location: Dobbertin, near Parchim/Mecklenburg, DDR.

Schinkel designs (until 1831) four parish churches in northern suburbs of Berlin:
Elisabeth-Kirche vor dem Rosenthaler Tor, Berlin/DDR, Invalidenstrasse near Pappel-Platz. Executed, 1832–1834; interior gutted during World War II; restored.
Nazareth-Kirche auf dem Wedding, Berlin/West, intersection Müllerstrasse and Schulstrasse. Executed, 1832–1834; later additions; interior altered; gutted during World War II; restored.
Pauls-Kirche auf dem Gesundbrunnen, Berlin/West, Badstrasse. Executed, 1832–1834; later additions and renovations, 1889–1890 and 1911; interior gutted during World War II; restored.
Johannes-Kirche am Kleinen Tiergarten, Berlin/West, Alt-Moabit. Executed, 1832–1834; additions by Stüler and Bartning; interior gutted during World War II; restored.

1829 Schinkel designs a city palace at the Opernplatz for Prince Wilhelm of Prussia, son of Friedrich Wilhelm III and later Kaiser Wilhelm I. Several schemes projected until about 1832. Executed after designs by Carl Ferdinand Langhans, 1833–1834; known as the Kaiser-Wilhelm-Palais; gutted during World War II; facade restored. Location: Berlin/DDR, Bebelplatz.

Schinkel designs another city palace for Prince Wilhelm at the Pariser Platz, Berlin; not realized.

Schinkel designs the remodeling and expansion of the city palace for Prince Albrecht of Prussia, son of Friedrich Wilhelm III, in Berlin, Wilhelmstrasse. Executed, 1830–1833; known for its interior stairs and balcony of exposed cast-iron; used as Reichsleitung-SS in the 1930's; severely damaged during World War II; ruins razed, 1946.

Schinkel prepares first design for a city palace at the Pariser Platz for Wilhelm Friedrich Graf von Redern (1802–1883), later Generalintendant der Königlichen Schauspiele. Final design (inspired by the Palazzo Pitti) executed, 1830–1833; exterior altered, 1891; demolished, 1905, and replaced by the Hotel Adlon.

Schinkel participates in the restoration and rebuilding of the Nikolai- und Sophien-Kirche, Berlin.

Schinkel's friends Jakob L. F. Mendelssohn-Bartholdy (1809–1847) and Karl Friedrich Zelter (1758–1832) revive the St. Matthew Passion by J. S. Bach at the newly completed Singakademie in Berlin.

1830 Schinkel designs the Sternwarte (observatory), Berlin-Friedrichstadt, Charlottenstrasse, for Alexander von Humboldt. Demolished, 1913.

Schinkel submits proposals for the restoration of the Klosterkirche at Neuruppin/Mark Brandenburg.

Schinkel designs new gatehouses for the Neues Tor, Berlin. Executed 1836; razed after World War II.

3 August
Royal opening of the completed Museum am Lustgarten on the occasion of the sixtieth birthday of Friedrich Wilhelm III.

Schinkel receives a royal stipend in recognition of the successful completion of the Museum. He travels to the Rhine provinces and northern Italy accompanied by his family.

November
Completion of the Friedrich-Werdersche Kirche.

16 December
Schinkel is promoted to the rank of Geheimer Oberbaudirektor. He replaces Johann Albert Eytelwein as the official in charge of Prussia's Oberbaudeputation and is assisted by a staff of very competent architects and engineers.

1831 *13 March*

Schinkel celebrates his fiftieth birthday. He is honored by members of the Architekten- und Ingenieur-Verein in Berlin with a special festival in recognition of his services as an architect. This celebration continues after his death in 1841, the first official annual *Schinkelfest* being held in 1845; in 1852 it is expanded to include an annual architectural competition and the presentation of a scholarly paper. The *Schinkelfest* is still held each year in Berlin.

January–March

Schinkel prepares designs for a new building for the Allgemeine Bauschule and Oberbaudeputation in Friedrich-Werder, Berlin.

29 March

Plans for the Allgemeine Bauschule are accepted by Friedrich Wilhelm III upon the urging of Peter Christian Beuth. The building, known as the Bauakademie after 1848, housed the school of architecture and the offices of the Oberbaudeputation, as well as Schinkel's private apartment; space for shops was rented at the street level. Construction supervised by Emil Flaminius, 1832–1836; dedication ceremonies, 1 April 1836. The "Schinkelsches Museum" was located in Schinkel's private atelier on the second floor, 1841–1861. (On the sesquicentennial of his birth in 1931 this collection was reorganized and installed as the Schinkel-Museum in the former Kronprinzen Palais; since 1966, in the restored Alte Museum.) Courtyard of Bauakademie enclosed and stairway added, 1874–1875; exterior renovated and ornament cleaned, 1939; damaged during World War II; structure secured and rubble cleared away, 1948–1950; demolished, 1961. Fragments of the exterior terra-cotta ornament preserved in the Staatliche Museen zu Berlin, DDR.

1 June

Public opening of the Museum am Lustgarten.

August

Schinkel visits the spa of Marienbad.

Schinkel designs the Glienicker Brücke between Klein-Glienicke and Potsdam. Executed, 1834; replaced by iron bridge, 1907.

Schinkel designs the Hauptwache (main guardhouse) in Dresden/Saxony. Completed, 1833, under the supervision of Josef Thürmer; interior gutted during World War II; restored; now preserved as a historic monument.

Schinkel prepares designs for the Augusteum, the main university building in Leipzig. Executed, 1831–1836; interior gutted during World War II; present condition unknown.

September–November

Cholera epidemic in Berlin; among its victims is the philosopher Friedrich Hegel (dies 14 November).

1832 *22 March*
Death of Goethe at Weimar.

Spring
Completion of the Packhof complex along the Kupfergraben in Berlin.

Schinkel designs the renovation and expansion of Schloss Erdmannsdorf/Silesia, in neo-Gothic *Burgenstil*, for Friedrich Wilhelm III. Present condition unknown.

June–August
Schinkel makes an official inspection trip to Silesia and visits Kraków to consult with Graf Potocky regarding plans for Schloss Kresznowice, near Kraków.

25 August
Schinkel is honored by the kingdom of Bavaria with membership in the Königlich Bayerische Akademie der Künste.

1833 Schinkel designs Schloss Babelsberg near Potsdam for Prince Wilhelm of Prussia. Executed, 1834ff., under the supervision of Crown Prince Friedrich Wilhelm; enlarged by Heinrich Strack, 1844; later changes, but structure preserved; interior altered. Location: Potsdam-Babelsberg/DDR.

Schinkel designs the Römischen Bäder, an addition to the Gärtnerhaus complex (1829) at Charlottenhof, Schlosspark Sanssouci, with the active participation of Ludwig Persius, for Crown Prince Friedrich Wilhelm. Total project completed, 1835; preserved; restoration in progress. Location: Potsdam-Sanssouci/DDR.

July–September
Schinkel makes an official inspection trip to Saxony, Westphalia, and the Rhine provinces.

1834 *July–September*
Schinkel makes an official inspection trip through the eastern provinces and the Grand Duchy of Posen (Poznań). He revisits the Marienburg castle and urges the commencement of restoration work. He takes note of the vanishing natural resources of East Prussia, especially the Kurische Nehrung near Cranz and the forests near Warnicken, and suggests that the state protect these areas as nature preserves (Naturschutzpark), possibly the first request of its type in Germany.

6 August
Schinkel is made an honorary member of the Deutsche Gesellschaft zur Erforschung Vaterländischer Alterthümer, Leipzig.

12 October
Schinkel is made an honorary member of the Académie des Beaux-Arts (dans l'art de décoration théâtrale), St. Petersburg, Russia.

Schinkel designs a royal palace on the Acropolis in Athens for King Otto I of Greece (1832–1862), formerly Otto von Wittelsbach, son of Ludwig I of Bavaria; not realized. Portfolios of plans, sections, and general views of the projected palace in Athens and the later project for the imperial Russian palace Orianda (1838) were published as *Werke der höheren Baukunst für die Ausführung erfunden*, 2 vols., Potsdam, 1840–1842 (Athens) and 1845–1848 (Orianda).

Schinkel supervises the restoration of the Johannes-Kirche in Zittau/ Saxony. Executed, 1834–1837; preserved. He also restores the city hall of Zittau (orig. sixteenth century). Executed, 1840–1845; preserved.

Schinkel supervises the restoration of the Juliusturm, Spandau's oldest medieval bastion.

Eduard Gaertner (1801–1877) completes a six-panel oil painting, *Panorama von Berlin*, depicting the cityscape of central Berlin; now exhibited at the Schinkel-Pavillon, Schlosspark Charlottenburg, Berlin/West.

1835 *8 April*
Death of Wilhelm von Humboldt at Tegel, near Berlin; buried 12 April in the Humboldt cemetery at Schloss Tegel. Memorial column with statue by Thorvaldsen, after a design by Schinkel of 1829, is preserved.

4 May
Schinkel is made an honorary member and correspondent of the Royal Institute of British Architects, London.

July–August
Schinkel makes an official inspection trip to towns in the Prussian provinces of Pomerania, Altmark, and Neumark.

Schinkel prepares site plans for the area west of the Brandenburger Tor and Tiergarten, Berlin; not realized.

Schinkel proposes a master plan for the Berlin suburb of Köpenicker Feld; not realized.

Schinkel designs a new Bibliothek for Berlin, near the university north of the Unter den Linden; not realized. Second project, 1838–1839; not realized.

Schinkel designs the street signs for Berlin.

Schinkel assists the architect Emil Flaminius in designing the Schauspielhaus (municipal theater) for Frankfurt/Oder; design revised, 1839; executed, 1840–1842; destroyed during World War II.

Schinkel presents designs for a Gymnasium (high school) in Danzig.

Schinkel designs the partial remodeling of the interior of Schloss Weimar, the so-called Dichterzimmer including a Goethesaal. Executed after 1836; designs altered.

1836 *26 March*
Schinkel is made an honorary member of the Akademie der Vereinigten Bildenden Künste, Vienna.

1 April
Dedication ceremonies opening the Allgemeine Bauschule; Schinkel's family occupies the south wing of the second floor as private quarters.

24 June
Schinkel is made an honorary member of the Akademie der Bildenden Künste, St. Petersburg.

Schinkel designs the reconstruction and new additions to Burg Stolzenfels (original thirteenth-century castle destroyed by French in 1689) for Crown Prince Friedrich Wilhelm of Prussia. Executed, 1836–1842, with assistance of Friedrich August Stüler and Ludwig Persius after Schinkel's death; renovated after World War II; now historic monument and museum; open to the public. Location: Stolzenfels on Rhine River, south of Koblenz.

July–August
Schinkel visits the health resort of Hofgastein near Salzburg.

1837 Schinkel is handicapped by an injury to his hand.

July
Schinkel visits the health resort of Karlsbad.

Completion of Schinkel's Nikolai-Kirche in Potsdam (without dome); see 1826.

1838 *April–May*
Upon the request of the government, Schinkel assists the Norwegian architect, Christian Heinrich Grosch in designing three major buildings for the new university of Christiania (now Oslo). He prepares several drawings and supplies specifications. Executed, 1839ff.; the exterior articulation of these buildings resembles the Berlin Schauspielhaus.

May
Schinkel designs a large neo-Gothic Burgenschloss at Kamenz near Bautzen/Oberlausitz for Prince Albrecht of Prussia. Construction begun, 1840; completed, 1873; damaged during World War II; present condition unknown.

July–August
Schinkel combines a visit to the health resort of Bad Kissingen near Schweinfurt/Oberfranken with an official inspection trip through the western provinces of Prussia. He visits Fulda, Marburg, Köln, and Bonn; additional trip to Silesia.

Schinkel designs the Jagdschloss Granitz, a hunting lodge on the island of

Rügen for Fürst von Putbus. Executed, 1838; preserved; open to the public. Location: Lancken-Granitz, near Binz on Rügen/DDR.

Schinkel prepares designs for Schloss Orianda, a large pleasure palace and museum near Yalta on the southwest coast of the Crimea, for the Russian Czarina Alexandra Feodorowna, wife of Czar Nicholas I and daughter of Friedrich Wilhelm III (formerly Princess Charlotte of Prussia); not realized. Portfolio of plans, sections, and general views published, 1845–1848 (see 1834).

13 November
Schinkel is promoted to the rank of Geheimer Oberlandesbaudirektor in recognition of his lifelong service to Prussia and his international reputation as an architect of exceptional talents.

1839 Schinkel prepares plans for the restoration of the Klosterkirche in Berlin and the St. Nikolaikirche in Spandau.

Schinkel executes several large colored drawings depicting an ideal princely residence, presumably for the Crown Prince, preserved in the Staatliche Museen zu Berlin, DDR.

Schinkel is consulted regarding the expansion of the Bibliothek and the Tierarzneischule (veterinarians' institute) in Berlin.

July
Schinkel visits the health resort of Bad Kissingen.

1840 *17 June*
Death of Friedrich Wilhelm III in the Königliche Palais, Berlin; succeeded by his son, Friedrich Wilhelm IV.

Schinkel presents a master plan for Moabit, a northern section of Berlin; not realized.

July
Schinkel visits the health resort of Hofgastein near Salzburg in an attempt to cure his migraine headaches.

He visits Munich on his return trip to Berlin. There he executes his last design: the remodeling of a town house for his host, the sculptor Kirchmayer, for which he asks no payment.

7 September
Schinkel returns to Berlin.

8 September
During a walk in the Tiergarten with Carl Gropius, Schinkel discusses plans to again exhibit his *Panorama von Palermo*. In addition, he suggests the public exhibition of a large panorama featuring major historical monuments from ancient Egypt and Greece to medieval Germany.

9 September
Schinkel collapses and his prolonged final illness begins. His condition alternates between coma, semiconsciousness, and occasional moments of consciousness for the next thirteen months. He is half blind.

1841 *January*
Thorvaldsen visits Schinkel and is one of the last persons to communicate with him.

9 October
Schinkel dies at the Bauakademie in Berlin.

12 October
Funeral services for Schinkel are held in the Bauakademie. He is buried in the Dorotheenstädtischer Friedhof, the cemetery of the parish of the Friedrich-Werdersche Kirche. His remains were reburied at their present site in the same cemetery, 23 April 1843. The grave is marked by a granite stele with bronze capping, based on Schinkel's own design for a funerary monument for Sigismund F. Hermstädt of 1833. The stele was restored after being vandalized during World War II, and the grave site refurbished annually on the occasion of the *Schinkelfest* commemorating the anniversary of his birthday, 13 March. Location: Berlin/DDR, Dorotheenstädtischer Friedhof, Hannoversche Strasse near Oranienburger Tor.

Friedrich Wilhelm IV orders the portrait bust of Schinkel by Friedrich Tieck (1819) to be permanently exhibited in the peristyle of the Museum am Lustgarten. It is now in the National-Galerie, Berlin/DDR.

1842 *16 January*
Friedrich Wilhelm IV issues a royal order to the effect that Schinkel's artistic legacy (paintings, drawings, models, etc.) should be bought by the state. These were first exhibited in the Bauakademie and later formed the nucleus of the Schinkel collection, which is now in the Alte Museum, Berlin/DDR. Some important works are also preserved in the restored former Sommerhaus, now Schinkel-Pavillon, in the Schlosspark Charlottenburg, Berlin/West.

Bibliography

Ackerman, James S. *The Architecture of Michelangelo,* 2 vols. New York: Viking Press, 1961.

Adam, Robert. *Ruins of the Palace of the Emperor Diocletian at Spalatro in Dalmatia.* London, 1764.

Adler, Friedrich. "Friedrich Gilly, Schinkels Lehrer," *Zentralblatt der Bauverwaltung,* 1 (1881), 8, 17, 22.

———. "Schinkel Festrede: Die Bauschule zu Berlin von Karl Friedrich Schinkel," *Zeitschrift für Bauwesen,* 19 (1869), 463–475.

Adler, Leo. "Berlin," in *Wasmuths Lexikon der Baukunst,* 5 vols. Berlin: Wasmuth, 1929–1937, I, 458–476.

Architekten- und Ingenieur-Verein zu Berlin. *100 Jahre Schinkel-Wettbewerb.* Festschrift. Berlin: Architekten- und Ingenieur-Verein zu Berlin, 1955.

Banham, Reyner. *Theory and Design in the First Machine Age.* London: Architectural Press, 1960.

Bannister, Turpin C. "The Roussillon Vault," *Journal of the Society of Architectural Historians,* 27 (October 1968), 163–175.

Beenken, Hermann. *Schöpferische Bauideen der deutschen Romantik.* Mainz: Matthias Grünewald Verlag, 1952.

Behrendt, Walter Curt. *Alfred Messel.* Berlin: Bruno Cassirer, 1911.

———. *Modern Building: Its Nature, Problems, and Forms.* New York: Harcourt, Brace and Company, 1937.

Berckenhagen, Ekhart. *Alte Bühnenbilder: Zeichnungen und Stiche des 16. bis 19. Jahrhunderts* (Exhibition catalogue). Berlin: Ehemals Staatliche Museen, Kunstbibliothek, 1960.

Berlin im Jahre 1786: Schilderungen der Zeitgenossen. Leipzig, 1886.

Bibiena, Ferdinando Galli da. *Direzioni a'Giovani studenti nel disegno.* Bologna, 1731–1732.

Bibiena, Giuseppe Galli. *Architetture e prospettive.* Augsburg, 1740.

Börsch-Supan, Helmut. *Der Schinkel-Pavillon im Schlosspark zu Charlottenburg.* Berlin: Verwaltung der Staatlichen Schlösser und Gärten, 1970.

Broebes, Jean Baptiste. *Vues des palais et maisons de plaisance de S. M. le roy de Prusse.* Augsburg, 1733.

Collins, Peter. *Changing Ideals in Modern Architecture, 1750–1950.* London: Faber and Faber, Ltd., 1965.

Dehio, Ludwig. *Friedrich Wilhelm IV. von Preussen: Ein Baukünstler der Romantik.* Vol.

XXX of Kunstwissenschaftliche Studien. Munich: Deutscher Kunstverlag, 1961.
De Zurko, Edward Robert. *Origins of Functionalist Theory*. New York: Columbia University Press, 1957.
Die Bauverwaltung, 10 (October 1963). Issue on Berlin.
Doebber, Adolph. *Heinrich Gentz: Ein Berliner Baumeister um 1800*. Berlin: Verlag Carl Heymann, 1916.
———. "Zur Baugeschichte des Charlottenburger Mausoleums," *Zentralblatt der Bauverwaltung*, 32 (1912), 137–139.
Downing, Andrew Jackson. *Landscape Architecture*. New York, 1844.
Dronke, Wolfgang. "Die Neue Wache in Berlin," unpub. diss., Technische Hochschule, Berlin-Charlottenburg, 1931 (excerpt published in *Zeitschrift für Bauwesen*, 81 (1931), 44–52).
Durand, Jean-Nicolas-Louis. *Recueil et parallèle des édifices de tout genre anciens et modernes remarquables par leur beauté*, 3 vols. Venice, 1833 (1st ed., Paris, 1800).
Elling, Christian and Kay Fisker (eds.). *Monumenta Architecturae Danicae: Danish Architectural Drawings, 1660–1920*. Copenhagen: Den Gyldendalske Boghandel, 1961.
Ettlinger, L. "A German Architect's Visit to England in 1826," *The Architectural Review*, 97 (May 1945), 131–134.
Eylert, Rulemann. *Charakter-Züge und historische Fragmente aus dem Leben des Königs von Preussen Friedrich Wilhelm III*. Magdeburg, 1843.
Flaminius, Emil. "Über den Bau des Hauses für die allgemeine Bauschule in Berlin," *Allgemeine Bauzeitung*, 1 (1836), 3–5, 9–13, 18–26.
Fontane, Theodor. *Wanderungen durch die Mark Brandenburg*. Vol. V of *Gesammelte Werke*, 5 vols. Hamburg: Standard-Verlag, 1961 (1st ed., 4 vols., Berlin, 1862–1882).
———. *Fontane damals und heute*, ed. Hans-Ulrich Engel and Hans-Joachim Schlott-Kotschote. Berlin: Verlag für Internationalen Kulturaustausch, 1958.
Giedion, Sigfried. *Spätbarocker und romantischer Klassizismus*. Munich: F. Bruckmann A.-G., 1922.
———. *Walter Gropius: Work and Teamwork*. New York: Reinhold Publishing Corporation, 1954.
Giese, Leopold. *Schinkels architektonisches Schaffen: Entwürfe und Ausführungen*. Vol. I. *Die Friedrich-Werdersche Kirche zu Berlin*. Berlin: Der Zirkel. Architektur Verlag, 1921.
Gilly, David. *Sammlung nützlicher Aufsätze und Nachrichten die Baukunst betreffend*, 6 vols. in 3. Berlin, 1798–1806.
Goethe, Johann Wolfgang. *Goethes Werke*, Grossherzogin Sophie von Sachsen ed., 50 vols. Weimar: Verlag Böhlau, 1887–1918.
———. *Italienische Reise, 1786–1788*. Munich: Hirmer Verlag, n.d.
———. *Schriften zur Kunst*, ed. Christian Beutler. Vol. XIII of *Gedenkausgabe der Werke, Briefe und Gespräche*, ed. Ernst Beutler. Zurich: Artemis-Verlag, 1954.
Grimm, Hermann. "Schinkel als Architekt der Stadt Berlin," *Zeitschrift für Bauwesen*, 24 (1874), 414–459.
Grisebach, August. *Carl Friedrich Schinkel*. Leipzig: Im Insel-Verlag, 1924.
Gropius, Walter. *Apollo in the Democracy: The Cultural Obligation of the Architect*. New York: McGraw-Hill Book Company, 1968.
Hederer, Oswald. *Leo von Klenze: Persönlichkeit und Werk*. Munich: Verlag Georg D. W. Callwey, 1964.

Hegemann, Werner. *Das steinerne Berlin: Geschichte der grössten Mietskasernenstadt der Welt.* No. 3 of Bauwelt Fundamente. Berlin: Verlag Ullstein, 1963 (1st ed., Lugano, 1930).

Henselmann, Hermann, *et al. Über Karl Friedrich Schinkel.* Berlin: Verlag Bruno Henschel und Sohn, 1951.

Herrmann, Wolfgang. *Laugier and Eighteenth Century French Theory.* Vol. VI of Studies in Architecture, ed. Anthony Blunt and Rudolf Wittkower. London: A. Zwemmer, Ltd., 1962.

Hinz, Gerhard. *Peter Josef Lenné und seine bedeutendsten Schöpfungen in Berlin und Potsdam.* Berlin: Deutscher Kunstverlag, 1937.

Hitchcock, Henry-Russell. *Architecture Nineteenth and Twentieth Centuries.* Vol. XV of The Pelican History of Art, ed. Nikolaus Pevsner. Baltimore: Penguin Books, 1958.

Hittorff, Jakob I. "Historische Notiz über Carl Friedrich Schinkel," *Zeitschrift für Bauwesen,* 8 (1858), 98–106.

Johnson, Philip. "Karl Friedrich Schinkel im zwanzigsten Jahrhundert; wie wir den grossen Architekten nach der Bauhaus-Corbusier-Revolution sehen" (Festvortrag), *Schriftenreihe des Architekten- und Ingenieur-Vereins zu Berlin* (No. 13, 1961; reprinted as "Schinkel and Mies," *Program,* New York: Columbia University, School of Architecture [Spring 1962], 14–34).

Kachler, Karl Gotthilf. *Schinkels Kunstauffassung.* Basel: Volksdruckerei, 1940.

Kauffmann, Hans. "Zweckbau und Monument: Zu Friedrich Schinkels Museum am Berliner Lustgarten," in *Eine Freundesgabe der Wissenschaft für Ernst Hellmut Vits,* ed. Gerhard Hess. Frankfurt am Main: Fritz Knapp Verlag, 1963.

Kaufmann, Emil. *Architecture in the Age of Reason: Baroque and Post-Baroque in England, Italy and France.* Cambridge, Mass.: Harvard University Press, 1955.

———. *Von Ledoux bis Le Corbusier: Ursprung und Entwicklung der autonomen Architektur.* Vienna: Verlag Dr. Rolf Passer, 1933.

Klopfer, Paul. *Von Palladio bis Schinkel: Eine Charakteristik der Baukunst des Klassizismus.* Esslingen: P. Neff-M. Schreiber, 1911.

Koch, Georg Friedrich. "Karl Friedrich Schinkel und die Architektur des Mittelalters," *Zeitschrift für Kunstgeschichte,* 29 (1966), 177–222.

Kohlhoff, Wilhelm. *Denkmal der Liebe und Verehrung ihrem verewigten Lehrer H. David Gilly gewidmet von den stud. Mitgliedern der Bauakademie.* Berlin, 1808.

Krätschell, Johannes. "Schinkels gothisches Schmerzenskind, die Werdersche Kirche in Berlin," *Blätter für Architektur und Kunsthandwerk,* 1 (1888), 114–117.

Krieger, Bogdan. *Berlin im Wandel der Zeiten.* Berlin-Grunewald: Verlagsanstalt Hermann Klemm A.G., 1923.

Kugler, Franz. *Karl Friedrich Schinkel: Eine Charakteristik seiner künstlerischen Wirksamkeit.* Berlin, 1842.

La Font de Saint-Yenne. *L'Ombre du grand Colbert.* The Hague, 1749.

Lammert, Marlies. *David Gilly: Ein Baumeister des deutschen Klassizismus.* Berlin: Akademie-Verlag, 1964.

Laugier, Antoine. *Essai sur l'Architecture.* Paris, 1753.

Lavallée, Joseph, and Louis François Cassas. *Voyage pittoresque et historique de l'Istrie et Dalmatie.* Paris, 1802.

Le Corbusier. *Towards a New Architecture,* tr. Frederick Etchells. London: Architectural Press, 1946 (originally published as *Vers Une Architecture,* Paris: Editions Crès, 1923).

Levetzow, Konrad. *Denkschrift auf Friedrich Gilly.* Berlin, 1801.

Loos, Adolf. *Trotzdem, 1900–1930.* Innsbruck: Brenner-Verlag, 1931.

Lorck, Carl von. *Schinkel: Reisen in Deutschland.* Essen: Dom Verlag, 1956.

Mackowsky, Hans. *Häuser und Menschen im alten Berlin.* Berlin: Bruno Cassirer, 1923.

——— (ed.). *Karl Friedrich Schinkel: Briefe, Tagebücher, Gedanken.* Berlin: Im Propyläen-Verlag, 1922.

Mahlberg, Paul. *Schinkels Theater-Dekorationen.* Düsseldorf: Bagel, 1916.

Martin, Kurt. "Karl Friedrich Schinkel: Mittelalterliche Stadt am Wasser," *Museumsnachrichten,* Munich, Neue Pinakothek [1964], 148.

Meier, Günter (ed.). *Karl Friedrich Schinkel: Aus Tagebüchern und Briefen.* Berlin: Henschelverlag, 1967.

Merian, 12 (No. 11, 1959). Issue on Berlin.

Meyer, Gerhard R., *et al. Das Alte Museum, 1823–1966,* Festschrift zur Wiedereröffnung 1966. Berlin: Staatliche Museen, 1966.

——— *et al. Museumsinsel Berlin.* Weltstädte der Kunst. Munich: Süddeutscher Verlag, 1967.

Müther, Hans. "Schinkels Museum in Berlin," *Berliner Heimat: Zeitschrift für die Geschichte Berlins,* 2 (1959), 72–82.

Mumford, Lewis. *Roots of Contemporary American Architecture,* 2nd ed. New York: Grove Press, Inc., 1959.

Neil, J. Meredith. "The Precarious Professionalism of Latrobe," *Journal of the American Institute of Architects,* 53 (May 1970), 67–71.

Neumann, Max. *Menschen um Schinkel.* Berlin: Walter de Gruyter & Co., 1942.

Nicolai, Friedrich. *Beschreibung der königlichen Residenzstädte Berlin und Potsdam,* 3rd ed. rev., 2 vols. Berlin, 1786.

Oncken, Alste. *Friedrich Gilly, 1772–1800.* Vol. V of Forschungen zur deutschen Kunstgeschichte, ed. Deutscher Verein für Kunstwissenschaft. Berlin: Deutscher Verein für Kunstwissenschaft, 1935.

Ott, Brigitte. *Zur Platzgestaltung im 19. Jahrhundert in Deutschland.* Hamburg: the author, 1966.

Patte, Pierre. *Monumens érigés en France à la gloire de Louis XV.* Paris, 1765.

Peintre, Barbault. *Les plus beaux monuments de Rome ancienne.* Rome, 1761.

Percier, Charles, and P. F. L. Fontaine. *Palais, maisons, et autres édifices modernes, dessinés à Rome.* Paris, 1798.

Peschken, Goerd. "Die städtebauliche Einordnung des Berliner Schlosses zur Zeit des preussischen Absolutismus," in *Gedenkschrift Ernst Gall,* ed. Margarete Kühn and Louis Grodecki. Munich-Berlin: Deutscher Kunstverlag, 1965.

———. "Eine Stadtplanung Schinkels," *Archäologischer Anzeiger* (1962), 861–876.

———. "Neue Literatur über Andreas Schlüter," *Zeitschrift für Kunstgeschichte,* 30 (1967), 229–246.

———. *Schinkels Bauakademie in Berlin: Ein Aufruf zu ihrer Rettung.* Berlin: Deutscher Kunstverlag, 1961.

———. "Schinkels nachgelassene Fragmente eines architektonischen Lehrbuches," *Bonner Jahrbücher,* 166 (1966), 293–315.

———. "Technologische Ästhetik in Schinkels Architektur," *Zeitschrift des deutschen Vereins für Kunstwissenschaft* (No. 1/2, 1968).

———. "Zum für März geplanten Abbruch der Bauakademie in Berlin," *Bauwelt,* 9 (March 1961), 240–241.

Pevsner, Nikolaus. *An Outline of European Architecture*, 7th ed. rev. Baltimore: Penguin Books, 1963.

———. "Goethe and Strassburg," *Architectural Review*, 93 (1945), 154–159.

———. "Schinkel," *Journal of the Royal Institute of British Architects*, 59 (January 1952), 89–96.

Pinder, Wilhelm. *Deutsche Dome des Mittelalters*. Die Blauen Bücher. Königstein im Taunus: Karl Robert Langewiesche Verlag, 1955.

Plagemann, Volker. *Das deutsche Kunstmuseum 1790–1870*. Vol. 3 of Studien zur Kunst des 19. Jahrhunderts. Munich: Prestel-Verlag, 1967.

Pückler-Muskau, Hermann Fürst von. *Andeutungen über Landschaftsgärtnerei verbunden mit der Beschreibung ihrer praktischen Anwendung in Muskau*, ed. Theodor Lange. Leipzig: Verlag von Hans Friedrich [1911] (1st ed., Stuttgart, 1834).

[———]. *Briefe eines Verstorbenen: Ein fragmentarisches Tagebuch aus England, Wales, Irland und Frankreich, geschrieben in den Jahren 1826–1829*. 1830 (reprinted as *Fürst Pückler reist nach England*, ed. H. Ch. Mettin. Munich: List Verlag, 1965.

Pundt, Hermann G. "K. F. Schinkel's Environmental Planning of Central Berlin," *Journal of the Society of Architectural Historians*, 26 (May 1967), 114–130.

Rave, Paul Ortwin. *Berlin in der Geschichte seiner Bauten*. Munich-Berlin: Deutscher Kunstverlag, 1960.

———. *Das Mausoleum zu Charlottenburg*. Berlin: Verwaltung der Staatlichen Schlösser und Gärten, 1966.

——. *Das Schinkel-Museum und die Kunst-Sammlungen Beuths*. National-Galerie. Berlin: Ernst Rathenau Verlag, 1931.

———. *Genius der Baukunst: Eine klassisch-romantische Bilderfolge an der Berliner Bauakademie von Karl Friedrich Schinkel*. Berlin: Verlag Gebr. Mann [1939].

———. *Karl Friedrich Schinkel*. Munich-Berlin: Deutscher Kunstverlag, 1953.

———. *Karl Friedrich Schinkel: Schrifttum*. Beiheft zum Schrifttum der deutschen Kunst. Berlin: Deutscher Verein für Kunstwissenschaft, 1935.

———. *Karl Friedrich Schinkel Lebenswerk: Berlin. Erster Teil, Bauten für die Kunst, Kirchen, Denkmalpflege*. Berlin: Deutscher Kunstverlag, 1941.

———. *Karl Friedrich Schinkel Lebenswerk: Berlin. [Zweiter Teil], Stadtbaupläne, Brücken, Strassen, Tore, Plätze*. Berlin: Deutscher Kunstverlag, 1948.

———. *Karl Friedrich Schinkel Lebenswerk: Berlin. Dritter Teil, Bauten für Wissenschaft, Verwaltung, Heer, Wohnbau und Denkmäler*. Berlin: Deutscher Kunstverlag, 1962.

———. "Schinkel, ein Berliner und Europäer" (Festrede zum Schinkelfest), *Schriftenreihe des Architekten- und Ingenieur-Vereins zu Berlin* (No. 4, 1952).

———. "Schinkel, Karl Friedrich," in *Allgemeines Lexikon der bildenden Künstler*, 37 vols., ed. Ulrich Thieme and Felix Becker. Leipzig: Verlag von E. A. Seemann, 1907–1950. Vol. XXX (1936), 77–83.

———. "Schinkels Traum von einem Königspalast auf der Akropolis zu Athen," *Atlantis*, 6 (1934), 129–141.

Renan, Sheldon. *An Introduction to the American Underground Film*. New York: E. P. Dutton & Co., Inc., 1967.

Riemann, Gottfried. "Karl Friedrich Schinkels Reise nach England im Jahr 1826 und ihre Wirkung auf sein architektonisches Werk," unpub. diss., Martin-Luther Universität, Halle-Wittenberg, 1967.

Rietdorf, Alfred. *Gilly: Wiedergeburt der Architektur*. Berlin: Hans von Hugo Verlag, 1940–1943.

Schadow, Johann Gottfried. *Kunst-Werke und Kunst-Ansichten.* Berlin, 1849.

Schewick, Heinrich van. *Masse und Gewichte.* Berckers kleine Volksbibliothek. Kevelaer Rhld.: Verlag Butzon & Bercker, 1949.

Schiedlausky, Günther. *Karl Friedrich Schinkel.* Burg b. M.: August Hopfer Verlag, 1938.

Schinkel, Karl Friedrich. *Decorationen auf den königlichen Hoftheatern zu Berlin,* 5 pts. Berlin, 1819–1825.

———. *Entwurf zu einem Königspalast auf der Akropolis zu Athen,* 4th ed. Berlin, 1878.

———. *Sammlung architektonischer Entwürfe: Enthaltend theils Werke welche ausgeführt sind theils Gegenstände deren Ausführung beabsichtigt wurde,* 2 vols. Berlin, 1866.

——— and Peter Christian Wilhelm Beuth. *Vorbilder für Fabrikanten und Handwerker,* 3 vols. Berlin: Technische Deputation für Gewerbe, 1821–1837.

Schmitz, Hermann. *Berliner Baumeister vom Ausgang des achtzehnten Jahrhunderts,* 2nd ed. Berlin: Verlag Ernst Wasmuth A. G., 1925.

Schniewind, Carl. *Der Dom zu Berlin: Geschichtliche Nachrichten vom alten Dom.* Berlin: Warnick, 1905.

Sekler, Eduard F. "The Stoclet House by Josef Hoffmann," in *Essays in the History of Architecture presented to Rudolf Wittkower,* ed. Douglas Fraser. London: Phaidon Press, 1967.

Senator für Bau- und Wohnungswesen, Abt. Landes- und Stadtplanung Berlin. *Berlin: Planungsgrundlagen für den städtebaulichen Ideenwettbewerb "Hauptstadt Berlin."* Bonn-Berlin: Bundesminister für Wohnungsbau und Senator für Bau- und Wohnungswesen, 1957.

Serlio, Sebastiano. *Tutte l'opere d'architettura.* Venice, 1619.

Sievers, Johannes. [*Karl Friedrich Schinkel Lebenswerk:*] *Die Arbeiten von Karl Friedrich Schinkel für Prinz Wilhelm, späteren König von Preussen.* Berlin: Deutscher Kunstverlag, 1955.

Speer, Albert. *Erinnerungen.* Berlin: Verlag Ullstein GmbH., 1969.

Spiero, Sabine. "Schinkels Altes Museum in Berlin: Seine Baugeschichte von den Anfängen bis zur Eröffnung," *Jahrbuch der preussischen Kunstsammlungen,* 55 (1934), 41–86.

Staatliche Museen zu Berlin, National-Galerie. *Karl Friedrich Schinkel, 1781–1841* (Exhibition catalogue). Berlin: Staatliche Museen zu Berlin, 1961.

Staël [-Holstein], Madame de. *De l'Allemagne.* Paris, 1871.

Stahl, Fritz [Siegfried Lilienthal]. *Karl Friedrich Schinkel.* No. 10 of Berliner Architekturwelt. Berlin: Verlag Ernst Wasmuth, 1912.

Stuart, James, and Nicholas Revett. *The Antiquities of Athens.* London, 1762.

Stüler, August. "Über die Wirksamkeit Friedrich Wilhelms IV in dem Gebiete der bildenden Künste," *Zeitschrift für Bauwesen,* 11 (1861), 520ff.

Summerson, John. *Heavenly Mansions and Other Essays on Architecture.* New York: W. W. Norton & Co., Inc., 1963.

Sydow, Eckhart von. "Schinkel als Landschaftsmaler," *Monatshefte für Kunstwissenschaft,* 14 (1921), 239–245.

Treitschke, Heinrich von. *History of Germany in the Nineteenth Century,* 4 vols. New York: Robert M. McBride and Company, 1916.

Visionary Architects: Boullée, Ledoux, Lequeu (Exhibition catalogue). Houston: University of St. Thomas, 1968.

Waagen, Gustav Friedrich. "Carl Friedrich Schinkel als Mensch und als Künstler," in

Berliner Kalender auf das Schaltjahr 1844. Berlin: Königliche Preussische Kalender-deputation, 1843, pp. 303–428.

Wackenroder, Wilhelm Heinrich. *Werke und Briefe*. Vol. II, *Briefwechsel mit Ludwig Tieck, Pfingstreise von 1793*, ed. Friedrich von der Leyen. Jena: Verlag Eugen Diederichs, 1910.

Wolzogen, Alfred Freiherr von (ed.). *Aus Schinkel's Nachlass: Reisetagebücher, Briefe und Aphorismen*, 4 vols. Berlin, 1862–1864.

———. "Karl Friedrich Schinkel und der Theaterbau," *Bayreuther Blätter*, 10 (1887), 65–90.

Ziller, Hermann. *Schinkel*. Vol. XXVIII of Künstler-Monographien, ed. H. Knackfuss. Bielefeld-Leipzig, 1897.

Notes

Introduction

1. Goethe made this comment in a letter to the Boisserée brothers after Schinkel's first visit to his home in Weimar; see *Goethes Werke*, Grossherzogin Sophie von Sachsen ed., 50 vols. (Weimar, 1887–1918), XXVII, 137. Other references by Goethe to Schinkel as a man, a painter and an architect can be found cited in Paul Ortwin Rave, *Karl Friedrich Schinkel: Schrifttum*, Beiheft zum Schrifttum der deutschen Kunst (Berlin, 1935), p. 5.

2. Jakob I. Hittorff, "Historische Notiz über Carl Friedrich Schinkel," *Zeitschrift für Bauwesen*, 8 (1858), 106.

3. Oswald Hederer, *Leo von Klenze: Persönlichkeit und Werke* (Munich, 1964), p. 147.

4. Walter Curt Behrendt, *Alfred Messel* (Berlin, 1911), p. 119. Günther Schiedlausky, *Karl Friedrich Schinkel* (Burg b. M., 1938), p. 17, seems to have been more perceptive of the nature of Schinkel's attitude toward theoretical studies. He wrote: "Schinkel war das genaue Gegenteil eines Akademikers oder Eklektikers, der sich eng und ängstlich an hergebrachte Stilformen anschliesst, und hob sich dadurch weit über die beschränkte Schulauffassung des Klassizismus heraus."

5. Adolf Loos, *Trotzdem 1900–1930* (Innsbruck, 1931), pp. 110–111. This quotation is from his lecture "Architektur," parts of which were first published in *Der Sturm*, 42 (15 December 1910). Although the date of Loos's praise of Schinkel may seem early in the context of a general reappraisal of neo-Classicism among the first generation of twentieth-century architects, it was certainly not the first time that Schinkel had been lauded as the precursor of modern architectural thought; see Hermann Ziller, *Schinkel* (Bielefeld-Leipzig, 1897), the first modern monograph on Schinkel which includes extensive sections of his own writings. More important was the reassessment of Schinkel's work and the acknowledgement of its value as an inspiration to young architects by Hermann Muthesius both in *Stilarchitektur und Baukunst* (Mülheim-Ruhr: K. Schimmelpfeng, 1902), and also in his address ("Wo stehen wir") to the Deutsche Werkbund congress in 1911. For quotations of relevant passages, see Reyner Banham, *Theory and Design in the First Machine Age* (London, 1960), pp. 71–74.

6. Sigfried Giedion, *Spätbarocker und romantischer Klassizismus* (Munich, 1922), pp. 3–4; Nikolaus Pevsner, "Schinkel," *Journal of the Royal Institute of British Architects*, 59 (January 1952), 95.

7. Cf. Edward R. de Zurko, *Origins of Functionalist Theory* (New York, 1957), pp. 197–198; and Henry-Russell Hitchcock, *Architecture Nineteenth and Twentieth Centuries* (Baltimore, 1958), pp. 28–36.

8. Quoted by Regierungs-Baudirektor i. R. Fritz Schirmer, *Die Bauverwaltung*, 10 (October 1963), 9.

9. Philip Johnson's article, "Karl Friedrich Schinkel im zwanzigsten Jahrhundert," Festvortrag, *Schriftenreihe des Architekten- und Ingenieur-Vereins zu Berlin* (13 March 1961), was the first acknowledgement by a twentieth-century architect and critic of Schinkel's ability to coordinate all phases of art in creating a total environmental framework for his architectural designs. Johnson analyzed the impressive and sometimes neglected complex of the Hofgärtnerei near Potsdam, but did not discuss the schemes for Berlin in any detail. The Berlin architect and scholar, Dr. Goerd Peschken, has emphasized Schinkel's planning ability in two articles: "Zum für März geplanten Abbruch der Bauakademie in Berlin," *Bauwelt*, 9 (March 1961), 240–241; and "Eine Stadtplanung Schinkels," *Archäologischer Anzeiger* (1962), pp. 861–876. His interest in this aspect of Schinkel's work coincides with my own, and we were able to discuss our views during meetings in Berlin in 1960, 1966, and 1969. We were both originally stimulated by the suggestions of the most fervent scholar of Schinkel's work, the late Paul Ortwin Rave. Peschken's keen insight into the city planning problems of Berlin grew out of his chief interest, the work of Andreas Schlüter; see his "Die städtebauliche Einordnung des Berliner Schlosses zur Zeit des preussischen Absolutismus," in *Gedenkschrift Ernst Gall*, ed. Margarete Kühn and Louis Grodecki (Munich-Berlin, 1965), which establishes the importance of the site planning for Schlüter's palace. My article, "K. F. Schinkel's Environmental Planning of Central Berlin," *Journal of the Society of Architectural Historians*, 26 (May 1967), 114–130, attempted to expand our understanding of Schinkel's planning concepts and to relate these to his earlier work as a landscape painter.

10. The primary graphic sources used in the research for this study are the approximately four thousand original drawings by Schinkel preserved by the Staatliche Museen zu Berlin (DDR) and now kept in the newly restored Alte Museum. The primary literary sources are Schinkel's letters, diaries and commentaries, which have been collected in the following publications. Alfred Freiherr von Wolzogen, ed., *Aus Schinkel's Nachlass: Reisetagebücher, Briefe und Aphorismen*, 4 vols. (Berlin, 1862–1864), is the most comprehensive compilation, although the text was occasionally altered to suit the editor's style. Extremely valuable are Wolzogen's listings of Schinkel's works, awards, and promotions, notes on his family, and commentary on the specific nature of his projects, building programs, etc. Hans Mackowsky, ed., *Karl Friedrich Schinkel: Briefe, Tagebücher, Gedanken* (Berlin, 1922), utilized part of Wolzogen's record, expanded upon it, and added valuable new findings. Karl Gotthilf Kachler, *Schinkels Kunstauffassung* (Basel, 1940), added previously unpublished passages pertaining to Schinkel's philosophy and his aesthetic attitude toward art and architecture. Carl von Lorck, *Schinkel: Reisen in Deutschland* (Essen, 1956), concentrated primarily on Schinkel's letters and diaries pertaining to the larger context of his projects and added valuable observations regarding past misinterpretations, especially those of Wolzogen. His critical observations concerning similarities between Schinkel's writing style and the nature of his graphic documentation show a deep understanding of Schinkel's complex artistic personality. Günter Meier, ed., *Karl Friedrich Schinkel: Aus Tagebüchern und Briefen* (Berlin, 1967), is the most recent collection of important excerpts from Schinkel documents. It enriches some of Schinkel's descriptions of particular sites by using his own drawings as illustrations and also by the addition of supplementary notes by the editor. Schinkel's own publication, *Sammlung architektonischer Entwürfe*, 2 vols. (Berlin, 1866), combines his graphic and literary docu-

ments. His comments are short, but relevant, being compiled from individual portfolios (28 in number) which he issued intermittently from 1818 to 1840. As secondary sources, the best contemporary works are: Gustav Friedrich Waagen, "Carl Friedrich Schinkel als Mensch und als Künstler," in *Berliner Kalender auf das Schaltjahr 1844* (Berlin, 1843), pp. 303–428; and Franz Kugler, *Karl Friedrich Schinkel: Eine Charakteristik seiner künstlerischen Wirksamkeit* (Berlin, 1842). For general reference, biography and bibliography, see Paul Ortwin Rave, "Schinkel, Karl Friedrich," in *Allgemeines Lexikon der bildenden Künstler*, ed. Ulrich Thieme and Felix Becker (Leipzig, 1936), XXX, 77–83. A bibliography of four hundred works was compiled by Rave in 1935 in *Karl Friedrich Schinkel: Schrifttum.* For the most comprehensive coverage of Schinkel's work, see *Karl Friedrich Schinkel Lebenswerk*, 13 vols. to date (Berlin-Munich, 1939–1969). This series was originally produced by the Akademie der Baukunst, came under the direction of Paul Ortwin Rave in 1948 and, after his death in 1962, was continued by Frau Dr. Margarete Kühn. An excellent catalogue, *Karl Friedrich Schinkel 1781–1841*, Staatliche Museen zu Berlin (DDR), National-Galerie (Berlin, 1961), was published for the first major exhibition of Schinkel's original drawings after their return from the USSR.

I. Berlin before Schinkel's Time

1. For Berlin's history, including its characteristic communal structure, see Friedrich Nicolai, *Beschreibung der königlichen Residenzstädte Berlin und Potsdam*, 3rd ed. rev., 2 vols. (Berlin, 1786). Cf. Bogdan Krieger, *Berlin im Wandel der Zeiten* (Berlin, 1923); and Leo Adler, "Berlin," in *Wasmuths Lexikon der Baukunst*, 5 vols. (Berlin, 1929–1937), I, 458–476. See Senator für Bau- und Wohnungswesen, *Berlin: Planungsgrundlagen für den städtebaulichen Ideenwettbewerb "Hauptstadt Berlin"* (Bonn-Berlin, 1957), for data pertaining to planning and development.

2. Although rarely recognized as a significant factor in studies of urban planning, the peculiar geological conditions of the northern half of the island have played an important role in limiting the architectural development of this section of the city. Extensive subterranean deposits of *Kolke mit Faulschlamm und Torf* (ice deposits with muddy silt and peat) have been continually melting and shifting and have challenged architects from Andreas Schlüter to Alfred Messel in their design and calculation of foundation systems. According to Dipl.-Ing. Peter Neuendorff, building supervisor of the Neue Nationalgalerie (West Berlin), these *Kolke* deposits contributed to the failure of Schlüter's Münzturm in 1706, forced Schinkel to employ a foundation of 3,053 timber piles supporting a horizontal grid for his Museum in 1824 (see Rave, *Schinkel Lebenswerk: Berlin*, I, 44–46) and caused even greater complications during the construction of the Pergamon-Museum which began in 1906. See the geological study of the Spree River basin in Senator für Bau- und Wohnungswesen, *"Hauptstadt Berlin,"* Plate 16.

3. Hans Mackowsky, one of the most sensitive as well as prolific writers on the people and culture of old Berlin, summarized the difficulty of analyzing the city's early planning history in his classic work, *Häuser und Menschen im alten Berlin* (Berlin, 1923), in the preface of which (p. vii), he wrote: "Können wir das mittelalterliche Berlin nur aus geringen Überbleibseln und fragmentarischen Zeugnissen in unbestimmten Umrissen mehr ahnen als nacherleben, trägt in der Renaissanceperiode das Angesicht der Stadt die ungewissen Züge des Werdenden, so hat erst unter den preussischen Königen die Physiognomie Berlins gleichzeitig mit dem individuellen Charakter seiner Bewohner feste Form

und Prägung erhalten. Berlin als Kulturbegriff, so hoch oder so niedrig man ihn einzuschätzen gewillt ist, besteht erst seit dieser Zeit, war niemals individueller, greifbarer und selbstsicherer als damals."

4. Constructed under Joachim II, Margrave of Brandenburg (1535–1571).

5. Friedrich Wilhelm had spent his youth in Holland and, as a consequence, continued close ties with that country during his reign.

6. Nicolai, *Berlin und Potsdam*, I, 151; other references to the Unter den Linden occur on pp. 171–172. For a comprehensive discussion of the avenue, see Krieger, *Berlin*, pp. 186–260.

Until 1872, the date of the adoption of the metric system in Germany, the standard units of measure in the Kingdom of Prussia and Anhalt were the *Meile*, the *rheinländische Rute*, *Fuss* and *Zoll*. Equivalents to the metric system and to the Anglo-American units of mile, yard, foot and inch are as follows:

1 preussische Meile	= 2000 rh. Ruten
	= 7532.485 meters or 7.532 kilometers
	= 4.681 miles
1 rheinländische Rute	= 12 rh. Fuss
	= 3.77 meters
	= 4.117 yards
1 rheinländischer Fuss	= 12 rh. Zoll
	= 31.39 centimeters
	= $12\frac{3}{4}$ inches
1 rheinländischer Zoll	= 2.615 centimeters
	= $1\frac{1}{16}$ inches

This data is based on Heinrich van Schewick, *Masse und Gewichte* (Kevelaer Rhld., 1949), esp. pp. 3 and 26.

7. Goerd Peschken, "Die städtebauliche Einordnung des Berliner Schlosses," p. 358, suggests that Johan Maurits van Nassau, owner of the famed Mauritshuis in The Hague, was the planner of the original Linden and supports his view by citing similar planning schemes executed by him in Kleve and Sonnenburg.

8. Nicolai, *Berlin und Potsdam*, I, 171.

9. The Linden Allee terminated in the east at the Opernplatz and did not extend to the river.

10. For a detailed history of the development of Friedrichstadt, see Nicolai, *Berlin und Potsdam*, I, 180–208.

11. The municipalities of Berlin, Cölln, Friedrich-Werder, Dorotheenstadt and Friedrichstadt were united to form Berlin, the capital of Prussia, on 1 January 1710.

12. Today, an almost straight-line continuation of the Unter den Linden extends a distance of twelve kilometers to the west, reaching as far as the Havel River. Thus, its influence on greater Berlin far exceeded that of Friedrichstrasse.

13. The supervisor for the construction of residential buildings along the streets of Friedrichstadt under Friedrich Wilhelm I was a Colonel Derschau, who had been temporarily relieved of his military duties in order to conduct this work. Traditionally, during the reigns of Friedrich Wilhelm I and Friedrich II, native architects and surveyors were drawn from the ranks of the military. The best known were Johann Arnold Nering (1659–1695), Philipp Gerlach (1679–1748) and Georg Wenzeslaus von Knobelsdorff (1699–1753).

14. Many of the facades were patterned after designs by the young architect, Nering, mentioned in the previous note. Since a considerable number of the military garrison of Berlin were quartered in the upper floors of private residences in the town, one soldier to each dwelling unit, the uniform attic spaces with steeply pitched roofs became a conspicuous feature of these row houses.

15. Nicolai, *Berlin und Potsdam*, I, 183.

16. Madamé de Staël, *De l'Allemagne* (Paris, 1871), pp. 81–82.

17. It is significant that the planning and execution of the Rondeel in 1732–1734 antedated that of the Circus in Bath by twenty years (though the encircling row houses were not completed as shown in Figure 9). Its conception also preceded the theoretical formulation for such a town-planning element in the writings of La Font de Saint-Yenne, *L'Ombre de grand Colbert* (The Hague, 1749), pp. 25–27, and Antoine Laugier, *Essai sur l'Architecture* (Paris, 1753), pp. 189, 256–260. See Wolfgang Hermann, *Laugier and Eighteenth Century French Theory* (London, 1962), pp. 133–140, for a concise summary of current French town-planning ideas.

18. Werner Hegemann, *Das steinerne Berlin: Geschichte der grössten Mietskasernenstadt der Welt*, 1st ed., Lugano, 1930; reprinted as No. 3 of Ullstein Bauwelt Fundamente (Berlin, 1963).

19. The *Stadtmauer* was demolished in 1866–1868. In 1961 the wall dividing East and West Berlin was erected following, in part, the line of the eighteenth-century customs wall.

20. Peschken's careful reconstruction of the sight lines from the portal to the avenue can be found in his "Die städtebauliche Einordnung des Berliner Schlosses," pp. 359–361, figs. 244, 248.

21. From Jean Baptiste Broebes, *Vues des palais et maisons de plaissance de S. M. le Roy de Prusse* (Augsburg, 1733). I agree with Peschken's observation (in "Die städtebauliche Einordnung des Berliner Schlosses," p. 352) that Broebes' drawing of the palace complex may have been partly his own conception since no graphic records of it by Schlüter's own hand exist. Broebes was a teacher of engraving at the Berlin Akademie at that time. In a renewed discussion with Dr. Peschken in September 1969, he suggested that the author of this project may have been the Swedish court architect, Nicodemus Tessin the Younger (1654–1728), who had been in the service of Elector Friedrich Wilhelm during the reconstruction and expansion of Schloss Stettin in 1688. Tessin's indirect yet lasting influence in Berlin would be felt in the works of one of his students, Johann Friedrich Eosander, known as Freiherr von Göthe (1670–1729), who was Schlüter's successor as Prussian court architect from 1707 to 1713.

22. Designed in 1696, cast in iron by Johann Jacoby in 1700. The statue was removed during World War II, and, since the barge carrying it sank in the Havel River, it was preserved. In 1951 it was re-erected on a new pedestal in the forecourt of Schloss Charlottenburg in West Berlin. A copy stands in the vestibule rotunda of the Bode-Museum in East Berlin.

23. The sequence of accents along the eastern approach route to the Schloss in Berlin—city gate, street, bridge, statue and cour d'honneur—may have been a calculated attempt to imitate a similar processional sequence in Paris: the approach to the Louvre via the rue Dauphine, the Pont Neuf with the statue of Henry IV and along the Quai du Louvre to the palace. Compare Figure 12 with an engraving of 1725, "Louis XV and Marie Leczinska crossing the Pont-Neuf," in *Paris and Its People*, ed. Robert Laffont (London: Methuen

and Co., Ltd., 1958), fig. 348. The tendency to imitate French prototypes was already evident in the major facade of the Zeughaus, which was based on a design by François Blondel (see n. 24, below).

24. The Zeughaus was begun by Arnold Nering in 1695 after designs by François Blondel, the renowned French architect who served as envoy to the Prussian court in 1657–1658. See Goerd Peschken, "Neue Literatur über Andreas Schlüter," *Zeitschrift für Kunstgeschichte*, 30 (1967), p. 237, n. 20, for the most recent clarification of its inception. Work on the building was continued by Martin Grünberg and Schlüter and completed by Jean de Bodt in 1706.

25. One cannot say with certainty when the Linden Allee became known as Unter den Linden, but the latter term was commonly used by the beginning of the nineteenth century.

26. *Berlin im Jahre 1786: Schilderungen der Zeitgenossen* (Leipzig, 1886), p. 148.

27. Nicolai, *Berlin und Potsdam*, I, lxx.

28. *Ibid.*, 232–233; this census was for the year 1784.

29. The building was originally a town house, built in 1663, remodeled in 1732 by Gerlach as a residence for Crown Prince Friedrich (and thus traditionally known as the Kronprinzen Palais), and occupied by Friedrich Wilhelm III from 1793 to 1840.

30. Friedrich Wilhelm III visited Paris in 1815 on the occasion of the signing of the second Paris treaty following Napoleon's defeat. In 1819 his daughter Charlotte married the future Czar Nicholas I of Russia (1825–1855). During his visit to St. Petersburg, Friedrich Wilhelm must have become aware of current building programs in Russia's capital and perhaps also in Helsinki where a number of Prussian-trained architects worked for the court. Schinkel himself designed a small chapel for the gardens of Peterhof in the 1820's, and in 1838 he received a commission from the Czarina to design a resort palace at Orianda on the southwest coast of the Crimea. This project, his last major work, was never realized.

31. La Font de Saint-Yenne, *L'Ombre du grand Colbert*, pp. 25–30. The perimetrical squares which became a distinctive feature of Friedrichstadt were not realized in Paris.

32. Mackowsky, ed., *Schinkel*, p. 180.

33. Fritz Stahl, *Karl Friedrich Schinkel* (Berlin, 1912), p. 45.

34. Emil Kaufmann, *Von Ledoux bis Le Corbusier* (Vienna, 1933), p. 61. Hegemann, *Das steinerne Berlin*, p. 181, makes this rash judgment: "Auf dem wichtigen Gebiet des Städtebaues hat Schinkel beinahe ganz versagt. Er hat schöne Einzelstücke geschaffen . . ." Even Rave sometimes questioned Schinkel's effectiveness as a planner; see *Schinkel Lebenswerk: Berlin*, II, 9: "Sein Anteil bei der räumlichen Gestaltung der schnell wachsenden Stadt [Berlin] selber [war] nicht sehr bedeutend gewesen."

35. I discussed this idea with Dr. Gropius in February 1968. In speaking of the origin of the term *Gesamtkunstwerk*, he emphasized Richard Wagner's intention to fuse all the arts—poetry, music, acting, dancing, painting—in a grandiose and all-embracing union. In some respects, this kind of comprehensiveness has been anticipated by Philipp Otto Runge (1777–1810) who proposed a "synaesthetic" fusion of all the arts and referred to his romantic landscape paintings as "musical poems." A published summary of Dr. Gropius' thoughts on the subject can be found in "Tradition and Continuity in Architecture," *Program*, Columbia University, School of Architecture (New York, Spring 1964), pp. 4–23; reprinted in his *Apollo in the Democracy* (New York, 1968). His comments are particularly appropriate since two of his forebears, Wilhelm Ernst Gropius and his son Carl Wilhelm, were lifelong friends and supporters of Schinkel. Their relationship is

described by Kugler, *Schinkel*, pp. 137–151, and Rave, *Schinkel Lebenswerk: Berlin*, I, 163–164. See also S. Giedion, *Walter Gropius: Work and Teamwork* (New York, 1954), pp. 7–8.

II. Schinkel's Training in Berlin

1. The quoted phrase is from Sir John Summerson's essay on J. M. Gandy in *Heavenly Mansions and other Essays on Architecture* (New York, 1963) p. 121. Although Latrobe was seventeen years older than Schinkel, his position as the first professional architect in the United States and the difficulties he encountered in this office are strikingly similar to the situation of his younger Prussian contemporary; see J. Meredith Neil, "The Precarious Professionalism of Latrobe," *Journal of the American Institute of Architects*, 53 (May 1970), 67–71.

2. Fontane's brief biography of Schinkel, written about 1862, is the only source which details some childhood characteristics and experiences; it appears in Fontane's *Wanderungen durch die Mark Brandenburg* (Hamburg, 1961), pp. 45–47. See also my Appendix, 1781–1801.

3. This telling characterization of Berlin's enlightened spirit derives from a poem by Erdmann Wirckers, dedicated to Friedrich I, King *in* Prussia (1701–1713), which reads in part: "Die Fürsten wollen selbst in deine Schule gehn,/Drumb hastu auch für Sie ein Spree-Athen gebauet."

4. Gilly was the first civilian architect to work for Prussia's royalty (see n. 13, chap. 1) and one of the first professionally licensed architects in Prussia (1770). He assumed his post in Berlin in 1786.

5. Rave, "Schinkel," in *Allgemeines Lexikon*, XXX, 77. The Bauakademie and the Gewerbeakademie (founded 1821) were combined in 1879 to form the nucleus of the modern Technische Hochschule, now called the Technische Universität.

6. For an appreciation of the high esteem in which David and Friedrich Gilly were held as teachers, see Konrad Levetzow, *Denkschrift auf Friedrich Gilly* (Berlin, 1801). See also Wilhelm Kohlhoff, *Denkmal der Liebe* . . . (Berlin, 1808); and Friedrich Adler, "Friedrich Gilly, Schinkels Lehrer," *Zentralblatt der Bauverwaltung*, 1 (1881), 8, 17, 22.

7. Marlies Lammert, *David Gilly: Ein Baumeister des deutschen Klassizismus* (Berlin, 1964).

8. *Ibid.*, p. 73.

9. David Gilly's best-known publication is a series of essays entitled, *Sammlung nützlicher Aufsätze und Nachrichten die Baukunst betreffend*, 6 vols. in 3 (Berlin, 1798–1806), which was a standard work on architectural engineering and practical building techniques in Prussia until ca. 1850. See Hermann Schmitz, *Berliner Baumeister vom Ausgang des achtzehnten Jahrhunderts*, 2nd ed. (Berlin, 1925), p. 320, for a more comprehensive listing of Gilly's writings.

10. Waagen, "Schinkel," p. 317, maintained that Schinkel learned little more than architectural drawing from David Gilly. Since no thorough study of this critical period in Schinkel's life has been made, subsequent biographers have accepted Waagen's assumption.

11. "Gilly, à Berlin" was the only German subscriber to *Voyage pittoresque et historique de l'Istrie et Dalmatie*; redigé d'après l'itinéraire de L. F. Cassas par Joseph Lavallée (Paris, 1802). This work contains views of several sites which Schinkel also visited and sketched during his trip through Istria.

12. Nering's Orangerie of 1685, the semicircular building shown in Selter's plan (see Figure 13), had been transformed into a customs warehouse, the Neue Packhof, in 1748 because additional storage facilities were needed for Prussia's expanding trade. The Alte Packhof remained southwest of the palace on the western bank of the Kupfergraben.

13. For contemporary commentary, see *Berlin im Jahre 1786*, pp. 19–21, 25–26.

14. Hermann Schmitz, *Berliner Baumeister*, p. 68.

15. For Soane's project, see Emil Kaufmann, *Architecture in the Age of Reason* (Cambridge, Mass., 1955), fig. 41. For Boullée's Projet du Pont de la Place Louis XV (no date) and Ledoux's Pont de la Loue, Chaux, 1773–1779, see *Visionary Architects: Boullée, Ledoux, Lequeu* (Exhibition catalogue; Houston: University of St. Thomas, 1968), Plates 38 and 78.

16. In 1786 Louis XVI had ordered that all houses and shops be cleared from several bridges in central Paris. The simple forms of these bridges, thus shorn of their incrustations, probably impressed Gilly during his visit to Paris in 1797–98.

17. Besides the contemporary work by Levetzow (see n. 6, above), the best recent works on the younger Gilly are Alste Oncken, *Friedrich Gilly, 1772–1800* (Berlin, 1935), and Alfred Rietdorf, *Gilly: Wiedergeburt der Architektur* (Berlin, 1940–1943).

18. Wilhelm Heinrich Wackenroder, *Werke und Briefe*. Vol. II, *Briefwechsel mit Ludwig Tieck, Pfingstreise von 1793* (Jena, 1910), p. 192. See Schmitz, *Berliner Baumeister*, p. 40, for Heinrich Gentz's moving tribute to Friedrich Gilly as expressed in his memorial inscription on Gilly's gravestone at Karlsbad, which reads in part: "Ein Liebling des Himmels und der Menschen, Ein Künstler der edelsten Art." Schinkel visited this gravesite in 1803, en route to Austria, and recorded it in its total setting in a pen-and-ink sketch.

19. In contrast to Gilly's drawing of abstracted, individual parts of Schloss Friedensstein in 1797, Schinkel's words describe his impressions of the total site. During a brief visit there with Beuth in April, 1826, he saw this Schloss at Gotha thus: "Dienstags früh fuhren wir weiter, hielten uns ein Stündchen in Erfurt und ein anderes in Gotha auf. In Gotha stiegen wir auf die Terrasse des Schlosses, die eine herrliche Aussicht hat, wie denn überhaupt Gotha die schönste Schlossanlage in den sächsischen Herzogthümern besitzt." Quoted from a letter to his wife, Susanne, as published in Wolzogen, *Aus Schinkel's Nachlass,* II, 140.

20. See Oncken, *Friedrich Gilly*, p. 30, for commentary on the contents of this library. Almost all of the great eighteenth-century archaeological publications were included.

21. Waagen, "Schinkel," p. 318.

22. The text of the letter can be found in Wolzogen, *Aus Schinkel's Nachlass*, I, 172–176. The theater is not identified. The use of awnings on cast-iron poles, sketched at the upper left, would be adopted by Schinkel in his 1827 design for a Kaufhaus on the Unter den Linden.

23. Oncken, *Friedrich Gilly*, pp. 133–135, supplies a list of drawings among which are those considered copies by Schinkel of Gilly's designs. Waagen, "Schinkel," p. 318, verifies the fact that copying the young Gilly's drawings was one of the basic exercises Schinkel performed as a beginning student under the direction of David Gilly.

24. The numerous stages in the creation of the monument to Friedrich II, from the initial proposal by Freiherr von Heinitz in 1787 to the final realization by Rauch in 1851, are outlined by Adolph Doebber, *Heinrich Gentz: Ein Berliner Baumeister um 1800* (Berlin, 1916), pp. 34–36; see also Schmitz, *Berliner Baumeister*, pp. 59–62, for a summary of the entries in the competition of 1797. Gilly's written commentary on his own entry can be found in Rietdorf, *Gilly*, p. 57.

25. Although Friedrich Gilly did not establish personal contact with some of the revolutionary architects of Paris until 1797, it is likely that his father's library contained a number of contemporary publications which featured designs by these men (see n. 20, above), e.g., the album of engravings compiled by Armand-Parfait Prieur and Pierre-Louis van Cleemputte containing the winning designs for the Prix de Rome (Paris, 1790–). Sir John Summerson, in a comment that accompanied Nikolaus Pevsner's "Schinkel," implied, no doubt (the critical line is missing in the text), that Gilly's gate was based on Sir John Soane's entrance arch at Tyringham, completed in 1796; see also Hitchcock, *Architecture Nineteenth and Twentieth Centuries*, p. 16. Upon closer investigation, it seems that Gilly, possibly inspired by Gentz who had recently returned from Rome, used the Arch of Janus as his prototype; see Plate 21 in Barbault Peintre, *Les plus beaux monuments de Rome ancienne* (Rome, 1761). Another depiction of the Arch of Janus would have been available to him in the Piranesi etching of 1771, one of the *Vedute di Roma*.

26. Brigitte Ott, *Zur Platzgestaltung im 19. Jahrhundert in Deutschland* (Hamburg, 1966), p. 24.

27. Unless otherwise noted, all statements pertaining to the memorial church project are based on information in Rave, *Schinkel Lebenswerk: Berlin*, I, 187–202, and Wolzogen, *Aus Schinkel's Nachlass*, III, 188–207. Though Wolzogen, followed by others, gives the date 1819 for the final design, I agree with Rave that the entire project should be dated 1814.

28. For Goethe on Strassburg, see "Von Deutscher Baukunst," in *Schriften zur Kunst*, ed. Christian Beutler (Zurich, 1954), pp. 16–26. See also Nikolaus Pevsner, "Goethe and Strassburg," *Architectural Review*, 93 (1945), 154–159. Paul Ortwin Rave, *Genius der Baukunst* . . . (Berlin, [1939]), pp. 7–16, summarizes some major currents of German intellectualism and philosophy which contributed to Schinkel's admiration for medieval art and architecture. See also Georg Friedrich Koch, "Karl Friedrich Schinkel und die Architektur des Mittelalters," *Zeitschrift für Kunstgeschichte*, 29 (1966), 177–222, for an analysis of specific medieval monuments, including Strassburg, which influenced Schinkel's early conceptual designs as well as his philosophy of architecture.

29. For a contemporary comment on the drawing and reference to its exhibition in the palace, see Johann Gottfried Schadow, *Kunst-Werke und Kunst-Ansichten* (Berlin, 1849), p. 118. Schinkel was probably first introduced to the Strassburger Münster through the sketches which Friedrich Gilly had made on his visit there in 1797; see Rietdorf, *Gilly*, pp. 76–77, figs. 64–67. Schinkel's own analysis of the church, written during his second visit to Strassburg in July, 1824, can be found in Mackowsky, *Schinkel*, pp. 113–115. In accord with Schinkel's activities as a preservationist and restorer of historical monuments (e.g., cathedral of Cologne, castle at Marienburg), the rendering shows the west facade of the Strassburger Münster with both spires, as it would appear if finished.

30. For an illustration of the Heiligegeist-Kapelle, see Paul Ortwin Rave, *Berlin in der Geschichte seiner Bauten* (Berlin, 1960), Plate 3; for Kloster Chorin, see Wilhelm Pinder, *Deutsche Dome des Mittelalters*, Die Blauen Bücher (Königstein im Taunus, 1963), Plate 88.

31. Schinkel drew a view of the cathedral complex of Pisa in 1804/05, and the cathedral's characteristic cupola also appears in several conceptual designs of his early career. It should be noted, however, that Schinkel changed the profile of the dome for his presentation drawing of the north flank of the church (illustrated in Rave, *Schinkel Lebenswerk: Berlin*, I, Plate 97), in which one may also detect a certain affinity of the side elevation with the cathedral of Milan, an Italian Gothic building which also appealed to

him. The arcade which surrounds the memorial church in Schinkel's drawing may also have had its source in the Campo Santo at Pisa, though its particular character may have been inspired by late medieval marketplaces surrounded by arcaded facades, typical of provincial cities in the Mark Brandenburg and Pomerania (e.g., Stralsund).

32. In Goethe, *Schriften zur Kunst*, p. 716.

33. P. O. Rave, "Schinkel: Ein Berliner und Europäer" (Festrede zum Schinkelfest), *Schriftenreihe des Architekten- und Ingenieur-Vereins zu Berlin* (No. 4, 1952), p. 9.

34. Hitchcock, *Architecture Nineteenth and Twentieth Centuries*, p. 198, interpreted Schmidt's design thus: "The two front towers flanking the gabled entrance bay are set close against the dome to provide a very Baroque sort of composition—this is really, therefore, a sort of Sant'Agnese in Agone or Karlskirche carried out with a G. G. Scott vocabulary of Neo-Gothic elements." This interpretation appears too labored. Perhaps Schmidt, who had won the competition for Berlin's city hall in 1857 and had been a professor at the Kunst-Akademie in Vienna since 1859, was one of those present at the Schinkelfest in Berlin on 13 March 1869 when the auditorium was decorated with a "Transparentbild [von Schinkels Entwurf] von dem grossartigen gothischen Dome . . . welchen er als Denkmal der Befreiungskriege für den Leipziger Platz projectirt hatte." ("Schinkelfest am 13. März 1869," *Zeitschrift für Bauwesen*, 19 [1869], 459).

35. Even Alfred Messel depended on Schinkel in his design for the Wertheim department store, 1896–1904, erected coincidently at the same site. Messel's work, however, was a creative act of assimilation, recognizing both the existing local building tradition and the emerging Jugendstil. See Behrendt, *Alfred Messel*, pp. 79–80, 104.

36. It was still common in Gilly's day to present contemporary buildings by several views in elevation; see Charles Percier and P. F. L. Fontaine, *Palais, maisons, et autres édifices modernes, dessinés à Rome* (Paris, 1798).

37. Peschken notes in "Die städtebauliche Einordnung des Berliner Schlosses," p. 358, that no survey of Berlin prior to Selter should be used for scholarly research due to lack of accuracy. I should add that even some of Schinkel's own site plans, especially those which appeared as engravings in his *Sammlung*, are not completely accurate.

38. See Wolzogen's excellent assessment of Schinkel's professional problems in *Aus Schinkel's Nachlass*, III, xiv.

39. Rulemann Eylert, *Charakter-Züge und historische Fragmente aus dem Leben des Königs von Preussen Friedrich Wilhelm III* (Magdeburg, 1843), p. xvii. Friedrich Adler, "Schinkel Festrede; die Bauschule zu Berlin von Karl Friedrich Schinkel," *Zeitschrift für Bauwesen*, 19 (1869), 466, characterized Schinkel's reaction to the king's wishes in the choice of style for the Friedrich-Werdersche Kirche thus: "Er erfüllte den Königlichen Befehl, eine 'gothische' Kirche zu errichten, mit aller Treue gegen den hohen Herrn, aber auch mit aller Treue gegen sich selbst."

40. In collaboration with Peter Christian Beuth, the director of the newly founded Technische Deputation für Gewerbe, Schinkel published his ideas in *Vorbilder für Fabrikanten und Handwerker*, a series of essays and engraved plates which appeared between 1821 and 1837.

In 1862, Theodor Fontane (*Wanderungen durch die Mark Brandenburg*, p. 54) evaluated Schinkel's impact on the arts and crafts thus: "Das ganze Kunsthandwerk—dieser wichtige Zweig modernen Lebens—ging unter seinem Einfluss einer Reform, einem mächtigen Aufschwung entgegen. Die Tischler und Holzschneider schnitzten nach Schinkelschen Mustern, Fayence und Porzellan wurden schinkelsch geformt, Tücher und Teppiche wurden schinkelsch gewebt. Das Kleinste und das Grösste nahm edlere

Formen an: der altväterische Ofen, bis dahin ein Ungeheuer, wurde zu einem Ornament, die Eisengitter hörten auf, eine blosse Anzahl von Stangen und Stäben zu sein, man trank aus Schinkelschen Gläsern und Pokalen, man liess seine Bilder in Schinkelsche Rahmen fassen, und die Grabkreuze der Toten waren Schinkelschen Mustern entlehnt."

In the early twentieth century, Behrendt (*Alfred Messel*, p. 131) assessed Schinkel's position as a pioneer of aesthetics in the building crafts: "In diesem Sinne ist Schinkels Persönlichkeit für Berlin bedeutungsvoll gewesen, deren schulbildender Einfluss sich fast durch zwei Generationen wirksam erwiesen hat. Der Segen, den die disziplinierende Kraft dieses Beispiels gestiftet hat, offenbart sich nicht allein in der Baukunst, sondern in allen mit ihr in Beziehung stehenden Gewerben. Der hohe Wert solcher Traditionen liegt darin, dass sie unbewusst Kulturarbeit fordern."

During a personal interview in February 1968, Walter Gropius discussed this aspect of Schinkel's career and acknowledged his influence on Peter Behrens as well as his own philosophy at the Bauhaus.

41. Wolzogen, *Aus Schinkel's Nachlass*, III, 363.

42. Important documentation and numerous related illustrations may be found in Schinkel's *Sammlung architektonischer Entwürfe*, VIII, Plate 53/54, and Rave, *Schinkel Lebenswerk: Berlin*, II, 88–95. Rave publishes the full text of Friedrich Wilhelm III's instructions. Among countless similar official writings, this document appears to be the classic example of a typical communique which demonstrates vividly the low level of the trivial and bureaucratic which confronted Schinkel and thwarted many of his plans as a state architect. It reads in part: "Der Stil, in dem die Tore zu Frankfurt am Main, namentlich das Bockenheimer, Friedberger und Allerheiligen Tor gebaut sind, hat Mir immer gefallen, und Ich bin daher willens, nach einem von diesen oder nach einer Komposition aus allen dreien, jedenfalls in diesem Genre, das Potsdamer Tor von Berlin bauen zu lassen, und damit die Laternenträger der vormaligen Opernbrücke in Verbindung zu bringen. Die genannten Frankfurter Tore sind in Kupfer gestochen leicht zu beschaffen, und der Geheime Oberbaurat Schinkel soll, wenn solches geschehen ist, den Auftrag erhalten, nach dieser jetzt ausgesprochenen Idee die Zeichnung zu diesem neuen Tore zu entwerfen."

43. Kugler's analysis is in *Schinkel*, pp. 38–39. Cf. Goerd Peschken, "Eine Stadtplanung Schinkels," p. 863; and Ott, *Zur Platzgestaltung im 19. Jahrhundert in Deutschland*, pp. 38–39.

44. Although a final authorization for the construction of this tower was not given, and Schinkel could not provide this vertical focal point at the termination of the Leipziger Strasse, a kind of substitute was built by Hermann Friedrich Waesemann between 1861 and 1869 in the heart of old Berlin. His design for a new Rathaus incorporated a tower of ninety-seven meters (restored in 1952) which is clearly visible in any view through the Brandenburger Tor and acts effectively as a visual connecting link between the Tiergarten area and the core of the city.

45. For Lenné's position and designs, especially the landscaping of the Tiergarten, see Gerhard Hinz, *Peter Josef Lenné und seine bedeutendsten Schöpfungen in Berlin und Potsdam* (Berlin, 1937).

46. Wolzogen notes that he referred to Schinkel as "my son"; see *Aus Schinkel's Nachlass*, I, 51–52, n. 3.

47. Remarks pertaining to Gentz's career are based on Adolph Doebber's *Gentz*.

48. Royal stipends for travel and study abroad had been awarded to Knobelsdorff, Gentz, and Friedrich Gilly. They were initiated by Friedrich II and temporarily discon-

tinued under Friedrich Wilhelm III. Schinkel did not receive assistance for his tour of 1803–1805. Later, however, upon completion of the Museum am Lustgarten in 1830, the king presented him with a stipend which enabled him to revisit Italy, this time accompanied by his family.

49. For Schinkel's itinerary, see Wolzogen, *Aus Schinkel's Nachlass*, I, 105–129. A map comparing the routes of Goethe and Gentz may be found in Doebber, *Gentz*, Plate 5. See also Heinrich Gentz, "Briefe über Sizilien," *Neue Deutsche Monatsschrift*, 3 (Berlin, 1795).

50. Gentz wrote in 1792: "Die Szena [des Theaters von Taormina] ist sehr konserviert . . . Es ist auf einen Fels gebauet und alle Zugänge sind in den Fels gehauen. Die grossen weitläufigen Felsen-Gänge, die von allen Seiten her zum Theater führen, geben diesem Theater einen Vorzug über alle, die ich kenne. In der Lage übertrifft es bei weitem alle. Schöner und glücklicher konnte diese wohl nicht gewählt werden. Von dem hohen Felsentheater herab übersahen die Zuschauer das herrlichste Land von der Welt, und gerade ihm gegenüber steht der Etna mit seinem rauchenden Gipfel und schliesst diese Szene, die malerischste, die man sich denken kann" (Doebber, *Gentz*, p. 24).

The following is Schinkel's reaction to the same site in 1804: "Auf dem Gipfel ragen die Trümmer des alten Theaters von Taurominium hervor. Mächtiger als jemals ergriff mich der Eintritt in dies Theater. Ich sah vor mir das Proscenium, über ihm und durch seine Öffnungen eine unendliche Ferne. Rechts stürzen sich wilde Gebirge hinab; an ihrem Fuss liegt unter Orangen und Palmen Taormina; ein Weg windet sich an der Felswand empor zum Castell auf dem Gipfel; mit einem Kloster steigt ein langer Hügel aus der Stadt hinab in's Meer, das wir tief und dumpf unter uns rauschen hörten; im Hintergrund hebt sich der Aetna in seiner ganzen Majestät empor und streckt sich weit hinaus in die Ebene Catania's; das Meer beschliesst den Horizont.—Es ward uns schwer, den bezaubernden Ort zu verlassen; welchen Eindruck musste das Schauspiel auf einem Theater bei solchen Decorationen machen!" (Wolzogen, *Aus Schinkel's Nachlass*, I, 110).

51. His travels to Italy and Sicily in 1786–1788 not only constituted a dramatic turning point in the life of Germany's greatest literary genius, but also inspired artists and intellectuals to see the Greek and Roman antiquities firsthand; see Goethe, *Italienische Reise* (Munich, n.d.).

52. Nikolaus Pevsner, *An Outline of European Architecture*, 7th ed. rev. (Baltimore, 1963), p. 356.

53. This and subsequent quotations are from Doebber's discussion of the monument in *Gentz*, pp. 34–37. The terms *Kaufladen* or *Kaufhaus* as used here by Gentz and also by Schinkel in his project of 1827 should not be translated, as they sometimes are, as "department store." The buildings contained retail shops and stalls leased to individual independent sellers, as in the traditional European market, and were not establishments of a single parent company.

54. The comments of a contemporary observer, Baron von Lamotte, are recorded in *Berlin im Jahre 1786*, pp. 25–26: "Die Aussicht verhindern zum Beispiel die Buden an der . . . Hundebrücke und bei der Hauptwache der Artillerie. So oft ich in diese Gegend nach der Neustädter Brücke [Opernbrücke] zu gewähren würde . . . sich hinter solchen elenden Hütten verbergen muss."

55. The Kronprinzen Palais has been under reconstruction since 1968 according to the later designs of Heinrich Strack; see Appendix under 1824.

56. Schinkel, too, opposed the use of freestanding colonnades as decorative elements. However, when colonnades or arcades had a specific purpose, he admired their usefullness

and supported their application. During his visit to Padua in July 1803, he observed (in Wolzogen, *Aus Schinkel's Nachlass*, I, 30): "Padova hat, wie die mehrsten Städte dieses Theils von Italien, die vortreffliche Einrichtung der Arkaden vor allen Häusern, so dass man bei dem schlechtesten Wetter trocken und reinlich durch alle Theile der Stadt gehen kann; es soll sich diese Einrichtung von den alten Tyrrhenern [Etruskern] herschreiben, die ehemals diese Gegend bewohnten."

57. Doebber, *Gentz*, p. 27.

58. Peschken feels that Schinkel may have used the power of his new position as supervisor of design for royal and state commissions in the Oberbaudeputation to overrule Gentz's proposals (private discussion). For Doebber's interpretations, see *Gentz*, pp. 81–83, and "Zur Baugeschichte des Charlottenburger Mausoleums," *Zentralblatt der Bauverwaltung*, 32 (1912), 137–139. See P. O. Rave, *Das Mausoleum zu Charlottenburg* (Berlin, 1966). See also n. 8, chap. iv.

59. Goethe, *Italienische Reise*, p. 143.

III. The Lessons of Italy

1. Lorck, *Schinkel*, p. 38. See Wolzogen, *Aus Schinkel's Nachlass*, III, 388, for Schinkel's definition of *Barock* as a synonym for *geschmacklos*.

2. Wolzogen, *Aus Schinkel's Nachlass*, I, 133. Besides Bramante, however, Schinkel included Michelangelo, Palladio, and Schlüter among the sixteen outstanding architects whose portrait-reliefs adorned the main entrance of his Bauakademie; see Rave, *Genius der Baukunst*, p. 50.

3. Wolzogen, *Aus Schinkel's Nachlass*, II, 106. Schinkel's admiration for Giulio Romano was inspired not by his architecture but by his decorations for the Palazzo del Te.

4. He was especially critical of Joseph Lavallée and Louis François Cassas, *Voyage pittoresque et historique de l'Istrie et Dalmatie* (Paris, 1802); see Wolzogen, *Aus Schinkel's Nachlass*, I, 53.

5. Mackowsky, *Schinkel*, p. 32.

6. Wolzogen, *Aus Schinkel's Nachlass*, I, 166.

7. Hittorff, "Historische Notiz über Carl Friedrich Schinkel," p. 100.

8. Wolzogen, *Aus Schinkel's Nachlass*, I, 52.

9. Though the balcony may belong to the Villa Malta, its placement in the composition is purely theatrical. The quality of the drawing suggests that it may have been added later.

10. Clemens von Brentano called Schinkel the greatest landscape painter since Claude Lorraine; see Max Neumann, *Menschen um Schinkel* (Berlin, 1942), p. 54. In a letter from Rome of September 1804 (Wolzogen, *Aus Schinkel's Nachlass*, I, 141–142), Schinkel stated his reaction to the reputation he was gaining as a painter: "Koch, von den Ihnen bekannten, flüchtigen Skizzen unserer sicilianischen Reise eingenommen, hat mir eine Menge Künstler in's Haus geführt, welche sie ansehen und copiren, . . . die mich gegen meinen Willen und meine Bestimmung mehr als Landschaftsmaler, denn als Architekt beurtheilen." Although by far the greatest number of Schinkel's graphic records of his first Italian journey are line drawings, one can readily cite a few finished watercolors and tempera paintings in which he did dramatize the pictorial effects of his subjects. Among them are the splendid *Ansicht des Campo Vaccino (Forum)*, Rome, 1803/04, and the *Ansicht der Kirche von Pirano* in Istria, 1803, both in the Schinkel collection, Staatliche Museen zu Berlin.

11. Wolzogen, *Aus Schinkel's Nachlass*, III, 353. ·

12. Wolzogen, *Aus Schinkel's Nachlass,* I, 87. At the end of the nineteenth century another northern architect would be attracted by the simple cubic structures of southern Italy and bring back sketches of them; see Eduard F. Sekler, "The Stoclet House by Josef Hoffmann," in *Essays in the History of Architecture Presented to Rudolf Wittkower* (New York, 1967), p. 238 and figs. 43, 44.

13. For Schinkel's study of Poussin, see Wolzogen, *Aus Schinkel's Nachlass*, III, 43, 54; and Kugler, *Schinkel*, pp. 122–123. An unpublished drawing by Schinkel after Poussin exists in the Schinkel collection, Staatliche Museen zu Berlin, Kupferstichkabinett und Sammlung der Zeichnungen, Inventory No. W.XVb/41.

14. Considering his acute observations during his extensive visit to Italy and the degree of maturity which the Hofgärtnerei displays, it is unlikely that Schinkel derived his primary inspiration from the publications of J.-N.-L. Durand or other French works, as Hitchcock suggests in *Architecture Nineteenth and Twentieth Centuries*, p. 34. However, this is not to say that Schinkel avoided Durand categorically; see Giedion, *Spätbarocker und romantischer Klassizismus*, Plates 46, 48, for a plausible influence of Durand's museum facade scheme on Schinkel's own design of 1822.

15. Speech delivered during the annual Schinkelfest in Berlin on 13 March 1961; printed as "Schinkel and Mies," *Program*, Columbia University, School of Architecture, pp. 14–34.

16. For Hittorff's comments, see his "Historische Notiz über Carl Friedrich Schinkel," pp. 105–106; for von Klenze's evaluation, see Hederer, *Leo von Klenze*, pp. 140–147. A recent and typically more critical assessment of Schinkel's project can be found in Peter Collins' *Changing Ideals in Modern Architecture, 1750–1950* (London, 1965), pp. 88–89. Schinkel's original watercolor presentation drawings have been lost since World War II.

17. Two sites were offered: the Acropolis and an area on the plain northeast of the hill. Obviously, Schinkel chose the more challenging one. It should be kept in mind that in 1834 the Acropolis was covered with the remains of many centuries of post-Hellenic construction and that Schinkel's knowledge of the ancient monuments was gained solely through printed sources.

18. The letter is published in Wolzogen, *Aus Schinkel's Nachlass*, III, 333–335.

19. Hederer, *Leo von Klenze*, p. 147.

20. In a letter to David Gilly in December 1804 (Wolzogen, *Aus Schinkel's Nachlass*, I, 167), Schinkel commented on the effect of climate on building forms in southern Italy and Sicily: "Auch in Rücksicht der Distribution ist die Architektur dieser Länder weiter von der unserigen entfernt. Das, was wir gewöhnlich bei Wohnhäusern Platzverschwendung nennen, tritt immer stärker auf, je südlicher die Länder sind. Offene Hallen, von Pfeilern und Arkaden getragen, und weite Corridore, die auf allen Seiten zu breiten Altanen oder Weinlauben führen, nehmen den grössten Theil eines Hauses ein. Bei der geringen Zeit, die man dort in den Zimmern zubringt, dienen diese Räume zum Verkehr und zur Arbeit in der Schwüle, da sich in ihnen die durchstreichende Luft abkühlt."

21. Wolzogen, *Aus Schinkel's Nachlass*, III, 335. For Schinkel's growing antagonism toward Baroque axiality, see his comments in Wolzogen, III, 373–374.

22. The reason given for the rejection of Schinkel's plan was that no water was available on the Acropolis; see Hermann Ziller, *Schinkel*, Vol. XXVIII of Künstler-Monographien, ed. H. Knackfuss (Bielefeld-Leipzig, 1897), p. 80. For Schinkel's assessment of the accepted design for the palace by Friedrich Gärtner, built in 1836–1841, see Mackowsky, *Schinkel*, pp. 181–182.

23. Wolzogen, *Aus Schinkel's Nachlass*, I, 35.

24. See Schinkel's letter to the Berlin publisher, Unger, of August, 1804, in Wolzogen, *Aus Schinkel's Nachlass*, I, 132–135. Due to Unger's death and the unsettled state of Berlin's economy upon Schinkel's return in 1805, the drawings were not published.

25. For the definitive analysis of the Campidoglio, see James S. Ackerman, *The Architecture of Michelangelo*, 2 vols. (New York, 1961), I, 54–74.

26. Schinkel's view is almost identical to that of Piranesi's etching of 1756, though the techniques are quite dissimilar.

27. Wolzogen, *Aus Schinkel's Nachlass*, III, fold-out sheet opposite p. 264, col. III, F. The horse trainers already appear in the first version of January 1823; see Figure 76. The inclusion of these sculpture groups was probably also in response to the existing parapet sculpture of the Zeughaus and Schloss.

28. The drawings obviously could not predate Schinkel's trip to Italy. The three have never been discussed as a group and the few references to the individual sheets have been inconclusive in determining their meaning or purpose; see Ott, *Zur Platzgestaltung im 19. Jahrhundert in Deutschland*, p. 80, n. 127. They were certainly not meant to be included in Schinkel's intended publication of his Italian architectural studies. At least one (Figure 46) has been considered of so little value that Ott, p. 42, remarks: "Man wünscht, der Entwurf wäre nicht von Schinkel."

29. The site of St. Vitus cathedral in Prague especially impressed Schinkel. Upon his arrival in the city in 1803, he wrote: "Der schöne gothische Dom im Hofplatz der Burg hat mich häufig gereizt, mit Mühe und Schweiss die Stufen des Bergs zu ersteigen" (Wolzogen, *Aus Schinkel's Nachlass*, I, 48). Having traveled through Saxony, he may also have noted the similar siting of the cathedrals of Meissen and, especially, Erfurt, with its impressive broad flight of stairs rising beside it.

30. Sebastiano Serlio, *Tutte l'opere d'architettura: Il secondo libro di prospettiva* (Venice, 1619), fols. 44–47. In *Dom auf einer Anhöhe* the incongruous wing to the left of the domed structure closely resembles Serlio's designs for town houses in *Il settimo libro*, especially the elevations on p. 37.

31. See Ferdinando Galli da Bibiena, *Direzioni a'Giovani studenti nel disegno* (Bologna, 1731–1732). The son and grandson of Ferdinando worked in Berlin in the second half of the eighteenth century; see Ekhart Berckenhagen, *Alte Bühnenbilder* (Berlin: Ehemals Staatliche Museen, Kunstbibliothek, 1960), pp. 5–8.

32. Goethe's *Faust* must always be adapted and condensed when produced. His first play, *Götz von Berlichingen*, contains fifty-four scenes and over forty named characters.

33. Also known as *Dom über einer Stadt*. A copy of this work by August W. Ahlborn of ca. 1815 is in Schloss Charlottenburg, Berlin. Another version, presumably by Schinkel, was destroyed during the fire at the Crystal Palace in Sydenham near London in 1936.

34. Giuseppe Galli Bibiena, *Architetture e prospettive* (Augsburg, 1740), Pt. II, Plate 10; original engraving ca. 1705.

35. Fontane, *Wanderungen durch die Mark Brandenburg*, p. 48.

36. For Schinkel's work for the stage, see his *Decorationen auf den königlichen Hoftheatern zu Berlin*, 5 pts. (Berlin, 1819–1825). For his relationship to Graf von Brühl, see Waagen, "Schinkel," pp. 340–341.

37. For a comprehensive discussion of Schinkel's panoramas, see Kugler, *Schinkel*, pp. 18, 137–152. For a chronological listing and descriptions of the lost panoramas, see Wolzogen, *Aus Schinkel's Nachlass*, II, 344–346.

38. See Wolzogen, *Aus Schinkel's Nachlass,* III, 408–409. The etching has been retouched with ink and wash.

39. In discussing this aspect of current developments, Sheldon Renan writes in *An Introduction to the American Underground Film* (New York, 1967), p. 228, that artists today "want to work in many media, and to combine many media in one work . . . want their work to be environments, to be big as life, and in many cases, literally to be life."

40. Mackowsky, *Schinkel,* p. 192.

IV. The Transformation of Central Berlin

1. Such enlightened minds as Wilhelm von Humboldt and Friedrich Karl von Savigny had been able to motivate the establishment of the capital's first university in 1810. In that same year, Madame de Staël published *De l'Allemagne,* in which (pp. 82–84) she wrote:

"Aucun spectacle en Allemagne n'égalait celui de Berlin. Cette ville, étant au centre du nord de l'Allemagne, peut être considérée comme le foyer de ses lumières. On y cultive les sciences et les lettres, . . . et l'on sait rassembler les gens de talent de toutes les classes.

". . . on doit trouver, même dans tout ce qui tient aux manières, plus d'usage du monde à Vienne qu'à Berlin. Néanmoins la liberté de la presse, la réunion des hommes d'esprit, la connaissance de la littérature et de la langue allemande, qui s'était généralement répandue dans les derniers temps, faisaient de Berlin le vraie capitale de l'Allemagne nouvelle, de l'Allemagne éclairée.

"Les écrivains philosophes ont eu souvent d'injustes préjugés contre la Prusse; ils ne voyaient en elle qu'une vaste caserne, et c'était sous ce rapport qu'elle valait le moins: ce qui doit intéresser à ce pays, ce sont les lumières, l'esprit de justice et les sentiments d'indépendence qu'on rencontre dans une foule d'individus de toutes les classes . . ."

For an eye-witness account of Berlin's cultural life during these years by one of the city's most distinguished artists, see Johann Gottfried Schadow, *Kunst-Werke und Kunst-Ansichten,* esp. pp. 88–131.

2. As a member, and later the chief, of this office (which was charged with the supervision of civil and governmental building projects), Schinkel's position was somewhat similar to that of a royal architect in France. As early as 1816 the king became his chief patron and the dispenser of funds for major architectural projects in Berlin. He would never bestow the patent of nobility upon Schinkel, nor elevate him to the official position of a royal architect per se. Nevertheless, Schinkel did enjoy royal privileges of special sorts: he was entrusted with the education of the crown prince in art and architecture, he received two royal travel grants in later years (1826 and 1830), and he was honored with royal citations in recognition of his outstanding accomplishments as a civil servant. As such he also reached the highest position within the prescribed framework of Prussia's near equivalent to the English Office of Public Works. In 1838 he became Oberlandesbaudirektor (almost a ministerial rank) of the kingdom of Prussia.

3. For the most comprehensive documentation and analysis of literary and graphic sources for the Neue Wache, see Rave, *Schinkel Lebenswerk: Berlin,* III, 140–171. There are only a few written comments by Schinkel (see Item 1 under "Schrifttum," p. 171), in contrast to the considerable number of extant drawings, more than for any other project on which he worked. See also Wolfgang Dronke, "Die Neue Wache in Berlin," unpub. diss., Technische Hochschule, Berlin-Charlottenburg, 1931; excerpt published in *Zeitschrift für Bauwesen,* 81 (1931), 44–52.

4. The Neue Wache functioned for exactly one hundred years as the headquarters of the royal guard of Prussia's kings and emperors. The guard was dissolved in 1918 and the building became a center for various civic functions. In 1930 it was decided to transform the building into a national memorial to the Unknown Soldier of World War I (Reichsehrenmal). Among the architects competing for this commission were Ludwig Mies van der Rohe, Peter Behrens, and Hans Poelzig. The competition was won by Heinrich Tessenow. In 1960 the newly restored building was rededicated as the Mahnmal für die Opfer des Faschismus und Militarismus. See Appendix under 1816 for more complete information.

5. Le Corbusier, *Towards a New Architecture*, tr. Frederick Etchells (London, 1946), p. 11.

6. Rave, *Schinkel Lebenswerk: Berlin*, III, 144.

7. Although Rave, *Schinkel Lebenswerk: Berlin*, III, 145, suggests that he may have considered two alternative locations, one adjacent to the Finance Ministry, the other in the center of the grove, Schinkel's perspective drawing (see Figure 56) reveals quite clearly that the latter section was intended for the display of the king's captured cannons.

8. The mausoleum has been commonly attributed to Gentz. However, recent research by Peschken has established that the original design was conceived by Schinkel; see "Technologische Ästhetik in Schinkels Architektur," *Zeitschrift des Deutschen Vereins für Kunstwissenschaft* (No. 1/2, 1968).

9. Related to his concurrent use of Egyptian forms for the stage design of Mozart's *Zauberflöte*; for illustrations, see August Grisebach, *Carl Friedrich Schinkel* (Leipzig, 1924), pp. 54–55.

10. Krieger, *Berlin im Wandel der Zeiten*, p. 128: "Der gute alte König . . . stand fast täglich am Fenster, wenn die Wachtparade vorbeimarschierte . . ."

11. The metric scale at the top was added after 1872 by an unknown hand; the passage at the lower right by Schinkel, dated 21 June 1816, was added after Friedrich Wilhelm's renewed requests for revisions.

12. See plan and longitudinal section of Neue Wache, second planning stage, Rave, *Schinkel Lebenswerk: Berlin*, III, Plate 151. Schinkel's own comments are in his *Sammlung*, I, 1: "Der Plan dieses, ringsum ganz freiliegenden Gebäudes ist einem römischen Castrum ungefähr nachgeformt, deshalb die vier festeren Ecktürme und der innere Hof. Letzterer ist nützlich, um die Oekonomie gegen den ringsum laufenden Platz zu verbergen, auch nimmt er den Abfall sämtlicher Bedachungen auf, und führt das Regenwasser von den Dächern unmittelbar in den, unter dem Gebäude fortlaufenden, überwölbten Kanal."

13. See Rave, *Schinkel Lebenswerk: Berlin*, III, 154, for a transcription of the handwritten passage.

14. In his *Denkschrift* (see Rave, *Schinkel Lebenswerk: Berlin*, III, 153), Schinkel had also suggested that the old customs warehouses, situated to the south along the Kupfergraben, be relocated and the area improved by landscaping the canal's banks for promenades.

15. The Pfaueninsel in the Havel River was the first royal estate in Prussia to be patterned after Erdmannsdorff's English landscape design at Schloss Wörlitz (1769–1773). Its gardens and parks, which included numerous pavilions, were remodeled by Peter Joseph Lenné in 1816. In addition, Schinkel may have recalled Heinrich Gentz's third project for a monument to Friedrich II (1806), which was planned for the same area as the Neue Wache and featured a small park in the style of English prototypes. Gentz had asked Schinkel to assist him in completing final presentation drawings for this project; see Doebber, *Gentz*, Plate 16 and pp. 37–38.

16. Even as late as 1843 Waagen would have to remind Friedrich Wilhelm IV, an amateur architect of sorts, to improve the area of Schinkel's Neue Wache; see his "Schinkel," p. 353: "Bei der Pietät Sr. Majestät des Königs gegen die Mahnen Schinkels steht indess zu hoffen, dass die empfindliche Lücke, welche das Gebäude jetzt, zumal in seiner Umgebung, etwas ärmlich und mager erscheinen lässt, gleich so vielen andern mit der Zeit ausgefüllt werden wird."

17. Quoted in *Merian*, 12 (No. 11, 1959), p. 80. Issue on Berlin.

18. The dimensions of this canvas are impressive: 2.49 × 3.74 meters. It is also known as *Parade Unter den Linden* or *Parade vor dem Opernplatz*.

19. Schinkel appears in top hat directly above and slightly to the right of the head of the young lady holding a parasol.

20. Kugler, *Schinkel*, p. 41.

21. According to Rave, this plan had been totally neglected in architectural literature for 120 years. He discussed it in *Schinkel Lebenswerk: Berlin*, II, 11–12, 17, and included a transcription of Schinkel's Commentaries which appear on the right-hand side of the drawing. These references are keyed by color, now somewhat faded, to existing and proposed buildings and old and new planting. See *ibid.*, III, 83–86, for further references to this scheme. According to Rave and confirmed by my own inquiries, there exists no official document or correspondence relating to this project. Consequently, it can be assumed that the plan was unsolicited and therefore found no acknowledgement or response from Friedrich Wilhelm III.

22. Mackowsky, *Schinkel*, p. 97.

23. Other important maps or aerial views of Berlin prior to 1800 had been executed by Memhard, 1648 (see Figure 2); La Vigne, 1685; Schultz, 1688 (see Figure 4); Walter, 1737; Schmettau, ca. 1748; and Schneider, 1798 and 1802.

24. One is reminded of Niels Eigtved's ingenious scheme for the transformation of Frederiksstaden (1749), in the heart of Copenhagen, which combined numerous building types, among them a large hospital complex, into one of Europe's most successful urban units; see Christian Elling and Kay Fisker, eds., *Monumenta Architecturae Danicae: Danish Architectural Drawings, 1660–1920* (Copenhagen, 1961), p. 17 and Plates 41–53.

25. See Wolzogen, *Aus Schinkel's Nachlass*, II, 60.

26. Monbijou was originally the property of Graf von Wartenberg. Built in 1703 by Eosander von Göthe, Schlüter's successor, it was later enlarged by Knobelsdorff for Queen Sophie-Dorothea, mother of Friedrich II.

27. Although the specific purpose of Schinkel's circular structure is not known, he may have intended it as a national shrine, similar in symbolic content to the Bavarian Walhalla. He had submitted designs for this memorial to the Wars of Liberation in 1815. The project was sponsored by Ludwig I, King of Bavaria, and finally realized by Leo von Klenze from 1830 to 1842. One is also reminded of Friedrich Gilly's concept of the "Pantheon des Weltalls," the symbolic-philosophical connotation which he attached to his monument to Friedrich II. Schinkel, in his design for the Museum, used a rotunda or Pantheon form in the center and defined its purpose as a silent focus within the sacred realm of his shrine dedicated to the arts.

28. The criticism of Ott, *Zur Platzgestaltung im 19. Jahrhundert in Deutschland*, p. 42, reads as follows: "Vor dem 'Pantheon' [sic] werden beide Baumwände von dem Spreeknie in ungleicher Länge beendet. Das Portal IV liegt nicht in der Mitte der Fassade, die überhaupt unsymmetrisch ist. Es ist hier also eine recht freie und unbarocke Perspektivwirkung entworfen—doch es ist dies wohl mehr ein Spielen mit dieser Möglichkeit,

nicht ein ausschlaggebendes Kennzeichen für Schinkels Kunst."

29. Hegemann's criticism of this distinctive type of Berlin housing of the *Gründerjahre* after 1871 is in *Das steinerne Berlin*, esp. pp. 200–207.

30. For general references, see Wolzogen, *Aus Schinkel's Nachlass*, III, 170–187; and Schinkel, *Sammlung*, I, 1–2.

31. Rave assigned the drawing to Schinkel; see Rave, *Schinkel Lebenswerk: Berlin*, I, 79. Peschken questions this attribution in a private letter of June 1967. For Langhans' theater and Schinkel's plans to remodel its interior in 1813, see Rave, *Schinkel Lebenswerk: Berlin*, I, 79–87.

32. Schinkel's letter to Graf von Brühl, Generalintendant of the royal theaters, published in Wolzogen, *Aus Schinkel's Nachlass*, III, 170–174, reads in part: "Eine so vollständige Bearbeitung des Plans erfordert aber Zeit und grosse Mühen aller Art, und es könnte sich wohl zutragen, dass bei unserm beiderseitigen besten Willen für die Sache, die Arbeit so ausfiele, dass Allerhöchsten Orts wegen einzelner Anstösse mittelst eines Bleistiftstrichs das Resultat vieler angestrengt durchwachter Nächte vernichtet würde, und nun von neuem Zeit und Mühe aufgewendet werden müssten, woraus die Förderung des Werkes nicht erwachsen kann . . . wie durch Missverstehen, oder, was noch weit schlimmer ist, durch Vermischung meiner Ideen mit anderen, jahrelange Arbeiten und die schönsten Hoffnungen zertrümmert wurden, und ich viele solcher Jahre nicht mehr ungenutzt zu verlieren habe."

33. According to Nicolai (*Berlin und Potsdam*, I, 201), the church had been partially modeled after the centralized Protestant temple at Charenton, a work of Salomon de Brosse.

34. Nicolai, *Berlin und Potsdam*, I, 202. Friedrich II considered himself a dilettante architect. According to Krieger, *Berlin*, p. 130, his private libraries contained two copies of *Architecture de Palladio divisé en quatre livres . . . avec des notes d'Inigo Jones . . . trad. de l'Italien*, 1726. In 1736, Friedrich sent Georg W. von Knobelsdorff on a study tour to Italy, where the architecture of Palladio left the most profound impression on him. During later years, however, the state-sponsored buildings under Friedrich II suffered from the king's frequently changing tastes. While St. Hedwig's cathedral (1745–1773) by Jean-Laurent Le Geay follows Serlio's version of the Pantheon, Friedrich directed Georg Christian Unger and Johann Boumann the Younger to design the old Bibliothek (1775–1780) in the style of Fischer von Erlach's Hofburg in Vienna. In regard to the twin churches at the Gendarmenmarkt, a certain resemblance to the domes of Greenwich Naval Hospital by Sir Christopher Wren has been suggested by Rave, *Berlin in der Geschichte seiner Bauten*, p. 30.

35. Rave, *Schinkel Lebenswerk: Berlin*, I, 131.

36. The choragic monument of Thrasyllos in Athens, which he probably knew from Stuart and Revett, was supposedly the model for this arrangement.

37. For the particular place of Gilly's project in the context of late eighteenth-century architecture, see Hermann Beenken, *Schöpferische Bauideen der deutschen Romantik* (Mainz, 1952), pp. 41–43. Cf. Oncken, *Friedrich Gilly*, esp. pp. 1–10, 42, 63–77.

38. The painted backdrop was executed by Carl Gropius, who had previously co-operated with Schinkel in the design of panoramas. An engraving of the design was included in Schinkel's *Sammlung*, I, Plate 14. For additional references and contemporary commentary regarding the opening of the Schauspielhaus, see Rave, *Schinkel Lebenswerk: Berlin*, I, 120–121.

39. This opinion differs from that of Pevsner, *Outline of European Architecture*, p. 375,

who writes: "Gilly's National Theater for Berlin [was] clearly a conception of the Goethe age."

40. For example, Giedion's analysis of Schinkel's Lustgarten project in *Spätbarocker und romantischer Klassizismus*, p. 125: "Der Platz des 'Lustgartens' beim Berliner Schloss zeigt wieder drei unverbundene Bauten. Den Rückhalt, den die weite Fläche am Schlüterschen Schloss findet, lässt sie, die fast doppelt so gross als der Münchener Königsplatz ist, doch nicht zerfliessen. Es ist Schinkels Verdienst, dass er das Alte Museum 1823, unter grossen Mühen in weitmöglichste Entfernung rückte, denn die Schlütersche Wand konnte niemals ein Gegenüber in der Säulenstellung Schinkels finden. Auf diese Weise bedrückt nicht eine Gestaltung die andere und jeder Bau kann Individuum in seinem Reich bleiben. Ausserdem wird durch die grosse Entfernung ein Platz in romantischem Sinn geschaffen und eine eigentliche Raumbildung verhindert. Dass es Schinkel gar nicht um einen einheitlichen Platzraum zu tun war, kann man auch aus den späteren Entwürfen für das Friedrichsdenkmal, 1829, ersehen . . ."

41. "Schinkel im zwanzigsten Jahrhundert," p. 11.

42. For an illustration of Gentz's project, see Doebber, *Gentz*, Plate 16 and pp. 37, 76.

43. For Schinkel's part in the planned remodeling of the stables and academy building in 1822, see Rave, *Schinkel Lebenswerk: Berlin*, I, 14–24. For the supposed encouragement of the crown prince to change the plans to an independent museum structure, see Ludwig Dehio, *Friedrich Wilhelm IV. von Preussen: Ein Baukünstler der Romantik* (Munich-Berlin, 1961), p. 38 and Plate 9. I reject this allegation on the basis that Friedrich Wilhelm's activities as a dilettante architect never reached this degree of comprehensive and original planning; see *ibid.*, Plate 24, for a project of barbarous egocentricity and mediocre draftsmanship. In support of my view, see Peschken's excellent appraisal in "Schinkels nachgelassene Fragmente eines architektonischen Lehrbuches," *Bonner Jahrbücher*, 166 (1966), esp. pp. 314–315.

44. The drawings are listed in Rave, *Schinkel Lebenswerk: Berlin*, I, 41; the introductory letter and supporting material are published in Wolzogen, *Aus Schinkel's Nachlass*, III, 217–232.

45. See Wolzogen, *Aus Schinkel's Nachlass*, III, 241–244, for the objections of Hofrath Hirt.

46. Wolzogen, *Aus Schinkel's Nachlass*, III, 250. The building cost in modern terms would be about $3,500,000. After the addition of some funds for the decorative program of the Museum and several eliminations, such as the apartment block, the official figure stood at "884.000 Thaler, 29 Silbergroschen und 8 Pfennige."

47. Rave, *Schinkel Lebenswerk: Berlin*, I, 37.

48. For the best analysis of the Museum, see Sabine Spiero, "Schinkels Altes Museum in Berlin," *Jahrbuch der preussischen Kunstsammlungen*, 55 (1934), 41–86. For Schinkel's own comments, see Wolzogen, *Aus Schinkel's Nachlass*, III, 217–298. Cf. Rave, *Schinkel Lebenswerk: Berlin*, I, 12–78, and II, 17–19, 106–128. See also the *Festschrift* published for the Museum's reopening, *Das Alte Museum: 1823–1966*, ed. Gerhard R. Meyer *et al.* (Staatliche Museen zu Berlin, 1966), containing an excellent essay by Gottfried Riemann, "Schinkels Altes Museum: Zu seiner Bedeutung und Geschichte."

49. Waagen, "Schinkel," p. 370.

50. Schinkel, *Sammlung*, No. 6 (1825), "Erläuterung." In his rather brief comments on the Museum, Schinkel precisely stated the dimensions of the building, which was not typical of him. The Museum measures 86.35 × 54.50 meters. The overall measurements of the Schloss were 113.2 × 189 meters; the Zeughaus plan is 88.67 meters square. All these

buildings have interior open courts. In the case of the Museum, the courts were primarily for additional light for the surrounding galleries.

51. For Schinkel's remodeling of the old Domkirche, see Carl Schniewind, *Der Dom zu Berlin: Geschichtliche Nachrichten vom alten Dom* (Berlin, 1905), pp. 31–33, 70–81. See also Rave, *Schinkel Lebenswerk: Berlin*, I, 214–220.

52. Wolzogen, *Aus Schinkel's Nachlass*, III, 244–249, "Schinkel's Votum vom 5. Februar 1823 zu dem Gutachten des Hofraths Hirt."

53. Schinkel's frescoes were badly damaged in 1945 and could not be restored in the recent rebuilding of the Museum. See Hermann Fürst von Pückler-Muskau, *Andeutungen über Landschaftsgärtnerei verbunden mit der Beschreibung ihrer praktischen Anwendung in Muskau*, ed. Theodor Lange, 2nd ed. (Leipzig [1911]), pp. 181–194 (1st ed., 1834), for a contemporary assessment of the frescoes.

54. Hittorff, "Historische Notiz über Carl Friedrich Schinkel," p. 102.

55. For these discussions, see Wolzogen, *Aus Schinkel's Nachlass*, III, 232–247. In addition, Schinkel justified the large basement as profitable for storage, study rooms, and the apartment of a caretaker. It is noteworthy that the substructure of the building today houses the offices of Museum staff as well as various archives and collections, among them Schinkel's own drawings.

56. The buildings east of the Kupfergraben and south of the Schlossbrücke remained an eyesore until they were finally razed during the reign of Friedrich Wilhelm IV; see *Die Werderschen Mühlen und der Mühlengraben*, a watercolor by F. W. Klose, in Krieger, *Berlin*, facing p. 60.

57. Fritz Stahl, *Karl Friedrich Schinkel* (Berlin, 1912), p. 45.

58. See chap. i, n.2. There exists an intermediary plan in the Deutsches Zentralarchiv, Historische Abteilung II, Merseburg, almost identical to Figure 78, but showing the Museum closer to the Kupfergraben.

59. Rave, *Schinkel Lebenswerk: Berlin*, I, 45.

60. The full text of Schinkel's marginal notes has been published by Rave, *Schinkel Lebenswerk: Berlin*, II, 112–113.

61. Wolzogen, *Aus Schinkel's Nachlass*, III, 8.

62. Rave, *Schinkel Lebenswerk: Berlin*, II, 113.

63. See Rave, *Schinkel Lebenswerk: Berlin*, II, 113, and Ott, *Zur Platzgestaltung*, p. 39, who simply accepts Rave's characterization of Schinkel's first landscaping scheme as "biedermeierliche Nettigkeit."

64. Schinkel's repeated use of column screens, in sketches, stage designs and buildings, goes back to his early training. A drawing of 1802 entitled *Halle am Meer*, perhaps a *Schulzeichnung* for the Bauakademie, is similar in concept to Peruzzi's frescoes at the Villa Farnesina (see Grisebach, *Schinkel*, Plate 7). His interest in this particular motif is also reflected in his diaries. In 1824, during a visit to San Zeno Maggiore in Mantua, he commented on a painting by Andrea Mantegna entitled *Madonna Enthroned*, noting that the entire composition was framed by a columned hall through which one could look outside, into the distance (Wolzogen, *Aus Schinkel's Nachlass*, II, 111). Schinkel's drawing of the upper vestibule of the Museum, executed in 1828 and published in the seventeenth installment of his *Sammlung* in 1831, is the last and most refined example of a motif which he had admired since his youth.

65. The new Staatsrat building incorporates Schlüter's Portal V, a relic salvaged from the damaged Schloss, which was demolished in 1950–1951. The symbolic association of a part of the old Prussian palace and the modern government of the German Democratic

Republic is explained by the fact that Karl Liebknecht addressed the populace of Berlin from the balcony of this portal in 1919.

66. Other museums at the northern end of the Spree island (known as the Museumsinsel) which did not interfere with Schinkel's customs warehouses are the Neue Museum, 1843–1855, by August Stüler and the National Galerie, 1866–1876, by Johann H. Strack. For a recent comprehensive study of the Museum island and the history of its buildings and collections, see Gerhard R. Meyer *et al.*, *Museumsinsel Berlin.* Weltstädte der Kunst (Munich, 1967).

67. Wolzogen, *Aus Schinkel's Nachlass*, III, 225.

68. Rave, *Schinkel Lebenswerk: Berlin*, III, 107–125, traces the chronology of the building history and of major design and planning phases from 1823 to 1830.

69. Kugler, *Schinkel*, p. 51.

70. The pedimental sculpture was designed by Schinkel and executed in gypsum cement by August Kiss. It included allegorical figures representing shipping and agriculture and symbols denoting the Havel and Spree rivers.

71. See Rave, *Schinkel Lebenswerk: Berlin*, III, 114, 116.

72. L. Ettlinger, "A German Architect's Visit to England in 1826," *Architectural Review*, 97 (May 1945), 131.

73. Waagen, "Schinkel," pp. 403–404.

74. It should be noted that Rave and Peschken attempted to reconstruct an intermediary site plan of the Packhof, which dated from 1825 and improved upon the earlier versions; see Rave, *Schinkel Lebenswerk: Berlin*, III, 112–113, and Plates 106, 107. Schinkel did not publish this scheme in his *Sammlung*, where the changing character of the site and architecture of this complex was treated only in the beforementioned extremes.

75. Schinkel's critical reference to the transformation of the Piazza del Popolo by Giuseppe Valadier appears in Wolzogen, *Aus Schinkel's Nachlass*, I, 261: "Die Piazza del popolo fand ich sehr verändert, indess viel zu modern für Rom, und die neue Architektur vom Architekten Valadier sehr ordinair." His travels in France and England, April–August 1826, have been documented in lengthy diaries and numerous letters; see *ibid.*, II, 137–165; III, 1–150. An excellent recent study of Schinkel's visit to England and its influence on his later works is Gottfried Riemann, "Karl Friedrich Schinkels Reise nach England im Jahr 1826 und ihre Wirkung auf sein architektonisches Werk," unpub. diss., Martin Luther-Universität, Halle-Wittenberg, 1967. Among other important contributions, this work contains a new and more accurate transcription of Schinkel's diaries from England.

76. Waagen, "Schinkel," p. 380. Subsequent remarks by Schinkel are from Wolzogen, *Aus Schinkel's Nachlass*, III, esp. 41–93, 113–114.

77. For Fürst Pückler's critical remarks, see his *Andeutungen über Landschaftsgärtnerei*, p. 180, including this penetrating statement: "Wie oft habe ich den Engländern bei den ungeheueren Summen, die sie täglich für die Kunst fast ohne Erfolg verschwenden, gewünscht, dass ein ihm gleicher Geist ihren so guten Willen und ihr so vieles Geld durch sein Genie befruchten möchte! Welche Schätze hat nur Herr Nash in dieser Hinsicht verschwendet, und was würde Schinkel damit geschaffen haben!" At the same time, he commented sympathetically and with great insight on the planning aspects of Regent's Park; see also his *Fürst Pückler reist nach England*, ed. H. Ch. Mettin (Munich, 1965), p. 17. This work was originally published anonymously in 1830 as *Briefe eines Verstorbenen:*

Ein fragmentarisches Tagebuch aus England, Wales, Irland und Frankreich, geschrieben in den Jahren 1826–1829.

78. In order to appreciate fully the difference between Beuth's and Schinkel's reactions to the industries of modern Britain, compare Beuth's letter of 1823 in Wolzogen, *Aus Schinkel's Nachlass*, III, 139–151, and Schinkel's diary entries on Birmingham, *ibid.*, p. 71. Cf. Ettlinger, "A German Architect's Visit to England in 1826," pp. 131–134.

79. Unfortunately, Schinkel's reaction to English factory buildings has been frequently misinterpreted by English-speaking scholars. For a typical example, see Lewis Mumford, *Roots of Contemporary Architecture*, 2nd ed. (New York, 1959), pp. 6–7, where he states: "When Schinkel beheld the cotton factories of Manchester, he properly hailed them as the source of a new architecture." The warehouses at St. Katherine's Docks in London, 1824–1828, by Thomas Telford, are a somewhat more successful solution. Although Schinkel does not mention them specifically, he may have seen these large cubic brick buildings under construction when he visited the Thames docks.

80. For an illuminating study of the origin and dissemination of low-rise segmental brick vaults, see Turpin C. Bannister, "The Roussillon Vault," *Journal of the Society of Architectural Historians*, 27 (October 1968), 163–175.

81. Wolzogen, *Aus Schinkel's Nachlass*, III, 141. Fürst Pückler, during his visit to Leeds, 1 October 1827, wrote about the local factories as enthusiastically as did Beuth. For his romantic descriptions, including many misconceptions about the life of factory workers, see *Fürst Pückler reist nach England*, pp. 103–105.

82. For a comprehensive study of the various designs and planning stages of this structure, see Leopold Giese, *Schinkels architektonisches Schaffen: Entwürfe und Ausführungen*. Vol. I, *Die Friedrich Werdersche Kirche zu Berlin* (Berlin, 1921). For Schinkel's own publication of his designs, see his *Sammlung*, No. 8 (1826), Plates 49–52 (the preferred classical version), and No. 13 (1829), Plates 79–84 (the alternate version in the medieval style). Schinkel wrote of the latter version: "Es wurden unter noch mehreren anderen Entwürfen, die ich damals bearbeiten musste, auch einer im Mittelalterstil verlangt, und dieser Entwurf erhielt die Genehmigung [des Königs]." See Rave, *Schinkel Lebenswerk: Berlin*, I, 254–300, for invaluable references and illustrations of various schemes which led to the final design of this church. Unless otherwise noted, subsequent quotations are from Rave.

83. Adler, "Schinkel Festrede," p. 466; Waagen, "Schinkel," p. 376.

84. Johannes Krätschell, "Schinkels gotisches Schmerzenskind, die Werdersche Kirche in Berlin," *Blätter für Architektur und Kunsthandwerk*, 1 (1888), 114–117.

85. His choice is reminiscent of the impressive facade of Sant' Andrea in Mantua, though Schinkel did not actually see this building until returning from his second trip to Italy, late in 1824.

86. For plans and preliminary sketches of this project, some of which have been erroneously attributed to Schinkel, see Johannes Sievers, [*Schinkel Lebenswerk:*] *Die Arbeiten von K. F. Schinkel für Prinz Wilhelm späteren König von Preussen* (Berlin, 1955), pp. 16–18, esp. figs. 8–10.

87. The text, entitled "Vorteile des anliegenden Planes," is published in Rave, *Schinkel Lebenswerk: Berlin*, II, 20.

88. Friedrich Wilhelm III was persuaded to approve the construction of the Bauakademie by Peter Christian Beuth, who argued that a new representative structure was needed to serve the combined functions of headquarter offices for the Oberlandesbau-

deputation, of which Schinkel was the director, and Berlin's school of architecture, of which Beuth was the director. It is clear that this new building, which also contained Schinkel's apartment, a library and exhibition rooms, was truly a monument to their lifelong friendship and their mutual efforts to improve the education of architects and designers of industrial products. Thus, it is not a coincidence that Eduard Gaertner painted Schinkel and Beuth side by side looking at the new building (see Figure 15) and that Friedrich Adler recalled in 1869 that it was Schinkel's favorite. For the two men's efforts in making the structure an expression of their own highest standards, see Rave, *Schinkel Lebenswerk: Berlin*, III, 38–58.

89. Waagen, "Schinkel," p. 411.

90. The first publication of the Bauakademie plans, elevations, sections and general exterior views appeared in No. 20 of Schinkel's *Sammlung*, 1833. The illustration used in my text is a preliminary drawing for the engraving. This is important since reproductions of the engraving from the *Sammlung* do not show a distinction in value or density between the dark blocks of the Bauakademie and Werdersche Kirche and the shaded areas for proposed improvements. Quotations from Schinkel's specifications are drawn from the text in No. 20 of the *Sammlung*. The best discussions of the Bauakademie are: Emil Flaminius, "Über den Bau des Hauses für die allgemeine Bauschule in Berlin," *Allgemeine Bauzeitung*, 1 (1836), 3–5, 9–13, 18–26; Adler, "Schinkel Festrede," pp. 463–475; Rave, *Schinkel Lebenswerk: Berlin*, III, 38–60, and *Genius der Baukunst;* Goerd Peschken, *Schinkels Bauakademie in Berlin* (Berlin, 1961), esp. pp. 10–15.

91. See Rave, *Schinkel Lebenswerk: Berlin*, I, 271–272, for previous efforts to improve these houses during the construction of the church.

92. While the main subject of the composition is the cupola above the chapel of the Schloss, designed by August Stüler and executed in 1845–1853, the sketch also vividly illustrates the visual ugliness which plagued environmental planners even in the nineteenth century. Only a dozen or so years had passed since Schinkel's death when Klose recorded the immediate vicinity of the Bauakademie. The ramshackle old mills still cover the canal (and would only be demolished in 1876) and posters are pasted over the walls of Schinkel's building—over the very bricks which had been so carefully laid in order to demonstrate excellence of technique to young masons. But, a work of superior architecture thus vandalized can still evoke admiration for its enduring qualities and one is reminded of Goethe's reaction to the plight of Palladio's buildings in Vicenza which he recorded during his visit in 1786: "Betrachtet man nun hier am Orte die herrlichen Gebäude, die jener Mann aufführte, und sieht, wie sie schon durch das enge, schmutzige Bedürfnis der Menschen entstellt sind, . . . wie wenig diese köstlichen Denkmale eines hohen Menschengeistes zu dem Leben der übrigen passen, so fällt einem denn doch ein, dass es in allem andern ebenso ist; denn man verdient wenig Dank von den Menschen, wenn man ihr inneres Bedürfnis erhöhen, ihnen eine grosse Idee von ihnen selbst geben, ihnen das Herrliche eines wahren, edlen Daseins zum Gefühl bringen will" (Goethe, *Italienische Reise: 1786–1788*, p. 51).

93. Rave, *Genius der Baukunst* is also valuable for its illustrations of details of the then (1939) recently cleaned terra-cotta ornament and his discussion of the subtle polychromatic effects which Schinkel achieved by using several types and textures of facing brick. These subtleties were apparently lost on the overly critical populace of Berlin, who referred to the Bauakademie in a contemporary jingle as: "Kasten dieser Stadt, ringsum glatt und platt."

94. For Schinkel's views, see Wolzogen, *Aus Schinkel's Nachlass*, II, 208, "Das Prinzip der Kunst in der Architektur."

95. Waagen, "Schinkel," p. 401. Actually, Schinkel's superb integration of architecture and ornament had been hailed earlier by the art historian and critic, Karl Friedrich von Rumohr, who wrote to Crown Prince Christian of Denmark in August, 1836: "Gestern war ich auch einige Stunden in Berlin und besah mir Schinkels neuesten Bau, die Bauakademie. In diesem hat er die Backstein-Konstruktion und -Ausführung mit Zuziehung von Terrakotta-Skulpturen auf eine Höhe der Vollendung gebracht, die mich entzückt hat. Nichts Antikes noch Mittelalterliches überstrifft sie. Die äussere Mauerbekleidung ist ein einziger Guss. Was in Konstruktion und Verzierung ganz Neues eben aus der Natur dieser Aufgabe gedacht, entworfen, ausgeführt worden, übertrifft jede Erwartung. Dieses Bauwerk ist unter denen Schinkels das einzige, das in der Zeichnung mir ganz missfallen, in der Ausführung hingegen wiederum das, so mir unter allen seinen Werken am meisten *gefallen* hat. —So wenig kann man auf Zeichnungen von Bauwerken sich verlassen" (Rave, *Schinkel Lebenswerk: Berlin*, III, 58.)

96. Jean-Nicolas-Louis Durand, *Recueil et parallèle des édifices de tout genre anciens et modernes remarquables par leur beauté*, 3 vols. (Venice, 1833); Schinkel's Bauakademie is shown in II, Plate 114, C.

97. This neglect cannot be explained solely by Friedrich Wilhelm III's lack of interest or the financial difficulties of the state. Rather, it is largely due to the curious organization of Berlin's municipal government, which allowed the chief of the Staatspolizei to overrule the Magistrat (city council) and often the king himself in matters of urban expansion. The establishment of new streets or city squares and even the standard layout of apartment houses with their characteristic "Berliner Zimmer" were subject to police regulations.

98. Fontane, *Wanderungen durch die Mark Brandenburg*, p. 52. The importance of Schinkel's work to the harmonious integration of the urban fabric, as noted by Fontane, was ignored by future planners of Berlin. If the period of Wilhelm II (1888–1918) produced such unrelated monumental structures as, for instance, the new Domkirche by Raschdorff and the Staatsbibliothek by von Ihne, the plans of the Third Reich were to outdo even the most grandiose projects of the imperial era of the *Gründerzeit*. Albert Speer's recently published memoirs (*Erinnerungen* [Berlin, 1969]) reveal how Schinkel's philosophy of sensitive planning integration had given way to concepts of gross representational grandeur, even megalomania, when Hitler projected the "north-south axis" in the mid-1930's.

99. Dr. Peschken will soon publish a comprehensive volume on Schinkel's *Lehrbuch* in the *Lebenswerk* series.

100. For a summary of the changing character of the Lustgarten after the erection of the new Domkirche, see Hans Müther, "Schinkels Museum in Berlin," *Berliner Heimat: Zeitschrift für die Geschichte Berlins*, 2 (1959), 72–82.

101. The badly damaged Schloss was demolished in 1950–1951; the remains of the Bauakademie were torn down in 1961. Gentz's Münzgebäude at the Werdersche-Markt had been demolished as early as 1886. The last Packhof building had vanished by 1938.

102. It should be noted that this combination, painter-architect, was apparently a rare phenomenon at the time. Although we know of Benjamin Latrobe's landscape sketches and the paintings of Leo von Klenze, Andrew Jackson Downing lamented in his *Landscape Architecture* (New York, 1844), p. 349: "The harmonious union of building and scenery is a point of taste that appears to be but little understood in any country; and, mainly,

we believe, because the architect and the landscape painter are seldom combined in the same person, or are seldom consulted together."

103. For the thoughts and sentiments of the most revered exponent of a humanistic architecture, the reader is referred to the essays of the late Walter Gropius, collected in *Apollo in the Democracy*. The subtitle of this book, *The Cultural Obligation of the Architect*, reflects the author's comprehensive view of the role of the architect in modern society.

104. Mackowsky, *Schinkel*, pp. 192–193.

Index